LIFE SURRENDERED IN GOD

The Author

LIFE SURRENDERED IN GOD

The Philosophy and Practices
of Kriya Yoga

ROY EUGENE DAVIS

With extensive commentary on
Patanjali's *Yoga Sutras*

CSA PRESS, Publishers
Lakemont, Georgia 30552

Second edition

Copyright © 1995 by Roy Eugene Davis

ISBN 0-87707-246-9

CSA Press, Publishers
Center for Spiritual Awareness
Lake Rabun Road, Post Office Box 7
Lakemont, Georgia 30552 (U.S.A.)
Telephone (706) 782-4723
Fax (706) 782-4560

Printed and manufactured in the United States of America

I salute the supreme teacher,
the truth, whose nature is bliss;
who is the giver of the highest
happiness; who is pure wisdom;
who is beyond all qualities and
infinite like the sky; who is beyond
words; who is one and eternal,
pure and still; who is beyond all
change and phenomena and who
is the silent witness to all our
thoughts and emotions—I salute
truth, the supreme teacher.

– Ancient Vedic Hymn

Preface

I wrote this book for God-surrendered devotees of the present era and for truth seekers centuries hence. It should not be taken merely as an interesting treatise to read once and put away. Repeatedly examine its meaning until understanding dawns in the mind as a result of direct, soul perception.

A comprehensive, philosophical overview is provided in the first two chapters to prepare the reader to better understand the commentary on the *Yoga Sutras*. Italics have generally been used only when a Sanskrit word is defined, and sometimes for special emphasis. Many Sanskrit words have by now entered into common usage in the West and do not need to be set apart by the use of italics.

The appended glossary can be referred to as often as necessary so that word meanings are clearly understood. Because of the frequency of use of key words and terms throughout the text, an index is not included. Subjects and themes can easily be located by referring to the table of contents.

Some repetition occurs because of the character of the subject matter, and to consistently remind the reader of essential principles and procedures. Rather than only write about the spiritual life, I have chosen to encourage readers to apply themselves to have their own experience of higher realities.

For optimum benefits, it is recommended that the reader examine the text to become familiar with it, then carefully read it through from the beginning. Repeated study should follow, with special attention given to the categories of cosmic manifestation in part one; the commentaries on the *Yoga Sutras* in part two; and the routines and procedures in part three. In this way the information presented will be a dependable guide to resolved participation, psychological transformation, and spiritual growth.

Because this is a handbook for devotees attuned to the Kriya tradition, most of the supporting quotes and references are taken from the *Bhagavad Gita*, with random comments by Kriya Yoga gurus. However, the exposition of basic principles and the guidelines will prove helpful to spiritual aspirants of any enlightenment tradition.

With the publication of this book, four decades have passed since I met my guru, Paramahansa Yogananda, and was initiated by him into the practice of Kriya Yoga. Since then I have traveled the world to share this philosophy and science of God-realization with thousands of individuals, many of whom are today steadily advancing on the soul liberation path. I can testify, from personal experience and my observation of the changed lives of those who live in accord with these principles, that the information in this book is valid.

Editorial changes made for this second edition include several revisions for the purpose of clarification, and some new additions to highlight certain themes.

Roy Eugene Davis

Lakemont, Georgia (U.S.A.)
June 30, 1995
(295 Dwapara Yuga)

CONTENTS

ILLUSTRATIONS

PART ONE

PHILOSOPHY

One Being, Life, Power and Substance

The Eternal Way

We are destined to be fulfilled in God. Coincidental with our outer sojourn in space and time, we are on an inner quest for ultimate meaning and purpose which will be completed when all considerations and conditions of limitation are transcended and we again rest in soul-satisfied realization of wholeness.

There is a natural way to live which allows progressive soul unfoldment. Revealed by saints and seers—and always known in the heart, the innermost core of us—it is the eternal way of right action which determines successful outcomes. Compliant adherence to causative principles innate to life itself is the certain way to know inner peace, enlightened understanding, and experience of God.

Our universe is orderly in its processes, has resources for our every physical need, and provides opportunities for experience and growth. If we are to be successful in life—and we should want to be—we need to ponder the reason for our being here, discover what it is, and do all we possibly can to fulfill our purposes. When we do this, we discover that an Intelligent Presence and Power exists which becomes increasingly real to us as we awaken through successive levels of insightful discovery to the final stage of revealed knowledge which is true enlightenment.

Nothing external to ourselves blesses or deprives us. Our own states of consciousness, mental states, and behaviors determine our perceptions, experiences, and circumstances. The principles of causation are impersonal. When we learn how to live effectively, and choose to do so, we demonstrate affluence: we flow in harmony with the rhythms of cause and effect and experience the supportive actions of evolutionary trends and forces. As self-responsible proficiency in constructive use of innate abilities improves, we also become increasingly receptive to the supportive, transformative, and redemptive influences of grace. The *Bhagavad Gita* 18:13,14:

> There are five factors involved in every action: the body, the ego, soul awareness, the impulse of desire which starts the action, and providence. Whatever a person undertakes to do, these five factors are involved. Because of these, if a person thinks that he alone is the doer, he is mistaken. A person who is selfless even in the midst of action is eternally free regardless of what occurs.

Body refers to the vehicle through which we express in the relative spheres. *Ego* is self-sense, our awareness of I-ness or individuality. *Soul awareness* determines how we view the world and relate to it. The *impulse of desire* impels behavior. *Providence* is the guardianship of God over creation and living beings. When egoism is dominant we often interfere with the providential support available to us. When we are surrendered in God, grace increasingly governs our behavior and determines our lives.

As human beings, we are a blend of divine essence, mind, and body. The body is of matter, "of the earth" (Latin, *humus*) while our essence is of God. Therefore, while expressing through the body divine qualities should be cultivated and enhanced. The driving tendencies which influence the mind are the forces to understand and regulate if we are to awaken to higher Reality and experience life as we are meant to experience it. Intentional living, constant desire to know God, and surrender in God comprise the direct approach to Self-realization. Discipleship is not merely for the purpose of enabling us to be good human beings, as useful as this is, or to live a relatively pain-free existence during this present life cycle. The purpose of focused involvement is to contribute to an acceleration of spiritual growth so that surrender in God is natural and soul liberation is spontaneous.

At our deepest level, behind the screen of mind and personality, is the pure, immortal, true Self we are. It is now what it has ever been and will be—pure, clear, bright, and complete. The Self we are, is God as us. Not everyone knows this about themselves and not all who intuitively feel it are able to immediately actualize it—to identify with it and live from it. No matter what your present conscious awareness of God is, with right attention and right action you can awaken to your divine nature and actualize it. Along with your right involvement, God's grace is the most influential ingredient in the enlightenment process. What a difference it makes when we are expressing all that we are capable of expressing! We then see the world through purified senses and flawlessly comprehend all that is examined. We experience peace of soul. We express health, harmony, and right action in all circumstances. We understand the rhythms and cycles of the universe and are able to attend to our duties without attachment to them or to their results. We function within the boundaries of time while grounded in timelessness.

Discipleship is easy for the surrendered devotee and difficult for the unsurrendered. And even when we want to be surrendered, we may have difficulty. The spirit may be willing but the flesh may be weak; that is, our aspiration may be legitimate but habits and mental conditionings may yet be influential. We may sincerely desire God-realization and have only a few personal restrictions, but be emotionally immature. The four major emotional habits to overcome on the discipleship path are *anger*, *resentment, willfulness*, and *self-pity*. These tend to influence us to engage in overt, or self-directed, destructive behavior. When angry, resentful, or willful, we may engage in addictive and harmful behavior. When overcome by self-pity we may remain small-minded and reclusive.

To Have Real Purpose in Life and Unfold Soul Capacities, Do These Things

To experience relative and absolute fulfillment, come to terms with life in relationship to your basic soul inclinations.

1. *Fulfill Your Duties and Be Happy* – Examine your basic psychophysiological constitution, personality and abilities, and determine your role in life. Then fulfill your duties and social obligations in a spirit of goodwill while cultivating the virtues and living a moral life. This, along with the three following guidelines will contribute to relative fulfillment and happiness. What-

ever your lifestyle, relationships, occupation, or profession, let your life be pure and your actions always constructive.

2. *Satisfy Legitimate Needs and Desires* – Provide a secure basis for your life and for your spiritual practices by satisfying all of your legitimate needs and desires. Housing, clothing, food, emotional support, supportive relationships, and ability to creatively express will liberate your mind from anxiety and provide the opportunity to become cultured as well as to fulfill higher aspirations. Emotional conflicts will be removed as you learn to function freely. Be comfortable, without attachments.

3. *Cultivate a Prosperity Consciousness* – To prosper is "to thrive, flourish, and be successful in all useful ventures." There is no spiritual value in being impoverished and there is no lasting happiness in being materialistic, but you should easily be able to have whatever you need to accomplish your purposes. An understanding relationship with our world is an indication of psychological health, and psychological health is necessary for success on the spiritual path. Whatever your role in life, be it one of simplicity or one in which you are more active and influential, so long as you are fulfilling your destined purposes you should be prosperous to the extent needed to fulfill those purposes.

4. *Remain Focused on the Goal of God-realization* – While attending to basic matters, be engaged in spiritual practices, yearning always for God-realization. To attend to outer needs while neglecting spiritual growth is to miss the mark in life. Responsible living provides the foundation for spiritual growth and spiritual growth makes it easier to fulfill personal obligations and achieve necessary goals.

**Philosophy, Religion
and Revealed Truth**

Philosophy—the rational investigation of the truths and principles of being, knowledge, and conduct—has three branches: natural philosophy, moral philosophy, and metaphysical philosophy. Such investigation should lead one to complete understanding of the subject. Philosophical inquiry can proceed by analytical examination, using the faculty of intelligence to determine conclusions until a shift from determination to intuition allows direct insight. Until direct insight is attained, philosophical conclusions will always be incomplete regardless of their usefulness as guiding influences in our lives. This is because the intellect is of the mind: it is the faculty of determination related to data. Intuition is the subjective side of intellect and allows direct perception unrelated to objective data.

Using mental faculties, we can speculate about our relationship with the world and God. This can be the first step in the acquisition of knowledge which can result in right behavior and the ability to examine esoteric (inner) causes of outer effects. The study of physics (the laws of nature) can awaken a desire to know the operations of the subjective side of life. Philosophical inquiry can lead to spiritual practice and soul unfoldment. For one intent on discovery, all legitimate questions must have answers and all correctly stated problems must have solutions, but answers and solutions found in the relative realm are incomplete. Philosophical inquiry must lead to contemplation and contemplation must lead to final insight. This is the desired end of philosophical inquiry.

The religious impulse is innate to the soul and causes every soul to sooner or later desire to know the meaning of life and experience God-realization and transcendence. Self-conscious people are, for the most part, preoccupied with actions and involvements related to physical survival and maintenance of the personality, little knowing that inner changes are steadily occurring which will one day result in spiritual awakening.

Various philosophical views have been offered in an attempt to explain the religious impulse. A primitive view is that the religious urge awakened when early man wanted to know the meaning of his dreams or of the forces of nature. A popular psychological opinion, first propounded some decades ago and still believed by many, is that man turns to religion in order to resolve neurotic conflicts. Not being able to resolve such conflicts, one turns outward and projects an external object—God as a parent figure, omnipotent and omnipresent—as a substitute for a father or mother. This theory has it that only neurotic people are religious and when they resolve their psychological conflicts they will no longer need their imagined god. This view does not explain why healthy-minded and otherwise happy people also desire to have a relationship with God and to understand the meaning of life.

Religious experiences are unlike ordinary perceptions—their characteristics indicate that something more than effects of personal causes are present. Besides the uniqueness of transcendence to varying degrees, there are three other possible characteristics: 1) a genuine religious or mystical experience involves a response of one's total being—it is a complete experience; 2) it is more intense and "real" than experiences at ordinary levels of human consciousness; 3) it involves an imperative to act. Once such an episode is experienced, we have no doubt but that something unusual and extremely useful has occurred, and we are impelled to behave in accord with higher values. Results vary with individuals. Some are left with a tangible awareness of the presence of a divine power and benevolence. Some experience varying degrees of ecstasy. Still others experience degrees of revelation, insight into life processes, and knowledge of higher realms. These three results may occur together.

While we may, or may not, choose to associate with a traditional, organized religious activity, if we are the least bit responsive to the soul urge to unfold, we cannot deny our religious impulse. We may then pursue religious or mystical experience without formal affiliation with group activities or rituals.

Social involvement in religious gatherings does, however, fulfill the emotional and spiritual needs of some people. One may derive support and encouragement, and acquire a reasonable philosophical education. Within the framework of traditional religious observances the resolved devotee can privately pursue metaphysical studies as well as engage in meaningful, personal devotional routines.

When we speak of the "oneness" of religions, what is really meant is the underlying unity of purpose, not the outer forms of custom and ritual which may obviously differ, or the philosophical belief systems which widely vary. Outer religious practices differ as much as do personalities and temperaments of individuals, and it is common for us to feel most comfortable with a religious philosophy which agrees with our personal views or satisfies our soul needs.

Behind all authentic religious-philosophical views and practices is the essence which provides the inspiration and spiritual nourishment, and it is this with which we should choose to identify. While respecting all authentic (truly inspired) traditions a devotee should pursue the inner way of surrender in God and righteous living.

The philosophical views presented in this text are those of seers who have experienced direct perception of Reality. The Sanskrit term used to describe the way to enlightenment (complete understanding) is *Sanatana Dharma*, which is translated as "the eternal way of righteousness" or "the eternal religion." True religion "binds" the soul to God, as the right practice of yoga results in "union" with God. The body of knowledge referred to as "revealed truth" comprises the philosophical system taught and lived by Vedic seers.

Veda is from the verb-root *vid*, to know. *Dharma*, from the verb-root *dhri*, means "to hold, to establish" and refers to duty, righteousness, law, and order. It is that to which we adhere or hold to maintain our course in life, and that which holds and maintains us. It also refers to the fundamental law of the nature of a thing which determines its activities. When our dharma, our fundamental nature, is in harmony with the fundamental laws of divine purposes we are said to be in harmony with God's will. This is why there is such a strong emphasis upon the necessity of doing one's duty in accord with universal laws. In this way we become harmonized with evolutionary purposes and experience the full support of God *in* and *as* nature in our righteous endeavors. This is what it means to be fully surrendered in God. If we are unaware of the facts of life and do not know how to live correctly, or are unable or unwilling to do so after having been informed, we cannot experience harmony and fulfillment until our understanding and behavior are adjusted.

Some history books state that approximately six thousand years ago (estimates vary) a group of people known as *Aryans* ("noble people") migrated from a region of what is now southern Russia, southward to parts of the Middle East and northern India, and were the progenitors of the wisdom of the Vedas. India was then already populated by various groups which had their own developed culture and modes of religious worship. As

centuries passed, cultural and religious practices became inter-
mixed until today what is known as Hinduism offers an extreme
variety of viewpoints and practices. However, the findings of more
recent investigations suggest that the land now known as India
was always the home of the people of Vedic times and that
migrations from India to other parts of the world have occurred.
As of this writing, the matter is still being debated.

The religious-philosophical system of the Indo-Aryans is generally known as Brahmanism or Hinduism—both words used by
foreigners. The river Sindhu, flowing from the Arabian Sea and
forming a part of the western boundary of India, was known by
the ancient Persians as the "Hindu" river. The Greeks, who came
later, borrowed this word and changed it to "Indos," which was
later converted into the English "Indus." They referred to the
country east of the "Indos" as India. Its inhabitants became known
as Hindus and their religious philosophy and practices, Hinduism. Early European travelers and Christian missionaries coined
the word "Brahmanism" because they found the brahmin caste,
the priesthood, dominating social and religious customs and practices. India is known to its inhabitants as *Bharata* or *Bharata-
varsha*, derived from Bharata, an ancient king of that country. It
is thought by some that India once extended far beyond its present
borders and included parts of Iran and Tibet.

The eternal way of righteousness is known wherever it is self-
revealed through conscious people and is not created or possessed
by any person or group. However, in our current era, this knowledge dawned in the East and from there was spread throughout
the planet. It is unfortunate that many people still think in
regional terms, forgetting that from where one presently resides
east and west are merely relative descriptive references to directions. Because of egoism and cultural influences some people are
protective of their own views and prejudiced towards views held
by others, whether near or distant. We hear someone say that
"Eastern" and "Western" truths are different—as if truth could
be categorized by geography. Cultural modes differ while what is
true remains true. And, since all people share a common origin
and a common sameness, the way to God-realization is the same
for all people.

Vedic knowledge, "revealed truth," spread by missionary

efforts of religious teachers, and merchants and travelers following trade routes. Seekers went to India to study philosophy, mathematics, astronomy, astrology, and medicine. Books were translated into Arabic and from that language into several European languages. From India the transmission of knowledge also spread through Tibet, China, and all of Asia. Religious teachings and practices were naturally modified when adapted to other cultures but the inner essence has always been available to sincere truth students. Everything that has been known, or will be known, can be known today by anyone who is sufficiently aware to comprehend it. Within every soul—within you and me—is complete knowledge of God and the ability to actualize it.

The Major Problem
and the Only Solution

As specialized units of pure consciousness with innate knowledge and almost unlimited capacities, why is it that we are not always aware of our true nature? Why are we not more knowledgeable and freely functional? The problem is unknowingness due to wrong identification. The solution is obvious—we must find a way to awaken, to become conscious and knowledgeable, and to express our innate capacities. Identified with mind and body, the soul falsely assumes itself to be these. Endowed with drives to express, the deluded soul looks outward and attempts to satisfy its needs in the objective realms, thus creating more complications and their resulting confusions.

Central to enlightenment traditions is the teaching that we need to return attention to the source, to God, and the unmanifest field of pure consciousness. How is this done? Beginning where we are, firmly resolved and imbued with faith, we enter into a process of needed inner transformation and spiritual growth. Three steps are essential to this process—*repentance, commitment,* and *right practice.*

To *repent* means to admit our shortcomings and turn to God. To be *committed* means to be firmly decided on a constructive course of action. To *practice* means to adjust behavior so that we are able to live according to our aspiration and commitment.

Without repentance, commitment, and right practice, discipleship is impossible. Without *repentance*, we remain as we are until forced by circumstances or the grace of God to change. Without *commitment* there will be no focus, no direction of attention, or definite sense of purpose. Without *right practice*, knowledge which can only result from experience will be absent. These three steps are the great essentials for spiritual growth. If these three processes cannot be accepted, one cannot be a disciple; to pretend to be a disciple, without surrendering to them, is to be dishonest. To refuse to be a disciple is to remain in a condition of spiritual ignorance. There is no possibility of spiritual growth without discipleship and no progress without surrender and practice. Grace can intervene and cause a conversion experience, but this is rare. In the course of time the force of evolution will result in gradual spiritual awakening, a slow process. For the majority of people, burdened with the weight of mental and emotional conflicts, only *repentance, commitment*, and *right practice* affords them the way to knowledge and freedom.

For the surrendered devotee, the enlightenment path is joyous, though sometimes difficult: joyous, because of ever-new episodes of learning and spontaneous discovery; sometimes difficult, because of the tenacity of ingrained habits and tendencies. For the unsurrendered but curious seeker, the path is challenging because of resistance to learning and following through with necessary procedures to modify behavior. Behavior must change if growth is to occur. Some behavior must be willingly modified to allow one to conform to the supportive influences of grace and some behavior will change spontaneously as a result of soul unfoldment.

It is important to remember that spiritual growth can occur while we remain true to our calling in life: the role we play because it is our duty or our service-oriented activity. So long as our vocation and our lifestyle is righteous and constructive, we can continue while deepening our spiritual practices. We do not have to withdraw from the world to grow spiritually. We only have to see the world in a new and better way, give attention to important matters, and abstain from relationships and involvements which are not worthy of us; which are in no way useful to us or to the wellness of society or the planet.

The Guru-Disciple Relationship:
Its Value and Requirements

The Sanskrit word *guru* means the "light" (*ru*) which removes "darkness" (*gu*). In the highest sense God is the guru because God's radiance removes unknowingness and provides understanding and realization. Because few disciples are able to proceed on the enlightenment path without assistance, an embodied teacher is helpful. *Guru* also means "teacher." A *Satguru* is a "truth teacher" established in perfect knowledge or truth ("*sat*").

From the guru a disciple learns practical lessons, philosophy, and definite procedures for removing inner restricting characteristics and for contemplating higher realities. The guru is also the vehicle through which subtle creative forces are transmitted to the disciple, which can contribute to soul awakening and success in spiritual practices and higher meditation.

The ancient axiom "when the student is truly prepared, the teacher comes into his life" is true. To seek a guru relationship before being adequately prepared will either be fruitless or disappointing. The student must be prepared for discipleship if instructions are to be understood and the transmission of grace is to occur. The four qualifications of discipleship are:

1. *Reasonable Intelligence* – Without ability to discern, the remaining three qualifications are not possible. Even devotees who do not engage in deep study of philosophical subjects must have a degree of intelligence in order to discern their own inner changes and the subtle superconscious states which unfold. The exercise of intelligence initially enables a devotee to partially discern the fact that the relative realms are transitory and there must be a changeless and permanent *Something* which is their cause and support.

2. *Renunciation* – As a result of discernment the devotee is able to understand that nothing of the relative spheres can long endure. One is then able to relate intelligently to the world without being attached to things or to experiences. Even actions judged to be good—such as charitable works, philosophical study, performance of duty, and religious ritual—are finite, as are their effects. Since enlightenment is the result of right endeavor and

not the effect of any mundane cause, it is only indirectly related to relationships and behavior. Righteous relationships and appropriate behavior contribute to mental and emotional poise and harmony with the environment, thus removing barriers to clear perception and focused spiritual practice. Human happiness is often the direct result of our actions; God-realization is more likely when actions have ceased. Since we cannot avoid necessary actions—those which are essential to our well-being and the performance of accepted duties—we can learn to be in the world but "not of it" while fulfilling our obligations. In this way we can be settled in renunciation.

3. *Yearning for Liberation* – The primary desire of the heart (soul) is to awaken in God. When we yearn for liberation of consciousness and help ourselves to the extent that we can, soul forces are enlivened, spiritual progress is more rapid, and we attract to ourselves supportive circumstances that assist us to final freedom in God.

4. *An Ethical Foundation* – The following "six treasures" form the basis of righteous living. Their practice prepares the inner faculties for the cultivation of higher knowledge and Self-realization. 1) *Calmness* as a result of soul-awareness and trust in God. Having faith in the teaching and trust in God, one can abide in mental and emotional calm regardless of outer or inner circumstances. 2) *Self-control*, essential for regulating thoughts, feelings, behavior, and sensory impulses. While these are spontaneously regulated when superconsciousness is influential, until superconscious influences are completely dominant the devotee must be self-disciplined by exercising self-control. 3) As a result of calmness and self-control the devotee becomes *settled in the Self*, inwardly stable to the degree that efforts to remain calm and in control are easy or nonexistent. 4) Thus inwardly settled the devotee is able to *endure changing conditions* with perfect detachment. 5) *Perfect concentration* is now possible, for the purpose of achieving all worthy goals and for success in meditation practice. 6) *Constant yearning* to know God and to experience soul freedom should prevail until one is fully supported by superconscious perceptions and God's grace. Until then, the devotee should remain focused on God and let the yearning of his heart inspire him to devotion and disciplined practice.

Hearing, reflection, and *meditation* are the three disciplines for the fully prepared disciple. Upon hearing the words of the guru the disciple should retain them in memory and reflect upon them. Instruction can also come through the written word. This is a kind of "hearing" because reading informs us. All instruction should be reflected upon until true knowledge is comprehended. Further, the devotee should meditate regularly to clear the mind of distractions and experience superconsciousness for the purpose of directly knowing and experiencing God.

The discipleship path is not always easy. If we are overly influenced by sensory impulses and attached to circumstances, things, and personal self-limiting beliefs, we will be challenged. Removing these restrictions is the purpose of discipleship.

How does one who is sincere on the enlightenment path find the guru? The first step is preparation. The universal law of correspondences is that when our desires conform to our receptivity, life presents us with our heart's desire. If the devotee has never had a guru relationship he will be led to the one which best suits his needs and that relationship will persist until the disciple experiences liberation of consciousness. It may be that the disciple will be led to renew a relationship which was started in a prior incarnation and will meet with the guru again, or be led to one of the guru's representatives if the guru is not accessible. If neither the guru or disciple-representatives are available, the seeker will be led to a qualified teacher who will provide necessary instruction and encouragement.

The true guru is God. A disciple should not attempt to overly personalize the guru relationship, find fault with the guru, or ignore the guru's instructions. The guru has already been through human conditions and is no longer interested in such matters, except for the purpose of showing the disciple the way to higher understanding and God-realization. Paramahansaji often said, "I am not the guru. God is the guru; I am only his servant. Some Western philosophers, lacking understanding, have said that truth students in the West cannot accept a guru-disciple relationship because their self-reliant attitude is incompatible with having to surrender egoism; therefore, perhaps another path is better for them. This is, of course, nonsense. Egoism must be surrendered if Self-realization is to be experienced. Hundreds of thousands of dedicated disciples in the West are proof that the way of righteousness, the way of surrender to God, is the way to inner peace and God-realization.

The Processes of Cosmic Manifestation

One Life, Being, Power, and Substance is responsible for the manifestation, maintenance, and transformation of nature. This Reality is referred to variously by sages and seers. A term commonly used is *Consciousness*—as self-existent, self-aware, and self-referring. Consciousness requires no object to support its existence; it is simultaneously the knower and the known. Consciousness can be known about by objective and subjective analysis, but it can only be fully comprehended by direct perception.

Thousands (some say hundreds of thousands) of years ago, sages contemplated the nature of Consciousness and discovered how and why the universe came into manifestation. They learned of fine and subtle interactions occurring throughout the field of nature, how souls become involved with matter, the laws of causation, and the way to enlightenment and final freedom. This understanding they shared with qualified students and communicated through oral and written transmission. A seer always affirms that what is taught is but a restatement of that which has always been available to know. There may be new discoveries but there are no new truths.

From the initial impulse within the unmanifest field of Consciousness, through to full material manifestation, the processes can be understood by examining the twenty-four categories of cosmic manifestation. This is the philosophical understanding known as *Samkhya*: the numbering or categorizing of the stages of Consciousness as it manifests and expresses. While explaining these processes, no suggestion is made that Consciousness is separated; only that aspects of Consciousness which become specialized for the purpose of making possible various functions in nature are examined and explained.

Consciousness alone expresses as all variations of life throughout the universe, from the Godhead to the physical realms. Consciousness as Existence is the Beingness, the inner Reality, of everything. Consciousness as Power expresses as all variations of force and energy in nature and makes possible all actions and forms. Where you are, where I am, Consciousness is the single Reality. Since knowledge of Consciousness is grounded in itself and we are units of mind-identified consciousness, knowledge of Supreme Consciousness, God, and nature is within us. All that we need to know to function effectively in this or any realm, is presently available because Consciousness is omnipresent.

If this view of life is new to you, many years may be required before complete comprehension unfolds. You may experience episodes of enlightenment during which you clearly comprehend the reality of God and the actions of cosmic processes. As you persist, your innate capacities will unfold and you will become a shining example of surrendered discipleship. Whatever your philosophical or religious background, an understanding of the processes of cosmic manifestation will clear your doubts and reveal the inner meaning of life. What was formerly concealed will be revealed and spiritual growth will be greatly accelerated.

The Unmanifest Field of Pure Consciousness *(Category One)*

The absolute, transcendental Reality underlying all manifestation is devoid of characteristics, yet contains within itself limitless possibilities. It is the source of every outer expression while remaining removed from that which it manifests; that is, its influences make possible the field of nature but its essential condition remains stable and self-complete. It causes all actions but is not itself acted upon. Devotees can become aware of it during interludes of spontaneous transcendence and train themselves to experience it at will by correctly practicing superconscious meditation. Though known, it cannot be described in words sufficient to satisfy the mind or intellect.

The unmanifest field is "something" even though sometimes referred to as a void. Its voidness is absence of modification, not absence of existence. While it remains outside of the boundaries of space-time, relative manifestations in the field of nature indicate its existence, as effects indicate their causes.

**The Godhead: Initial Manifest Being
and Its Field of Operation** *(Category Two)*

The Godhead is the first unfoldment from the unmanifest field of Consciousness. The origin of the word *God* can be traced via the Germanic languages to their Indo-European roots, in which a corresponding ancestor form means "the invoked one," from Sanskrit *hu,* meaning "invoke the gods." This is found in the *Rig Veda,* presently the oldest known religious scripture.

Unlike the unmanifest field which has no discernible characteristics, the field of God has attributes which can be examined, discussed, known about, and experienced. Complete knowledge of God, however, can only be directly known.

In the Godhead, three attributes or qualities prevail. These are the gunas, the results of the interplay of polarity, which regulate forces within the field of God and nature. *Guna* means "that which restrains or contains." These attributes make possible changes and transformations of forces. *Sattva,* is elevating and luminous; *rajas* influences change and transformation; and *tamas* contributes to heaviness or inertia.

Being also present in the field of nature they are influential in contributing to changes and transformations in mind and body as well as to changes in states of consciousness. Sattva guna returns forces in nature to the field of God. Rajas guna impels change and transformation. Tamas guna makes possible gross manifestation. On the spiritual path a devotee overcomes tamasic influences by engaging in purposeful actions, regulates rajasic influences by cultivating sattvic qualities, and finally transcends even the influences of sattva guna.

During preliminary superconscious meditation states, tamas guna can contribute to dullness, rajas to shifting perceptions, and sattva to focused contemplation. During transcendent states the gunas no longer influence.

**Movement in the Direction of Outer
Manifestation** *(Category Three)*

When the gunas, the regulating attributes within the field of the Godhead, are in a state of equilibrium the field of God is self-contained and the universe is nonexistent. When equilibrium is disturbed, the universe unfolds. The *Bhagavad Gita* 8:16-19:

> From the realm of Brahma [God as manifesting influence] through to the fullness of creation, all the worlds revolve again and again. Upon returning to the source there is no more rebirth. People who know day and night know that the day of Brahma (God manifesting) extends to a thousand aeons. All the manifest entities arise from the unmanifest field upon the coming of the day, and upon the coming of the night they dissolve into that very thing called the unmanifest. The aggregate of beings and elements, born again and again, is dissolved at the coming of the night, quite helplessly, and is produced again upon the arrival of the day.

A *day* of universal manifestation persists for billions of solar years and an equal "duration" is the occasion of nonmanifestation after creation is drawn back into the field of God.

Since the gunas permanently persist in the field of God, when one is influential the others are present with potential. This is why even sattva guna has to be transcended by the devotee, because so long as one's consciousness is supported by it, the possibility of rajasic and tamasic influences becoming instrumental remains. A devotee may feel, "Now that I am established in bliss consciousness and possessed of knowledge, I have attained." However, subtle awareness of being blissful and knowledgeable is evidence of nontranscendence, as is awareness of "I am experiencing this." Even the gods can fall from a high state of consciousness as a result of the influences of the gunas.

Because the soul is a unit of consciousness, we can direct attention inward to experience soul awareness, which is the same as God's awareness. In this way we can determine the nature of God and have faith to continue our spiritual practices.

Individualization and Self-Involvement of Consciousness *(Category Four)*

The *Word*, the primordial creative force endowed with intelligence, is the "self-begotten" of God. Everything else in the universe is an expression of this creative force. As it flows, it acts upon itself to express as the forces and aspects of nature. The sound-frequency of the Word is the result of the outflowing force and its inherent attracting influence. Tamas guna is influential in the outflowing movement and sattva guna is influential as the attraction back to the source. The result is a vibratory manifestation which gives rise to expressions of this force; hence, it is referred to as the Word (*Om*), the field from which all other vibrational aspects emerge and into which they eventually dissolve.

Acting upon itself this force unfolds four aspects which can be contemplated and discerned by a devotee:

1. *Creative Force* – The expressive, enlivening force which contributes to manifestation, maintenance, and transformation. It is the expression of cosmic power in the universe and in all animate forms, from atoms to man. By listening to Om, during meditation and at all times, one becomes attuned to this creative force and experiences unity with it. By contemplating it and following the inner sound back to its source, the meditator's attention is led to the field of God.

2. *Space* – The field in which events occur in contrast to infinite emptiness in which nothing occurs. Space-fields are pervaded by forces which allow circumstances to occur, resulting in curves and boundaries in space so that the "space" in which our universe expresses is different from other spaces in which other universes occur. Such spaces can interpenetrate without influencing each other, so an infinite number of space-time universes can emanate from the field of pure consciousness.

3. *Time* – Time coexists with space; hence the term space-time is used to refer to the field in which events occur. From our relative viewpoint time may seem to be a succession of moments, and may seem to be directional, flowing from past to present to future. Our time-direction may be peculiar to our present notion of time. There may be different directions of time, or time may be a field along with space in which events occur according to our perception of them. It may actually be possible to travel in various directions in the field of time, or to detach consciousness from the time-field and observe past, present, and possible futures from a neutral perspective.

4. *Fine Material Forces and Particles* – These forces and particles are the basis of manifest creation and have their origins in light, which has its origin in Consciousness. The universe is a play of cosmic forces and of electromagnetic field frequencies which have wavelengths and colors. We see but a minute fraction of existing frequencies in our environment—perhaps only one-billionth of the entire range. With instrumentation we can discern the existence of radio waves, gamma rays, microwaves, X-rays, and others. Atoms are not the smallest aspects of matter. They are units of matter, small universes influenced by electromagnetic fields and containing particles and fine forces which influence their actions.

By manifesting outwardly the Word externalizes or embodies itself. Originating in the Godhead, the Word is inseparable from God "as the power of fire to burn is really the fire itself."

The Sanskrit word for this primal field of nature is *maya*, from the verb-root *ma*—"to measure, to limit, to give form." It is form-producing and truth-veiling. It is the womb of creation and makes possible manifestation, which is why in some religious teachings it is referred to as Divine Mother, the feminine aspect of God which gives birth to the world.

Because manifestation veils Reality, it obscures the perception of Reality for the soul involved with it. Identified with the outer, we cannot perceive the inner. We are aware of effects but not the causes of effects. Our studies and spiritual practices are for the purpose of enabling us to understand and to perceive the inner side of life—the subjective fields which are not discernible through senses and mind.

The field of nature is not an illusion. It does exist. However, it is *illusory*—it is not what it appears to be when looked upon from the outside. With veiled powers of intuition and intelligence, the embodied soul, examining the outer field of nature and not comprehending the inner side, experiences misperception—falsely assuming the impermanent to be permanent and believing the field of nature to be the only reality because unable to discern and understand what is behind it. This inability to know the truth is referred to as delusion based on unknowingness: ignorance of the facts.

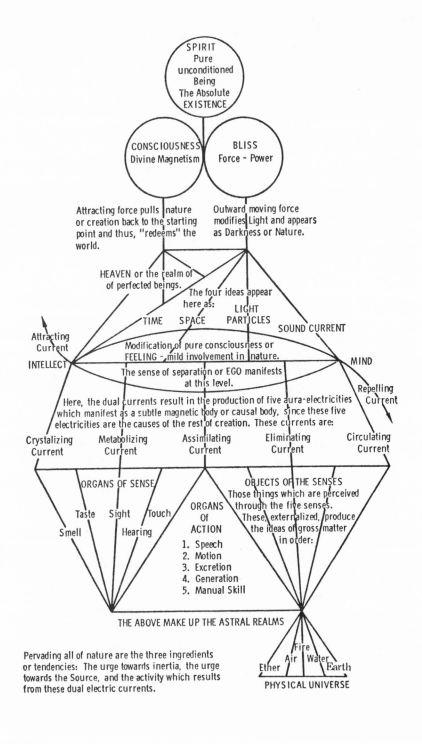

SPIRIT
Pure
unconditioned
Being
The Absolute
EXISTENCE

CONSCIOUSNESS
Divine Magnetism

BLISS
Force – Power

Attracting force pulls nature
or creation back to the starting
point and thus, "redeems" the
world.

Outward moving force
modifies Light and appears
as Darkness or Nature.

HEAVEN or the realm of
of perfected beings.

The four ideas appear
here as:

LIGHT
TIME   SPACE   PARTICLES

SOUND CURRENT

Attracting
Current

Modification of pure consciousness or
FEELING – mild involvement in nature.

MIND

INTELLECT

The sense of separation or EGO manifests
at this level.

Repelling
Current

Here, the dual currents result in the production of five aura-electricities
which manifest as a subtle magnetic body or causal body, since these five
electricities are the causes of the rest of creation. These currents are:

Crystalizing
Current

Metabolizing
Current

Assimilating
Current

Eliminating
Current

Circulating
Current

ORGANS OF SENSE

OBJECTS OF THE SENSES
Those things which are perceived
through the five senses.
These, externalized, produce
the ideas of gross matter
in order:

Taste   Sight   Touch

Smell   Hearing

ORGANS
Of
ACTION
1. Speech
2. Motion
3. Excretion
4. Generation
5. Manual Skill

THE ABOVE MAKE UP THE ASTRAL REALMS

Pervading all of nature are the three ingredients
or tendencies: The urge towards inertia, the urge
towards the Source, and the activity which results
from these dual electric currents.

Fire
Air   Water
Ether   Earth

PHYSICAL UNIVERSE

Born into the field of matter the soul so completely identifies with matter that it temporarily loses its ability to apprehend the fine aspects which make the manifestation of matter possible. Thus sense-bound, the soul is in need of being awakened from material consciousness to divine consciousness. Unless a sense-imprisoned soul awakens, it cannot fully comprehend the field of nature or the reality of God.

Philosophers with clouded understanding may vainly try to explain away the field of nature by simply stating that it does not exist! While expressing through a body and mind formed of the substance of nature they dismiss it as not "real." When seers say that the universe is not real they mean that it does not have independent existence and is not permanent as it presently expresses. They teach that the only thing that is Real is Consciousness which makes possible the realms in manifestation. They do not deny the existence of the universe: they merely point to *That* which is its cause and support. Simultaneous with the manifestation of the creative force is the expression of God which enlivens nature as well as tends to attract the field of nature back to the field of God. Awakening to this level of God-expression the soul rises free from unconscious involvement with the field of nature, with maya. This aspect of God is given many names. It is known as *Kutastha Consciousness*, "the one on the summit," the immutable Self of God which remains above, or removed from, objective realms. Within us, it is the witness consciousness which remains aloof from the changes of nature and remains untouched by the conflicting forces present in mind and body. It is the cause of grace: that which "redeems" the soul and the worlds. Its redemptive influence is known as the activity of the Holy Spirit and it is to this we surrender in order to be lifted from involvement with the senses and mental agitations.

Simplistic explanations for the purpose of world-manifestation have been offered from time to time to pacify unenlightened minds. "God was lonely," one story goes, "so he created the worlds to have companionship and to enjoy himself." Another story has it that God created the worlds to give souls an opportunity to choose a relationship with him, or to deny him and be punished. Such speculations reveal ignorance and insult our intelligence.

World manifestation is the result of "purposeless necessity."

Self-contained, Consciousness requires no purpose for doing what It does. It *is* and It *expresses*. The "necessity" is due to the fluctuations of the gunas in the field of God. In relative spheres nature can be said to have purpose because it supports souls on the awakening path.

Illumination of consciousness results in knowledge which liberates the soul. It can be useful to engage in philosophical analysis of God and the universe so long as such inquiry leads to higher understanding. It is futile, however, to stir shallow intellectual waters only for the purpose of providing stimulation to an already restless mind. For this reason seers often counsel their disciples to deepen their spiritual practices and avoid useless speculation about that which they are not presently able to comprehend. When asked to describe the nature of truth a seer may remain silent: eloquent testimony of That which is beyond the range of the senses.

When the primordial force out of which all matter emerges is expressive, sattva guna influences the production of the celestial realms which remain beyond the spheres of gross manifestation, including astral and causal realms. Celestial spheres are resting places for souls not yet involved with matter and for souls awakening from the realms of matter. Celestial realms are not the final destination. There, souls can continue their spiritual awakening or they can again become involved with matter, depending upon their inclinations and the influences of the gunas upon their states of consciousness.

From the celestial realms some souls flow into involvement with matter as a result of the influence of the gunas. They can then become fully deluded and have to awaken from that condition, or they can retain a degree of awareness and become involved with only causal and astral realms, never coming into involvement with the physical universe. If they flow into involvement with subtle or physical realms and retain conscious awareness, they are known as divine incarnations or avatars: manifestations of divine light and power. Their presence enlivens the natural order and their understanding provides souls in need of learning, the way to spiritual awakening and freedom. It is the understanding of such souls that is shared with you in these pages. What is here explained is not a philosophical belief system, but the revealed truth as shared by illumined souls settled in God-realization.

The Field of Cosmic Mind *(Category Five)*

Self-aware Consciousness modified by a degree of individuality pervades this field. The influence of tamas guna results in the modification of individuality. Rajas guna influences cause the production of the aspect of the Cosmic Mental Field which makes possible the processing of information. Sattva guna influences produce the aspect which makes discernment possible, the intellect. Cosmic Mind is a field with the aspects of awareness, individuality, mental processes, and intellect.

The light of Consciousness shining on the field of primal nature enlivens it, and the blending of light with primal nature results in the field of Cosmic Mind. This becomes a covering for Consciousness: a veil through which it can further manifest in the relative spheres. We say, then, that God expresses self-veiling power through the agency of self-manifesting creative force. Spirit and nature, dual aspects of manifesting Consciousness, express as the cosmic dance of creation. God is cause; nature is effect. God determines; nature produces forms making possible world manifestation.

The Mind-World Connecting Principles and Their Essences and Products
(Categories Six to Twenty-Four)

The essence of a thing is its fundamental cause and support. The spiritualized field of Cosmic Awareness has five expressions of aura electricities. From these are produced five subtle organs of cognition which make possible sensory perception, five subtle organs of action which make possible expression, and five subtle element-influences which make possible the manifestation of objective nature (the gross material elements and their forms).

Because of the interaction of attraction and repulsion (the influences of the attracting nature of God and the outflowing tendency), a magnetic field is produced in which the five aura-electricities appear. This forms the causal field from which fur-

ther relative fields are produced. The five aura-electricities manifest due to the influences of the gunas: two from the extremities,
the positive and negative poles (sattva and tamas); one from the
middle (rajas); and two from the gaps in between. The five aura-
electricities are the result, respectively, of: sattva, tamas, rajas,
sattva-rajas, and rajas-tamas.

These guna-influences produce the fine essences of all that is
further manifested. During superconscious meditative contemplation, when attention is withdrawn from sensory objects and
mental processes, these fine essences can be perceived as: sound
frequencies, the basis of mantra; lights, because each sound frequency produces light radiations; and tastes. Such contemplation is usually related to the chakras, through which fineessences
express in the astral and physical bodies.

The entire play of creation is nothing more than the manifestation of cosmic forces influenced by the gunas, the regulating
aspects of nature due to polarized creative force.

Disciples of the Kriya Yoga path learn of inner causes which
produce and support nature and practice helpful meditation techniques which enable them to become aware of, work with, and
transcend cosmic forces. Becoming proficient in practice, the devotee consciously unfolds soul capacities and is able to comprehend
the characteristics and actions of cosmic forces in manifestation
while continuing to experience progressive states of higher awareness. Outflowing forces result in:

1. *Mind and Sense Perceptions* – The positive electric
attributes of the five aura-electricities under the influence of sattva guna are the organs of sense perception: smell, taste, touch,
sight, and hearing. These, attracted by the negative pole of spiritualized awareness (the mind), produce a magnetic field, the
mental sheath. The mind is the abode of subtle sense perceptions. Sensory input is here received, perceived, and presented
to the intellect for interpretation. Because the mind is the dwelling place of subtle sense perceptions, it is possible to experience
vivid sensations during dreams (and during occasions of mental
imagery) without external influence.

2. *Astral Body and Organs of Action* – The neutralizing
attributes of the five aura-electricities under the influence of rajas

guna are the organs of action: speech, mobility (legs and feet), manual dexterity (arms and hands), elimination, and reproduction. Under the influence of rajas guna the aura-electricities produce the astral body, the sheath of life force or prana.

3. *Element-Influences and Objects of Perception* – The negative electric attributes under the influence of tamas guna are the causes of the manifestation of objective aspects of the aura-electricities, which enable the senses to perceive objects. These are the subtle senses of smell, taste, sight, touch, and hearing, enabling perception of external objects and the satisfaction of desire so that desires are neutralized.

These fifteen attributes, along with the faculty of intelligence and mind, enable the I-identified unit of awareness to function in the relative spheres. Together, these attributes and their fields constitute the fine material body used by the matter-involved soul. The soul, after having become involved with these influences, may retain them through a series of physical incarnations, and in subtle spheres, until they are no longer needed and finally discarded when the soul awakens to complete transcendental realization.

4. *Element-Influences and Physical Manifestation* – The five subtle element-influences (the objects of the senses) in combination produce the gross physical realms. From Shankara's treatise on *Self-Knowledge*:

> The world, filled with attachments and aversions, and the rest [all other characteristics common to the deluded condition], is like a dream; it appears to be real as long as one is ignorant but becomes unreal when one is awake. The world appears to be real as long as nondual Consciousness, which is the basis of it all, is not known. It is like any illusion, having no basis of its own. All the various forms exist in the imagination of the perceiver, the substratum being the eternal and all-pervading Consciousness whose nature is existence and intelligence. Names and forms are like rings and bracelets and Consciousness is like the gold from which they are formed. As the all-pervading space appears to vary on account of its association with various forms which are different from each other, and remains pure upon the dissolution of the form-giving qualities, so also the omnipresent Lord (Consciousness as creative

manifesting power) appears to be diverse on account of association with various form-building qualities and remains pure and one upon the dissolution of these qualities. Owing to its association with various restricting qualities and attributes, such ideas as differences, color, and category or status, are superimposed on Supreme Consciousness, as flavor, color, and worth are attributed to water [when it is so influenced]. The physical body, the medium through which the soul experiences pleasure and pain, is determined by past actions and formed out of the five great subtle elements which become gross matter when one-half portion of one subtle element-influence becomes united with one-eighth portion of each of the others.

Just as the three gunas exist together as manifestations of polarized creative force regardless of which one is dominant, so the five element-influences, products of the actions of the gunas, exist together as manifestations of the gunas regardless of which one is dominant. This is why it is said that one-half portion (the dominant manifestation) of each element-influence is united with one-eighth portion of the other element-influences. Ether, air, fire, and water influences exist in earth manifestation; ether, air, fire, and earth element-influences exist in water manifestation; ether, air, water, and earth element-influences exist in fire manifestation; ether, fire, water, and earth exist in air manifestation; and air, fire, water, and earth exist in ether manifestation. This is why matter can be transformed. Some masters can, by an act of will, transform matter. Mahavatar Babaji has poured water on fire and the fire increased in intensity. He said, "I look for the oil in water and call it forth."

The element-influences express in the physical realm as governing influences which determine the basic constitution of life forms and their functions. From this understanding the science of *Ayurveda* ("life-knowledge") evolved: an approach to wellness based on balancing element-influences of the mind and body. When element-influences are imbalanced an organism's constitution becomes disorganized. When element-influences are balanced, an organism's constitution remains well and function is optimal. When our constitution is balanced we experience radiant health, psychological wellness, and mental clarity.

The five gross physical elements; five subtle element-influences; five subtle organs of perception; five subtle organs of action; along with mind; the organ of discernment (faculty of intelligence); egoism; and the modified field of soul awareness which allows feeling, comprise the twenty-four principles of cosmic manifestation. The twenty-fifth principle is the field of pure consciousness. The cosmic body includes God as the Oversoul and all of the manifestations of the attributes of the gunas expressing in the field of nature. As cosmic processes are directed from the field of God, so our body processes can be directed from soul awareness. We can discover the reality of the universe, and God, by turning within and learning of the forces and attributes used by the soul while involved in the field of matter. By realizing our soul nature, we can comprehend God.

The Seven Spheres of Creation

Seven spheres of expressive creative force provide the fields of operation for cosmic processes and embodied souls. From the negative pole of nature, a creative force is repulsed that flows out to produce the worlds. From the positive pole an attracting influence keeps world-manifestation in balance and eventually redeems creation by pulling all forces of nature back to the source. Primal nature veils divine light rays and the attracting influence unveils them. The projecting power, through the action of tamas guna, produces forms. The transformative influence of rajas guna maintains nature. The purifying influence of sattva guna renders forms more capable of expressing the finer qualities of life:

1. *The Sphere of God* – This is referred to as the sphere of truth, of Reality. Souls which awaken to this sphere and reside therein can pass beyond it, remain in it, or be again sent forth into involvement with manifest creation if tamas guna becomes influential. If rajas guna prevails in soul awareness, the soul will perceive what occurs in the realm of God and relate to activities in this realm. If sattva guna prevails the soul will experience existence-bliss. Avatars come from the field of God into the field of nature to function in spheres or realms this side

of primal manifestation.

2. *The Sphere of the Holy Spirit* – The sphere expressed when the impulse to manifest becomes influential. The Holy Spirit, the enlivening influence of the Godhead, contributes to movement in the direction of further manifestation and regulates internal processes of creation. When conscious of this sphere, the awakening soul detaches from manifest realms and becomes increasingly aware of the realm of God.

3. *The Sphere of Spiritual Reflection* – This specialized manifestation occurs when rays of God's light shine on the field of primal nature. It is the sphere of Cosmic Individuality as well as the sphere of soul individuality—the sense of independent selfhood or existence apart from God—which contributes to further involvement with matter. Souls are not created; they are rays of God's consciousness involved with matter. This is the sphere of conscious souls referred to as gods, goddesses, or *devas*, "shining ones."

4. *The Sphere of Primal Substance* – The sphere of spiritual reflection and the sphere of primal substance are dual expressions of outflowing creative force. Spirit and nature mix to further the manifesting process. From here emanate aspects of creative force, including electromagnetism, gravity, and weak and strong forces. This is the realm of primal nature produced from Om, space, time, and fine essences of cosmic forces which are not yet matter but have potential to manifest as matter.

5. *The Sphere of Magnetism* – The causal realm with five aura-electricities which make possible further projections of cosmic forces enabling nature to fully manifest.

6. *The Sphere of Electric Attributes and Fine Matters* – The astral realm. Here are manifested the subtle organs of sense perception, organs of action, and element-influences.

7. *The Sphere of Material Manifestation* – The physical universe. The full projection of creative force as objective nature.

Within the body are seven primary vital places through which life forces flow to perform various functions. Located along the cerebrospinal pathway, they are commonly referred to as *chakras* ("wheels"), centers of vital, radiating forces. As one's states of consciousness are identified with these centers, so levels of awareness are determined. In accord with our prevailing states of consciousness, we perceive ourselves and our environment. A Kriya Yoga meditator learns to ascend through these chakras, withdrawing attention from external circumstances in order to explore inner realms. Awareness of the seven spheres of cosmic manifestation is experienced: the devotee apprehends the field of God and proceeds to awaken to liberation of consciousness. The seven spheres and the seven chakras represent the fourteen stages of creation. Identified with the chakras while attention is flowing outward, soul awareness remains objective. Ascending the chakras and experiencing progressive stages of release, the soul acquires access to subjective realms.

The Unveiling of the Organs
of Action and Perception

Souls, specialized units of God's consciousness, are screened by five coverings or sheaths.

1. *The Covering of Primal Nature* – The innermost sheath of the soul is referred to as the "heart." Experiencing the bliss of existence, the soul rests in supreme Self-satisfaction. Only a fine veil of primal nature then veils soul awareness.
2. *Knowledge Sheath* – Comprised of the manifestations of the magnetic-aura-electricities of the organ of intelligence which determines what is truth. This is the seat of perfect knowledge.
3. *Mental Sheath* – Where impressions and memory accumulate, confusing the mind and causing effects.
4. *Life Force Sheath* – The seat of the organs of action, comprised of life forces, the astral body.
5. *Physical Sheath* – Body of gross matter, nourished by food.

When a universe manifests as fine, gaseous, fiery, liquid, and solid matters, the visible world appears. From a singularity, a source-point without dimensions, the substance of the universe unfolds. All of the energy to be expressed in and as the universe is present in this original source-point and never increases or decreases; it only undergoes transformation.

When planets are suitable for the emergence of life, billions of solar years after their manifestation, Divine Attraction begins to unveil omnipotent energy which enlivens creation. When the cosmic sheath containing the organs of action is unveiled, the vegetable kingdom emerges. When the cosmic sheath containing the organs of sense perception is unveiled, simple organisms and higher life forms are evolved. When the cosmic sheath comprised of electrical properties which make possible the faculty of intelligence is unveiled, humankind emerges. When enlightened souls experience the unveiling of the innermost sheath, they express freely. They are liberated even though a final phase of awakening yet awaits them. When this sheath is transcended, souls complete their awakening to full enlightenment.

Reincarnation, Karma and the Fulfillment of Destiny

An awakening soul can progress spiritually while physically embodied and continue unfoldment in astral, causal, and celestial realms. Conditions are not always ideal for every soul. Life in the body may be terminated before much progress is made, sense attachments may result in bondage to objective realms, and psychological conflicts may inhibit mental and spiritual growth. Many people die to the world only slightly more conscious than when they were born into it; some even less so. Few dimly understand the nature and workings of the cosmos or know of their divine potential. Some, with partial understanding and feeble aspiration, are unable to focus on essentials for the purpose of quickening spiritual progress.

It is obvious, then, that upon departing this world unable to function in more subtle ones, we may be drawn back into a physical body for the purpose of improving our understanding and working out our salvation, our soul freedom.

Our awareness of being, however dim, is proof to us that we are more than mind or body. When alone and quiet we also know that when we depart the body we will continue to exist. Habitual states of consciousness determine our capacity to relate to environmental circumstances. This means that our present status corresponds to our states of consciousness. When our consciousness is clear and our understanding sufficient, we can function where we are with insight and choose to experience circumstances more suitable to our growth and expression.

Souls tend to be attracted to circumstances which conform to their states of consciousness or which offer an opportunity for the satisfaction of desires or the fulfillment of purposes. Unconscious souls move through space-time influenced by their whims, their conscious or unconscious desires, or by the forces of nature and the trends of circumstances. Living without understanding, they accumulate memories of pleasure, pain, success, failure, and the traumas of misfortune. These memories comprise the karmic condition—the storehouse of mental causes which modify attitudes and behaviors, and cause various effects.

Besides the karmic influences brought with us when we are born into a physical body, other factors can be influential. The basic psychophysiological constitution inherited from our parents somewhat contributes to how we function. Learned and acquired characteristics assumed during formative years add further influences, as do our ongoing involvements and life experiences. The more soul-centered we are, the less we are influenced by karmic patterns, environmental influences, or the opinions of others. The less soul-centered, the more likely we are to be influenced by our mental and emotional characteristics and outer influences.

As of this writing, the global human population is almost six billion, which is probably more than the total number of people to have ever lived on Planet Earth. Where are all these souls coming from? The astral and causal realms are teeming with trillions of souls, and souls can also come into the human condition through the various streams of more highly complex life forms evolving on the planet. There are other planets in the physical universe where souls are undergoing growth experiences.

The process of reincarnation requires no objective proof and there is no need for a beginning truth student to struggle to fully understand the process. What is more important is soul unfoldment and God-realization. Understanding of cosmic processes will unfold as spiritual growth occurs.

The way to avoid future complications is to learn to live in harmony with nature's laws and to be God-surrendered. In this way constructive habits are acquired, sensory impulses are regulated, karmic drives are neutralized or transformed into constructive behaviors, legitimate desires are fulfilled, and understanding of the operations of the mind is acquired. Such intentional involvement brings us into harmony with life's larger plan for us and grace becomes increasingly evident, assisting us to experience the fulfillment of our soul destiny.

Fate has to do with the almost certain effects of existing causes, unless these causes are modified or eliminated. If our states of consciousness are conditioned, effects are predictable.

Destiny has to do with soul fulfillment—of playing out a useful role in the world, experiencing circumstances which further our growth, and being impelled by God's grace to progress on the awakening path. It is the fulfillment of soul destiny that we should desire, not the satisfaction of egocentric desires.

With even a little spiritual awakening, grace becomes influential in our lives, adjusting events, providing learning opportunities, and impelling our continued soul unfoldment. We then may experience guidance, unexpected meetings with people which support our progress, and deserved but unearned elevations of consciousness. At such times we are aware that useful changes are taking place which we could not have contrived.

When we are in the stream of grace, help is given us in ways obvious and not always so obvious. When we are limited to conditioned human consciousness we share an attunement with others who are restricted. When we begin to experience more expansive states of consciousness, we share an attunement with souls whose perceptions are more cosmic.

The influence of the gunas upon our states of consciousness reflect as mental attitudes and personal behaviors.

The *Bhagavad Gita* 16:1-3:

> Courage, purity of mind, wise use of knowledge, concentration, generosity, self-control and right use of abilities, along with faithful study of scriptures and noble purpose; nonviolence, truth, freedom from anger, renunciation, tranquility, freedom from finding fault, compassion to all, freedom from envy; gentleness, quiet manner and faithfulness, vigor, forgiveness, persistence, selflessness, freedom from the desire to harm another, and freedom from excessive pride—these are the natural endowments of a person who is born with a divine nature.

Intentional endeavors should be supported by behaviors which are characteristic of spontaneous expressions of soul qualities. When sattva guna prevails in our consciousness we are impelled to behave like this. When sattva guna no longer impels and we are living from soul awareness, these are natural behaviors.

When tamas guna is dominant, and we are self-centered and restless, we behave accordingly. The *Bhagavad Gita* 16:4-24:

> A tendency to show off, arrogance, excessive pride, anger, harshness, and ignorance; these are the endowments of a person with a negative nature. The positive endowments are said to make for quick deliverance (from bondage to the senses); the negative endowments make for greater attachment and trouble. People who incarnate with a preponderance of positive endowments are sure to succeed, for they have a spiritual destiny. We have described the nature of divine beings; now let us consider the nature of those who are influenced by negative tendencies. Such people do not know (or seem to care about) the way of renunciation and freedom. Their consciousness is not pure, their conduct is not righteous, and they are slaves to darkness. Such people are materialists who do not comprehend the truth that the world has a spiritual basis. These people, because of their ignorance, are enemies of the world. They think in terms of destruction instead of orderly unfoldment and the perpetuation of the worlds. They are controlled by insatiable desire, full of hypocrisy, excessive pride and arrogance; they are deluded and have impure motives. The gratification of their desires is their highest aim in life. Such people seek wealth for wealth's sake. They feel themselves to be the doers of all action and do not turn within for higher guidance. Eventually they become bewildered and even more involved with delusion. These people, given to self-conceit, force, and pride, spend incarnation after incarnation in a dark, negative condition. The gateway to pain and seemingly endless delusion is threefold: lust (uncontrolled, passionate desire), anger, and greed. These three should be renounced if freedom is desired. A person who discards advice to be found in scriptures and is a slave to personal desires does not attain Self-realization, the highest goal. Therefore, let the words of the wise be the authority for determining what course of action should be taken and what should be avoided.

The *Bhagavad Gita* 17:7-19:

> By the foods we eat, and by our manner of giving, the level of understanding can be determined. Those who are on the upward way choose foods which promote life, vitality, strength, health, joy, and cheerfulness. Restless people are attracted to foods which are overly seasoned and overly stimulate the system. Lower types eat foods which are tasteless, stale, and unclean. High-minded people give according to scriptural law, without any expectation whatever of reward. They give wisely because they feel it their duty to make right use of the substance of this world. Restless people give selfishly for the sake of expected reward and for personal recognition. The lower types give grudgingly, if at all, without faith, and they try to acquire things for nothing, without making just compensation. Discipline of the body includes reverence for the spiritual teacher, pure intentions, cleanliness, control of vital energies, and nonviolence. Discipline of speech includes kind speech and truthfulness. Discipline of the mind includes silence at appropriate times, self-control, and high resolve. These are to be observed without any expectation of reward. Whatever we do to satisfy egoism is not of lasting value. Harming ourselves or others is destructive and evidence of ignorance.

Spontaneous behavior is the natural result of inner grace. But until grace is operational, until we behave righteously without having to think about it, we are advised to exercise self-discipline, live righteously, bring our lives into harmony with nature's laws, and do constructive things to contribute to the well-being of all life.

On the enlightenment path we are not merely interested in learning the extent to which mental conditionings determine states of consciousness and behavior; we want to discover, by observation and experimentation, what lies beyond the realm of the conditioned state. It does not require too much study to understand how social, cultural, and religious conditionings influence us and how to separate ourselves from such conditionings. We need to discover the deeper drives which influence us: the karmic impressions and life-urges which arise from the unconscious and influence our otherwise conscious behavior. For this we need to study the teachings of the seers and engage in introspective contemplation during superconscious meditation— going beyond superficial mental levels to the very core of life from which impulses arise. We need to learn to allow constructive impulses freedom to express, while restraining destructive impulses or redirecting their forces for constructive purposes.

One problem that may be confronted on the self-discovery path is that of maintaining our integrity in relationship to others. What is recommended is to be outwardly appropriate while inwardly committed to God-realization. Our lifestyle should enable us to fulfill our obligations while we continue our spiritual practices and explore higher states of consciousness. We should not be double-minded: we cannot be attached to outer relationships and surrendered in God at the same time. We can, however, enjoy relationships while surrendered in God. If our relationships force us to choose between them and righteous behavior, a decision will have to be made.

Awakening to Awareness of Immortality

When we were born into this world our soul forces identified with the physical body. The extent of our identification determines the degree of soul awareness.

Soul force flows into the medulla oblongata at the base of the brain. From there, it goes to the higher brain centers, downward through the spinal pathway. Soul force which is not utilized for body functions and mental operations may remain dormant. This dormant potential, gathered at the lower chakras, is kundalini.

When we are almost completely body-identified, we falsely assume ourselves to be a body, with a beginning at birth and a conclusion at physical death. We are sense-bound and limited by our conditionings. We are in material consciousness, primarily concerned with physical survival. Unenlightened people are subject to karmic influences and the effects of the gunas. They can be purposeful and have good intentions, or can be without higher purpose and exhibit egocentric characteristics. Many in material consciousness lead decent lives and accept on faith whatever happens: even the inevitability of death. "There is little point in questioning conditions," they say. "I might as well go along with it." If tamas guna prevails, they will be dull, sluggish, unintelligent, and for the most part unconscious. If rajas guna prevails, they will be assertive and productive, successful in accomplishing their purposes which are survival-oriented. If sattva guna prevails they will be decent and righteous, and may feel comfortable with a religious belief which sustains their faith. Their attention to duty and simple faith can take them far on the awakening path.

When soul force is somewhat awakened and active through the second chakra, one will exhibit a greater degree of curiosity about life and will be more compelled by sense urges. If tamas guna prevails the lower qualities are expressed and passion tends to rule behavior which may be destructive. If rajas guna prevails one will be more selective while still driven by sensory urges, wanting to "experience everything," becoming enchanted by and attached to relationships and experiences which satisfy the urge to gratify the senses. Here, even music, art, and beauty can be objects of fascination and attachment. If sattva guna prevails one will become cultured and have good taste, as well as be moderate in expressing through the senses. If a religious impulse is influential, tamas guna may influence one to become morbidly interested in lower psychic phenomena, magic, and sorcery. Rajas guna may influence one to become overly involved with time-wasting astral perceptions. Sattva guna will influence one to explore the inner workings of nature and desire further spiritual awakening.

When soul force is influential through the third chakra, one more easily understands the nature and operations of the mind, the laws of mental causation, and how to use executive abilities to accomplish purposes. At this level, as with the two preceding ones, soul-awareness is not yet pronounced and one may be inclined to want to master the world or control destiny. If tamas guna prevails, one will be self-centered and aggressive in behavior, accomplishing purposes without concern about how end results affect others or the environment. If rajas guna prevails, one will be successful in accomplishing purposes while still operating from an egocentric point of view, but will be law-abiding and fair in relationships. If sattva guna prevails, one will use executive abilities for entirely constructive purposes. Interest in metaphysics may be pronounced.

When soul force is active through the fourth chakra, comprehension of higher possibilities dawns in the mind and one desires to be a disciple on the spiritual path. The desire of the heart is, "Not my will, but God's will, be done." One is now ready to engage in sincere study and spiritual practices. If tamas guna prevails, one will tend to avoid responsible behavior. If rajas guna prevails, one may seek understanding but depart from the guru relationship when overly challenged to change, or because of falsely assuming that realization has been attained when it has not. If sattva guna prevails, one will be a devoted disciple and continue steadily on the path of inner transformation leading to Self-realization, conscious awareness of the soul nature.

When soul force is active through the fifth chakra, having attained a high degree of soul awareness the devotee continues to explore superconscious states and contemplates the categories of cosmic manifestation. The devotee becomes God-realized and understands everything from the field of God through to full manifestation of the universes. A knower of wisdom and truth, one lives in the world established in cosmic consciousness, experiencing ego-sense as a bubble in the sea of God's consciousness and observing the world process as a play of cosmic forces. This is the level of spiritual mastership. If tamas guna is influential, one can still err in judgments because God-consciousness is not yet complete. If rajas guna is influential, one may be attached to bliss consciousness and other perceptions possible in the field of God. If sattva guna is influential, the urge to completely merge in God and experience that which is beyond the field of God will be impelling. Even at this level, if the soul is still identified with a mind and body, the possibility of karmic influences, and the influences of the gunas, remains. When one is no longer compelled by karma or the gunas, one is "liberated while embodied."

When soul forces flow freely through the spiritual eye, the door to the inner realms can be traversed at will. Here the soul knows itself to be the all-ness of Consciousness even while perhaps aware of a degree of individuality. Neither karma nor the gunas can further influence at this level of realization. There is no possibility of again becoming blindly identified with matter because of inattention or need. This is the level of perfection. Souls at this level of realization may dwell in the sphere of God, transcend the field of God, or flow back into involvement with the field of nature because of God's will for them to participate in evolutionary processes. Soul awareness, remains permanent.

Beyond the sixth level, no description is possible. The seventh stage is transcendence, *nirvana* (the "extinguishing" of modifications of awareness).

Because states of soul awareness are independent of relationships with mind, body, and nature, higher states can be experienced while the soul is yet embodied. Therefore, soul liberation and full enlightenment should be accepted as possible during one's present life cycle. When duties in this world are fulfilled, at transition the soul will experience the sphere best suited to its awareness. If subtle karma is yet to be worked out or overcome, one may do this in higher astral spheres. If only tenuous karma remains, this may be worked out and transcended in causal spheres. Or it may be that the soul will experience the realm of God for a duration, then return to causal or astral spheres to conclude the process of purification.

Regardless of future involvements on the awakening path, the ideal is to remain surrendered in God and avoid attachments to anything but God.

Cosmic Time-Cycles, Sequential Ages, and Our Future in the Ongoing Process of Evolution

Oral traditions of many cultures and an increasing accumulation of archaeological information indicate that humankind has inhabited Planet Earth for many hundreds of thousands of years. Recorded history based on available evidence provides information about only the past twelve thousand years with any degree of accuracy. Catastrophic geological changes and shifting climate patterns have obscured or concealed evidence of the past and the passage of time has dimmed our memory of it. It is known that since approximately 10,000 B.C., following the glacial melting after the last Ice Age, organized societies emerged in India, the Middle East, parts of Europe, Egypt and lower Africa, and the Americas. Representatives of some of these groups were widely traveled by sea and land. Cultural influences were interchanged, resulting in transmission of knowledge which modified philosophical attitudes and influenced societal behaviors.

Our planet is ideally distanced (approximately 90 million miles) from the sun to enable nature to flourish and humankind to prevail. If earth were ten percent closer to the sun, surface temperatures would be unbearably hot; if ten percent more distant, temperatures would be too cold. Tremendous land mass changes have occurred due to volcanic activity, periodic Ice Ages, and sudden changes in weather patterns. Many old civilizations have been completely eliminated and others damaged. Continents continue to drift. Atmospheric conditions are changing because of industrialization, mass cutting of trees, pollution, and misuse of natural resources. In the past, changes occurring as a result of indifference and unwise use of its resources was localized. Today, because of population increases and their extensive environmental impact, imprudent behavior can have more unpleasant effects, contributing to the discomfort, unwellness, and insecurity of the planet's inhabitants.

We now examine the theory of cosmic Time-Cycles as rediscovered a little over 100 years ago by Swami Sri Yukteswar. This will enable us to understand the influences of fine forces upon the electrical properties of the mental field and its subtle organs of perception which make possible our understanding of the objective world, as well as to conceptualize and comprehend the Yugas or Ages—the eras of time in which world events occur.

We measure time in relationship to the movements of the planet's orbit around the sun and its rotation. The time it takes for earth to orbit the sun is a solar year of approximately 365 days; a day is the time required for the planet to turn completely on its axis. One twenty-fourth of a day is an hour and 1/60th of an hour is a minute. A further division by 60 results in the number of seconds in a minute. Some of the ancients calculated time in other ways. A lunar month is the time required for the moon to revolve around our planet, which is a few days less than the average month. The average potential life span for humans in our current Age is 120 years. Approximately 20 years separate each generation. Races also have their life spans: usually thousands of years before dying out or being assimilated into other racial groups. Humanity as a whole has life-waves, each evolving with the passage of time. These life-waves progress in intervals of thousands of years.

The duration when the universe is manifest is its Day and the duration of nonmanifestation is its Night.

The *Bhagavad Gita* 8:17-22:

> Those who know that the day of God is of the duration of a thousand Ages and that the night of God is a thousand Ages long, they are knowers of Day and Night. At the coming of the Day, all manifested things come forth from the Unmanifested and at the coming of Night they merge in that same Source. This very same multitude of existences, arising again and again, merges helplessly at the coming of Night and streams forth into being [again] at the coming of Day. But beyond the Unmanifested there is yet another Eternal Being who does not cease even when all creation is withdrawn. This is called the Imperishable. Souls which realize this condition never again become involved with outward creation. This Reality is the Supreme Essence of all life. In This all existences abide and It pervades all creation. It can be realized by steadfast devotion.

Fragmentary evidence of past civilizations reveal their relationship with cosmic cycles: among them the Mayan, Asian, Native American, and African. Shaiva philosophers whose oral history suggests thousands of years of progress, centuries ago evolved an elaborate explanation of world cycles based on astronomical observations. They knew of major planets and star systems and were advanced in mathematics, medicine, and language. Later, with the advent of writing they compiled extensive texts to preserve their knowledge.

Because of present lack of information, and the tendency for traditionalists to cling to unreasonable theories, many who today mention world cycles proclaim that we are currently passing through a Dark Age, *Kali Yuga*, during which there is little hope of improvement and a more certain possibility of impending global disaster. Partially awakened people, lacking the basic information provided here, or unable to comprehend it, continue to speak of our current era as a Dark Age. Pessimists and doomsday enthusiasts are enthralled with predictions of near-future catastrophe because of their personal lack of vision or meaningful purpose in life.

A 12,000 year sequence of cycles has been known to seers before and during the beginning of the present historical era. Later, for reasons we shall learn, their calculations were misinterpreted, resulting in general confusion about the cyclic patterns. In the *Manu Samhita*, an ancient text, it is written:

> Four thousand years, they say, is the Golden Age of the world. Its morning twilight has as many hundreds and its period of evening dusk is of the same length. In the other three Ages, with their morning and evening twilights, the thousands and hundreds decrease by one. That fourfold cycle comprising 12,000 years is called an Age of the Gods. The sum of a thousand divine ages constitutes one day of Brahma; and of the same length is its night.

The Ages are related to the precession of the equinoxes, the gradual backward increase in distance between the equinoctial points in reference to a fixed star, which is taken as Aries 0 degrees in the zodiac of the constellations. The ancients believed this star to be Alcyone, the brightest star of the Pleiades, one of several star clusters around which our sun revolves with its planets. Our solar system is located toward the outer edge of the Milky Way galaxy, which is trillions of miles across. Light, traveling at 186,000 miles a second, would require approximately 100,000 years to travel from one side to the other. Billions of suns (nuclear reactors) shine in our galaxy, many far larger than our own. And billions of galaxies share space in our universe, separated from us by multiplied trillions of miles.

The Babylonians referred to Alcyone as "the foundation stone." The Arabs named it "the immortal seal" and "the central one." Vedic astronomers referred to it as "the mother." The Greek word for it signifies "peace."

Sri Yukteswar first shared his interpretation of cosmic cycles in his small book, *The Holy Science*, published in 1894 at the request of Mahavatar Babaji. After years of careful study, Sri Yukteswar concluded that a 24,000 year cycle, the time it takes for the sun to return to its starting place, calculated as Aries 0 degrees, corresponded to the Ages referred to in the *Manu*

Samhita, with four descending Ages occurring during a 12,000 year period and four ascending Ages occurring during the subsequent 12,000 year period. There is a difference of opinion among astronomers about the actual time it takes for a complete cycle of the precession of the equinoxes to occur. Vedic astronomers concluded that 24,000 years is the most accurate, making allowances for occasional variations in speed.

Moons revolve around planets and planets in our solar system revolve around the sun. The sun moves in its orbit, with its planets, and all participate in an exchange of energies which influence magnetic fields. According to Vedic sources, our sun moves in its orbit toward, and away from, a "Center of Creative Power" located in the middle of our galaxy. The influences of the Center of Creative Power, acting upon the electrical properties of the mental field of humanity, contribute to an increase in perceptual abilities when our solar system is nearest to it. When further away the influences are less, resulting in a diminishment of intellectual powers. During the time-phase when intellectual capacities are at their peak, mankind as a whole is more enlightened and this reflects in society as a Golden Age condition. During the time-phase when intellectual capacities are diminished, the majority of earth's inhabitants experience a Dark Age. Between these extremes are periods of varying degrees of awareness and intellectual capacity, reflecting as sequential ascending and descending Ages.

The Creative Power Source is referred to in Sanskrit literature as *Vishnunabi* (the "navel of Vishnu"), also Brahma, the "universal magnetism" which regulates mental virtues or capacities. Sri Yukteswar taught that this Power Source acts upon life in proximity to it, using celestial bodies as distribution points through which its energies are channeled. In this way it regulates our mental characteristics. Each 12,000 year cycle brings about a complete change in the mental condition of the majority of people on the planet. There are always some souls which are so highly realized that they are not influenced by external forces. They remain the custodians of wisdom and function as teachers of the race. A 12,000 year phase during which one-half of the sun's orbit is completed is an Electric Time-Cycle. The full 24,000 year phase is an Electric Couple of two 12,000 year cycles, one descending and the other ascending.

A Dark Age is 1,200 years in duration, calculating 1,000 years as the duration of the Age itself, plus 100 years before and after as durations of mutation from one Age to another. This represents 1/20th of the sun's grand orbit. The mental ability of the average person during this cycle is but one-fourth developed, so that humans cannot comprehend anything but the most obvious external matters. They are then in material consciousness, able only to perceive the objective environment through the senses. Intellectual abilities are modest and intuition is not awakened.

The second ascending period of 2,400 years, when the sun moves through 2/20ths of its orbit, is the Electric Age: the era now unfolding. Intellectual ability at this time is sufficient to allow comprehension of fine forces in nature, electricities and their attributes, and the existence and operations of magnetic fields. As of this writing (1995) we are 295 years into an ascending Electric Age.

The last Dark Age concluded around A.D. 1700. Now past the 200-year morning twilight of our current Age, we are leaving behind Dark Age influences and undergoing rapid acceleration of soul awakening, resulting in dramatic changes in society, progress in scientific discovery, and transformation of philosophical and religious thought. During the final 200-year mutation period (100 years between the ending and beginning of the last Dark Age), researchers began to observe the existence of fine properties of matter. Around A.D. 1600 William Gilbert discovered magnetic forces and electrical properties. Kepler discovered significant laws of astronomy and Galileo produced the telescope. Drebbel of Holland soon after invented the microscope. Newton discovered the law of gravitation and the steam engine came into use for industrial purposes. The action of electricity upon the human body was discovered. During the morning twilight phase of our current Age, electricity was harnessed, the telegraph and telephone invented, air travel became common, radio and television opened the world to almost instant communication, atomic power was unleashed, satellites were sent into orbit, man walked on the moon, the solar system began to be explored by space probes and advanced telescopes, healing influences of electric currents and magnetism were investigated, and computers

CHART OF ELECTRIC TIME CYCLES

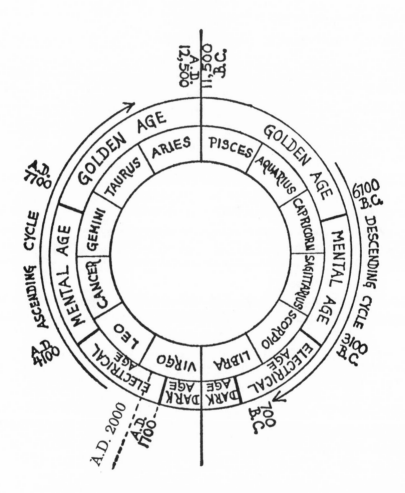

The Autumnal Equinox is now falling in Virgo; the Vernal Equinox is therefore now falling in Pisces. Because Western astrologers usually consider the Vernal Equinox to have major significance, they say we are now in the Piscean Age. According to Sri Yukteswar we will enter the Aquarius-Leo Age in A.D. 2499.

began to transform the way information was processed. There is more to come, for this is the Age of space exploration and quite possibly actual communication with people living on other planets in our galaxy and beyond.

The present Time-Cycle will continue until A.D. 4100, unfolding further advances in scientific fields and welcomed improvements on a global scale. War will be forgotten, poverty eradicated, new power sources will replace the use of fossil fuels, recycling of natural resources will be commonplace, global population will be stabilized, crime will diminish, food shortages will be nonexistent, people will live in harmony with nature's laws and be relatively disease-free, and an interest in spiritual matters will increase.

The third ascending period of 3,600 years, during which the sun passes through 3/20ths of its orbit, is called a Mental Age, during which the human intellect is able to comprehend the source of electric forces upon which creation is based, as well as the true nature of individual and Cosmic Mind. Telepathy is common, advanced intellectual powers are demonstrated, and the creative forces of mind and nature are used in entirely benevolent ways.

The remaining fourth period, during which the sun passes through 4/20ths of its orbit, is called an Age of Enlightenment, a Golden Age. During this phase intuitive abilities are pronounced and most people can comprehend the true nature of consciousness. This period of 4,800 years then merges into a descending period of similar length as the other Ages follow its decline.

The Golden Age is almost 10,000 years in duration, with the other Ages shorter and the Dark Age of two 1,200 year Ages opposite the Golden Age. Because of the trends of evolution each Dark Age becomes more evolved, thus the whole of mankind moves progressively in the direction spiritual maturity.

As civilizations rise and fall in relationship to electric influences by which all of nature is ruled, souls incarnate during the time-phases when their personal needs and karmic conditions can best be served. In this way, because of the law of correspondences (as within, so without), souls flow to circumstances most opportune for their learning, growth, and inclination to function. Many conscious souls born into the world during this ascending

Electric Age are here to participate with the evolutionary process and to continue their spiritual growth.

Among the general population are represented the various
stages through which mankind as a whole moves through the
Ages. We have among us many who are still in a Dark Age consciousness, others who somewhat understand electrical properties, some who are mental giants, and a few who are fully
enlightened. As the Ages advance, the percentages will change
to correspond to the prevailing times. Devotees on the enlightenment path who understand the influences of the Ages should not
be content to remain subject to them. They should attend to spiritual practices and learn to live in an inner state of grace so that,
for them, any time is an Age of Enlightenment regardless of
external circumstances. The Golden Age is also referred to as
Satya Yuga, (the "Truth Age"). The sage Ramana Maharishi, who
lived in South India during the first half of this century said, "A
wise person lives in Satya Yuga all of the time."

Seers who have studied the phenomenon of cycles further
assert that every 6,000 years mankind undergoes a minor dramatic change in the course of evolution, and every 12,000 years
a major one. We are now moving through one of these periods of
major change. It does not, however, mark a period of external
disaster, but one of internal transformation and constructive outer
modification. The 1980's were referred to by many saints as "the
hour of God" because it was a transition-phase into more intense
involvement with influential creative forces; a period of stress
because of rapid changes within people and adjustments in outer
circumstances. It will require another century, at least, before
we are fully under the impact of the transformative forces regulating the Electrical Age.

Legend has it that the fall of Atlantis, presumed by many to
be a myth, began around 11,500 B.C. just after the beginning of
the decline of the last Golden Age. Plato, in his *Critias*, described
the Golden Age of Atlantis. It was a philosophical democracy in
which the arts flourished and the sciences were cultivated in
great universities. Man had no enemies and war was unknown.
Gradually, because of declining influences from the Creative
Power Source, men began to lose their spiritual awareness and
their virtues. Personal ambition and corruption ensued and

nature's forces ran rampant. Atlantis is believed to have been devastated by cataclysmic earthquakes around 10,184 B.C., approximately 1,316 years after the beginning of the decent of the last Golden Age. Esoteric traditions teach that before the final devastation, some of the population migrated to other parts of the world, including India, Egypt, and Mexico, to establish new communities.

There is not necessarily a cause and effect relationship between man's corrupt behavior and natural disasters. Often they are coincidental because evolutionary forces are working simultaneously within the psyche of man and the field of nature. It is error to think that God punishes us for our folly. Any difficulties we experience due to errors in judgment are episodes of self-induced discomfort, regardless of whether the errors are conscious or unconscious.

The light of the last Golden Age lingered because poets and philosophers preserved an oral tradition and sometimes left written and symbolic records. The memories are also retained in the collective subconscious of the race.

It is of interest to know why many people are today mistaken about where we are in the sequence of the Ages. Sri Yukteswar's research revealed the reason for this error. Traditional sources claim that the Dark Age is 432,000 years in duration. In India, around 700 B.C. during the reign of Raja Parikshit, events occurred which contributed to the error. Prior to this time, Maharaja Yudhisthira, noticing evidence of a coming Dark Age, turned his throne over to his grandson and retired to the seclusion of the Himalayan mountains. He took his astronomers and astrologers with him, leaving no one in the remaining court who could correctly calculate the movements of celestial bodies. The astronomers did not want to contribute to fear and anxiety among the public by recording the Dark Age. They, instead, recorded it as the beginning of an ascending Electric Cycle. Around A.D. 499 the mistake in the almanac was discovered, but not the reason for it. The almanac recorded the duration of a Dark Age period of 1,200 years instead of two consecutive 1,200 year periods of descending and ascending cycles. The later astronomers then wrongly concluded that the Dark Age years were not really solar years but rather "years of the gods," with one such year calculated as a day and 1,200 years therefore as 432,000 solar years (1,200 times 360 days of a lunar year).

That which produced and sustains the worlds enlivens them with creative impulses to maintain the processes of transformation and growth. The *Bhagavad Gita* 4:7,8:

> Whenever there is a decline of righteousness and a rise of unrighteousness, I incarnate myself; for the protection of the good, for the destruction of the wicked, and for the establishment of righteousness, I incarnate myself from Age to Age.

This coming into expression of divine influence is not always in the form of a hero-spirit or avatar. It is generally evidenced as a creative thrust manifested simultaneously through a number of people all over the world, resulting in new ideas and useful actions which stimulate and refresh human consciousness. But avatars do incarnate, along with spiritually advanced souls which are still working out their freedom through spiritual practices and selfless service to the cause of evolution.

When we are desperate we often yearn for the coming of a savior, someone who will restore order and do for us what we have not been able to do for ourselves. While illumined teachers do become involved on the world scene, what is of equal importance is for all capable people to awaken to the realization of their divine nature and actualize it. In this way the "universal avatar," the divine reality of every soul, becomes increasingly evident and expressed.

Because of past Dark Age influences, collective human consciousness has been sleeping, but the situation is now changing. During the last two centuries an increasing number of souls have become sufficiently conscious to appreciate enlightened teachings, and a return to morality, social responsibility, and spiritual values is of primary importance to them. Knowledge is emerging and the way of discipleship is increasingly accepted as a valid approach to self-understanding and God-realization.

The learning process is still relatively slow because we are still in the dawning of an awakening era, and the majority of the world's population is still involved with egocentric, materialistic concerns. There has, however, been more change in the direction of higher values in the last two hundred years than in the preceding two thousand years, and the process is speeding up. Perhaps one person in a thousand is today sincerely asking the questions—Who am I? What is my source? What is the reason for my presence in the world? How can I know the truth?

We cannot understand what we are not capable of comprehending. This is why initial inquiry into the nature of God and the processes of life must be followed by right study and personal practice. Until we are fully involved with useful procedures we need frequent reminding. This is also why it is important today to spread by all available means, beginning with our own personal example to others, a *quantity* message of hope and faith to provide responsive souls with accurate information and encourage their spiritual education. From among those who are assisted in practical ways and are spiritually educated, some will be receptive to higher teachings and become disciples on the enlightenment path. This is the *quality* work. Both learning opportunities should be offered to serve the needs of everyone.

During the middle of the last century yogic teachings began to be taught more openly in India. Translations of Sanskrit texts attracted the attention of scholars and philosophers in Europe and America. During the final third of the last century several metaphysical religious groups were formed in America, which have since proliferated as hundreds of churches and teaching centers comprising the contemporary New Thought movement. Around the turn of the century the first wave of teachers of *Vedanta* (the "essence of the *Vedas*") visited the West. In 1920 Paramahansa Yogananda came from India to establish a firm foundation for yoga teachings. Later, more teachers came from India and other parts of Asia. The *dharma*, the way of righteousness, is being restored to provide the basis for the new era.

An Accelerated Path to God-Realization: Rediscovered and Now Available

Soul awareness is processed through mind and body. The more clear and orderly the mind and the more refined the brain and nervous system, the more easily soul consciousness can express. Noting that the influences of different Ages contribute to changes

in human mental function, seers concluded that it might be possible for a person to assist himself to play an intentional role in
accelerating inner transformation. In this way one might accomplish in a relatively short period of time what might otherwise
require centuries. Thus, advanced Kriya Yoga techniques were
evolved and refined.

In this process the crown chakra is taken as the central sun,
the mind as the moon, and the spinal pathway as the firmament
of the constellations. It was noted that subtle changes take place
in the human body during lunar months and solar years. Seers
then discovered that by revolving the moon (mind) around the
sun (crown chakra) they could cause beneficial changes in the
brain and nervous system. Thus, one revolution of the vital force,
directed mentally and assisted by a breathing technique, would
result in the equivalent of one solar year of evolution—this,
because the moon along with earth revolves around the sun during the course of a solar year. The practice of this meditation
technique cleanses the mental field by acting upon its electrical
properties, and by calming mental transformations and impulses
which contribute to their movements. By practicing this process
a few minutes each day, one is able to encourage inner changes
to occur in a few years, instead of remaining the effect of environmental influences through the centuries and the Ages.

The life-enhancing value of Kriya Yoga practice cannot be
appreciated until one becomes an Electric Age person, capable of
understanding the basis for its practice and willing to prepare to
learn it. Study this preliminary material often, to acquire an
understanding of the world-as-consciousness and the basic principles of righteous living. Follow through with careful and
repeated examination of all that follows, applying what you learn
to experience the results of actions which can contribute to total
wellness and spiritual growth. Constructive changes will occur
in your life and you will be a surrendered disciple on the enlightenment path. Grace will abound, your consciousness will expand,
and you will be led of God to fulfill your destiny in accord with
God's will for you.

Yoga: Philosophy and Practices

The principles of yoga are said to have been "revealed to man by the gods." This can mean that when humankind was ready for a major evolutionary unfoldment it was assisted by cosmic forces in the direction of further growth, that some devotees were taught from the inner planes, or that seers born with knowledge taught it to receptive persons.

For every person who sincerely desires to live in harmony with natural laws and experience God-realization, there is a way suitable to individual need. Yoga is experienced according to one's capacity and psychological temperament and the various classical yogic systems reflect this approach. What is recommended is that the devotee begin in whatever way seems best, or as the guru instructs, and continue with earnest endeavor. One should not be content to make a permanent lifestyle of the adopted approach to God; rather, one should be willing to learn and to grow. While techniques and procedures are helpful for the accomplishment of purposes, the ideal is to live spontaneously and intuitively from higher consciousness, in the flow of grace.

The following systems represent the essentials of yoga philosophy and practices:

Hatha Yoga – Complete training of the physical and vital natures of man to prepare body and mind to express superconsciousness. Sometimes called Sun-Moon Yoga because of the emphasis upon bringing into balance the polarities, the positive (sun) and negative (moon) forces in the body which flow through subtle channels (*nadis*). It is the kinetic or active flow of life force which enlivens the body and mind; the dormant aspect of life

63

force is the underlying potential, *kundalini*. Applying a regimen
of postures (*asanas*), life force regulation procedures (*pranayamas*), procedures for activating and regulating vital forces
(*mudras*), and meditation techniques, the practitioner prepares
the mind for higher superconscious experiences and God-realization. Hatha Yoga is more than a program of physical exercise,
although the procedures do contribute to flexibility and strength,
encourage glands and organs to function more efficiently, and
improve blood and lymph circulation. Starting with body cleansing routines and progressing to various practices, the practitioner succeeds in regulating and mastering sensory impulses in
order to live a balanced life and meditate successfully. Procedures are performed in a contemplative mood rather than by using
force impelled by impatient desire for results. The understanding should always be that practices are preliminary to transcendent states. The body is not to be exalted and the mind is not to
be supported by egoism. Instead, body and mind are to be purified so that all obstacles to soul expression are neutralized and
removed.

Karma Yoga – A necessary, conscious practice for every person, because living requires an understanding of relationships
and the ability to be creatively determined while remaining free
from attachments to inner causes and outer effects which might
contribute to less than optimum behavior. The way is to engage
in necessary and useful actions without compulsion or egoism
(self-centeredness). Thoughts are then ordered, emotions are
regulated, and purposes are achieved without attachments
either to the actions or their results. The impulse to express is
fulfilled, destructive drives are transformed into purely constructive ones, and egoism is dissolved while necessary and appropriate relationships and activities continue to be experienced.
Whatever action is pure, constructive, or righteous can be done
as service to God—as service to the cause of evolution. All relationships, work, and actions should be related to in this way.
One can then be happy, fulfill legitimate desires, relate to and
wisely use natural resources, and maintain an attitude of, "I am
not the doer; God is the doer; I am God's servant." By living in
this way, influential karma is neutralized, karma which might
bind one to future effects is weakened and removed, and one

remains free in the performance of duty.

Bhakti Yoga – *Bhakti* (love, devotion) is worship of God in whatever form appeals to the heart. The formless and nameless aspect of God without attributes can be the object of devotion, as can God with forms and names conceptualized by the devotee. One may cultivate an awareness of the presence of God at all times, or may worship formally or informally. However one begins, modes of worship as well as names and forms visualized, will eventually be transcended. Be a lover of God by seeing God as nature, in all circumstances, all people, and in the operations of your own mind and consciousness. Your mind and heart will be purified and divine qualities will be actualized.

Jnana Yoga – This is the wisdom (*gya-na*) way to God knowledge and enlightenment. By using the faculty of intelligence to contemplate the categories of cosmic manifestation and the operations of higher consciousness, everything this side of the field of God can be comprehended. Then, using intuition—the soul's capacity to "know by knowing"—revelation is possible. This is not an easy path for devotees because not all are endowed with keen powers of perception and discernment. The intellectual faculty may be clouded by tamas guna, or mental and emotional conflicts may interfere with concentration. When, as a result of yoga practices, the mind is somewhat purified, emotions are settled and intellectual discernment is easier.

Raja Yoga – The royal (*raja*) way of meditation for the purpose of experiencing superconscious states and illumination of consciousness. This process comprises the primary emphasis of this book, as explained in the commentaries on Patanjali's *Yoga Sutras*. While all yogic systems emphasize contemplation and surrender in God, the way of meditation offers specific procedures which enable the devotee to internalize attention, regulate mental processes, and arrange conditions so that superconscious states can be experienced and explored. Although various meditation methods may be taught by yoga teachers, the *Yoga Sutras* describe procedures one can use to facilitate spiritual growth for the purpose of realizing liberation of consciousness. Patanjali, who lived approximately two thousand years ago, did not innovate yogic meditation. He acquired information and presented it in a systematic manner, acknowledging that what he wrote had been long known and practiced by others.

Obstacles to success must be recognized, and overcome or renounced. Hatha Yoga devotees may become too body-centered instead of expansive. Karma yogis may fail to completely renounce the results of their actions, continuing to expect rewards for their good works, thus denying their reliance upon the formless Infinite. Devotees may remain at the level of sentimental, emotional worship. Seekers of knowledge may become proud of their partial understanding. Meditators may become fascinated with inner perceptions and ecstatic states, or be tempted to presume that they are more spiritually advanced than they are. Always have before you the high purpose of your spiritual practices, and continue with courage and faith until enlightened and free.

Subtle Anatomy and Physiology: Life Forces, Vital Centers, and Kundalini Activity

Before embarking on a program of meditation and examination of superconscious states, subtle anatomy and physiology should be learned. The disciple should be informed about the actions and influences of life forces in the body which have a direct relationship to mental states and states of consciousness. Thus educated, one will be able to proceed with accurate understanding of inner changes which occur as a result of practice.

Cosmic life force, expressing through the soul, flows into the mental field and physical body to animate them. Soul force manifests as five variations of frequency to perform specific functions:

1. *Udana Prana* – The aspect which directs vital currents upward. Seated in the throat. It contributes to speech and aids in spiritual growth by helping bring other forces upward. This is the aspect of life force which contributes to elevation of consciousness, lightness of the body, and to assisting the soul to depart the body during transition.

2. *Prana* – Seated in the chest. It regulates breathing, making possible the inspiration of oxygen (and of universal life force) and the expiration of carbon dioxide.

3. *Samana Prana* – Seated in the stomach and intestines. It regulates digestion, assimilation, and biochemical processes.

4. *Apana Prana* – Seated below the navel. It regulates elimination of waste products and is downward flowing.

5. *Vyana Prana* – All-pervasive. It regulates movements of vital forces, contributing to their distribution and actions.

When one or more of these aspects of life force are disturbed, mental and physical discomfort can manifest. Knowing this, yogis endeavor to maintain them in a condition of balance. Some contributing factors to disturbance of flows of life force can be stress, improper diet, insufficient sleep, mental discord, emotional conflict, sudden changes in environmental circumstances such as extreme heat or cold, bodily injury, failure to achieve goals, or the hearing of misfortune. Many of the recommendations for success in yoga contribute to maintaining the life forces in a condition of balance and normal operation.

Life forces are distributed through vital centers in the cerebrospinal pathway. The central channel through which they flow is *sushumna* (the astral channel in the spinal pathway), through which subtle and fine forces operate. It originates in the crown chakra and extends downward to the base chakra. Within sushumna are *vajra nadi*, *chitra nadi*, and *Brahma nadi*. These are, respectively, the channels representing astral, causal, and nonmaterial aspects and actions of vital forces. When prana is active at the astral level it contributes to dreams, hallucinations and visions, as well as to imaginal activities. When active at the causal level it contributes to more subtle perceptions. At the core of sushumna, Brahma nadi is the pathway through which awakened kundalini ascends. The practice of Kriya pranayama directly influences the actions of vital forces in the spinal pathway, awakening them and encouraging their upward flow.

Mingled with sushumna at the base chakra are two other major channels. These are *ida* (moon) and *pingala* (sun), which flow along the left and right sides of the spine. The left channel, ida, carries the negative current, which is feminine in character, nourishing, and cleansing. When the flow of prana is dominant through ida, air flows through the left nostril with greater force. During the nine days of the waxing moon phase, this prana influence is dominant at sunrise and sunset. At other times of the day it alternates with the sun breath.

The right channel, pingala, carries the positive current, which is masculine in character and electrical. It increases energy and vitality. When the flow of prana is dominant through pingala, air flows through the right nostril with greater force. During the nine days of the waning lunar phase, this prana is dominant at sunrise and sunset. At other times of the day it alternates with the moon breath.

When the flow of air is dominant through the left nostril, one is more inclined to right-brain activities which require imagination, visualization, and other "picture forming" mental processes. When the flow of air is dominant through the right nostril, one is more inclined to left-brain activities which require decision, action, outward involvements to produce desired effects, and intellectual analysis. When the flow of air through both nostrils is even and smooth, the two currents are harmonized and prana operates in the sushumna. Mental processes then become ordered, brain wave patterns become synchronized, and meditation and contemplation are easier to practice.

Of the vital centers in the body, seven are considered by yogis to be the most important, as all others are dependent upon them. These centers, or chakras, in the brain and spinal pathway are astral in nature and forces flowing through them regulate body functions as well as relate to psychological states and levels of soul awareness.

1. *Base Chakra* – The perineum, between the anus and genitals. The Earth Element prana frequency, influenced by Apana Prana. The prana frequency is sweet in taste, yellow in color, and has the sound of restless bees. The mantra is *Lam* ("lum"). The psychological state is restless and insecure, with need for security and self-preservation. Material states of consciousness. The Sanskrit name *Muladhara* means "foundation."

2. *Second Chakra* – In the sacral region of the spinal pathway. The Water Element prana frequency, influenced by Apana Prana. The prana frequency is astringent in taste, white in color, and has the sound of a flute. The mantra is *Vam* ("vum"). The psychological state is desirous and sensuous. Partial awakening of soul awareness. *Svadhisthan* means "abode of self" because kundalini is confined here.

3. *Third Chakra* – Opposite the navel. Fire Element prana frequency, influenced by Samana Prana. The prana frequency is bitter in taste, red in color, and has the sound of a harp. The mantra is *Ram* ("rum"). The psychological state is egoism. Soul abilities include creative use of mind and executive talents. *Manipura* means "the city of gems."

4. *Fourth Chakra* – Between the shoulder blades. The Air Element prana frequency, influenced by Prana life-current. The prana frequency is sour in taste, blue in color, and has the sound of a continuous peal of a gong. The mantra is *Yam* ("yum"). The psychological state is aspiration with mild discernment. Psychological characteristics are compassion and preparedness for discipleship. *Anahata* means "unstruck sound."

5. *Fifth Chakra* – Opposite the throat. The Ether Element prana frequency, influenced by Udana Prana. The frequency is pungent in taste, color is grey or misty with sparkling pinpoints of light, and has the sound of thunder or an ocean's roar; a cosmic sound. The mantra is *Ham* ("hum"). The psychological state is inspiration to knowledge. Soul awareness is "above the world of appearances" in understanding. *Vishudda* means "pure."

6. *Sixth Chakra* – Between the eyebrows. Transcending prana frequencies and superior to them. Cosmic forces are perceived here as a dark blue orb with a golden halo, centered by silver-white light. Gold is the frequency of Om; blue is the frequency of Cosmic Intelligence; white is the frequency of Spirit. Soul awareness here is "one with God." *Ajna* means "command." From this center lower ones can be regulated.

7. *Seventh Chakra* – Upper cerebrum. The "power station" in the body. It's radiance is brilliant white. Soul awareness here is pure. *Sahasrara* means "thousand-rayed." This chakra is sometimes symbolized as a lotus with a thousand petals.

Kundalini remains mostly at rest when the soul's interest is primarily outward and involved through the senses. When desire for higher understanding is present, especially when one sincerely yearns to know God, this force stirs and begins to release more vitality to flow upward to the brain, stimulating the chakras, awakening mental capacities, and enlivening the body. Discernible initial movements of this force are referred to as *shakti*: dynamic, creative life force in motion. The more obvious movement of kundalini contributes to rapid changes in psychological states, mental processes, and soul awareness.

There are exercises which can be used to coax the awakening of kundalini, which are best learned from the guru who is able to determine the disciple's preparedness for such practices. The more useful way for most people is to cultivate devotion, live a righteous life, and meditate long and deep.

Do not be afraid of spiritual awakening. Surrendered in God and living a balanced life, you have nothing to fear. No harm can come to a person who is surrendered in God and living righteously. Observe the recommended preliminary guidelines, live a moral life, be moderate and balanced, cultivate the virtues, be emotionally mature and rational, and prepare a firm foundation upon which your further growth can be based. This is the common-sense approach to spiritual growth.

Inner quickening can occur because of intense desire to know God and can be facilitated by the grace of God through the guru or someone in whom kundalini is awakened. When we are receptive and in proximity to a spiritually awakened person, we can receive a transmission of shakti which stirs our inner forces. When they circulate they accelerate transformation processes and incline us to spiritual fulfillment.

Especially when intent upon study and meditation, and when undergoing psychological adjustments, it is important to observe sensible health practices for wellness and to have abundant energy reserves. It is of equal importance to cultivate constructive mental attitudes and preserve emotional balance. Intensive involvement in life processes, concentration, meditation, and the inner changes which occur because of awakened vital forces, require that we maintain a prudent schedule of activity and rest to allow for restoration and maintenance of mind and body. Extremes of any kind are to be avoided. Our initial efforts to regulate sensory impulses, and our refusal to allow conditioned behaviors to be dominant, will eventually be replaced with effortless surrender and spontaneous spiritual growth as lower states of consciousness are replaced by higher ones and incomplete understanding is replaced by knowledge.

Psychological Transformation, Spiritual Growth, and Removal of Awareness from Attachments Which Limit Consciousness

Psychological transformation must occur along with spiritual growth. In yogic teachings, these processes are related to the chakras. Even reasonable success in becoming psychologically mature can contribute to ease of spiritual growth, and spiritual growth naturally contributes to psychological maturity. A wise devotee will give attention to both matters. An emotionally mature person may not necessarily be spiritually awakened and one who experiences preliminary success in meditation practice may not always be emotionally mature.

The following broad descriptions apply to most people. There will always be exceptions. For instance, there are many very young people who are emotionally mature and spiritually aware, and there are some older people who are immature and not yet spiritually awakened.

1. *Behaviors Common to First Chakra Awareness* – Because of clouded awareness, insecurity may be expressed, along with fearfulness, uncertainty, illusion, delusion, greed, and anger when needs are unmet or desires are unfulfilled. Young children often express these characteristics because they are adapting to a new environment in which circumstances are not understood.

2. *Behaviors Common to Second Chakra Awareness* – Because of awakened sense perception, expressions may include attempts to reach out, to "touch" the environment, to experience and relate to it, as increased sensitivity, sensuality, occasional confusion, fantasy and imagination, role playing, and pretending to be the hero or heroine of one's dreams. Adolescents often express these characteristics because they are learning to relate to the world and are exploring possibilities.

3. *Behaviors Common to Third Chakra Awareness* – Because of more pronounced self-identity, may be expressed as endeavors to demonstrate personal power, attain recognition, learn how to accomplish purposes, and sometimes as unbounded optimism and the feeling that anything is possible. Young adults often express these characteristics because they are becoming more indepen-

dent and are endeavoring to relate to the world on their own terms.

4. *Behaviors Common to Fourth Chakra Awareness* – Because of aspiration to be centered and balanced, may be expressed as changes in lifestyle, a change in direction in life, restlessness and uncertainty, a feeling that something important is missing in one's life, the development of conscience, and a real desire for soul happiness. Adults during middle age often express these characteristics because they have already experienced transition episodes and relationships and are ready to learn how to live a more meaningful life.

5. *Behaviors Common to Fifth Chakra Awareness* – Because of yearning to know the meaning of life, may be expressed as efforts to be more focused because it may seem that time in which to acquire true knowledge and to be emotionally mature may be running out. A possible problem can be unwise use of knowledge due to lack of emotional maturity and incomplete understanding. Adults nearing retirement age often express these characteristics because they are withdrawing from former responsibilities and beginning to turn their attention to what lies beyond.

6. *Behaviors Common to Sixth Chakra Awareness* – Because of desire to experience fulfillment of major purposes, emotional maturity and spiritual awareness may be expressed as behavior which is righteous and benevolent. At this stage we may see those who are older and wiser sharing their wisdom with others. They are at peace with themselves and with the world.

7. *Behaviors Common to Seventh Chakra Awareness* – Because this level represents completion, may be expressed as compassionate, selfless participation in assisting society and individuals in the direction of their highest good.

There are three major attachments which bind the soul to identification with creation. Yogis refer to them as "knots" to be transcended if soul freedom is to be known.

1. *Attachment to Outer Appearances* – Attachment to the realm of names and forms prevents spiritual growth. We have already examined the categories of cosmic manifestation and are

aware that outer appearances are made possible by the interactions of fine cosmic forces. We do not have to reject the world to renounce it. We have only to release our attachment to it. Although environmental radiations flow to our senses, there is nothing external with power to attach itself to us. We alone can determine our relationship with the world. Understand that sooner or later you will withdraw from the phenomenal realm either by choice or by involuntary transition. Therefore, it is far better to choose to be detached than to be forcibly disconnected with desires which may interfere with spiritual progress in subtle realms. Live in the world, enjoy it and be happy, and dissolve your attachments. In this way do you overcome the physical world.

2. *Attachment to Feelings* – To renounce attachment to feelings does not mean that we must become devoid of feeling, only that we should recognize sensation for what it is: evidence of perception. At a lower level, attachment to feelings can result in destructive and obsessive behavior. At a higher level, when one's life is reasonably balanced and noble aspirations prevail, one can be attached to beauty, pleasant sensations, and to the feeling generated by compassion. One may then be so powerfully driven to do good works—to help others, to shelter the homeless and feed the hungry, and to become so involved in humanitarian activities, including world enlightenment—that spiritual practices are neglected. The way to overcome this attachment is to appreciate beauty and all that is pure and righteous, and to serve the world and mankind as duty, letting wisdom prevail without emotional attachments to perceptions or actions. In this way do you overcome the astral sphere.

3. *Attachment to Inner Plane Perceptions* – One may be removed from attachments to outer spheres but still be attached to knowledge of the fine levels of creation, and to their perceptions and resulting influences upon states of consciousness. One may be attached to ecstasy, to the joy of merging in light and sound during meditation, or to visions of celestial spheres. One may enjoy feeling like a god or a goddess and be unconcerned about transcendence. The way to overcome this attachment is to accept what unfolds while remaining surrendered in God, letting grace clear soul consciousness and elevate it above the realm of created things. In this way do you overcome the causal sphere.

At every stage you will have to be alert and exercise your intelligence. This is the way to psychological maturity. Meditate regularly, using Kriya Yoga techniques and procedures to ascend the chakras and pierce these three "knots" of consciousness which bind soul awareness: 1) the three lower centers (attachments to outer appearances); 2) the heart center (attachment to feelings); 3) the spiritual eye center (attachment to inner plane perceptions).

Because yoga is the inner way to God-realization the only changes in lifestyle a devotee will have to make are those which enable one to live in harmony with the rhythms of nature, to fulfill legitimate purposes, and to contemplate God. There is no need to adopt social behaviors incompatible with one's present culture.

A visitor once said to Paramahansaji, "Your disciples all look like normal people." He replied, "Yes, outwardly, they are like other people. Inside, their hearts are different."

Let the "difference" of your *heart's desire* be the primary determining factor in your life as you proceed with your studies and spiritual practices. Let God be everything to you.

PART TWO

PROCEDURE

Text and Commentary
on Patanjali's Yoga Sutras

CHAPTER ONE

Concentration and
Superconscious States

1. Now, an explanation of yoga begins.

The word *now* indicates an auspicious or favorable occasion. What is to be taught is authoritative, of superior value, and based on traditional practices already tested and verified. After preliminary study of basic philosophical principles, the disciple should be ready to investigate subjective realms of mind, and to learn about and practice procedures which can provide experience of superconscious states which confer illumination of consciousness and soul liberation.

Unless a truth seeker has progressed from being a student to being a surrendered disciple on the spiritual path, without preliminary study and adequate preparation that discipleship requires, one will neither be able to meditate deeply nor understand the subtle processes of mental transformation that occur due to superconscious influences. The ideal disciple should be surrendered to God, respectful of the enlightenment tradition, and willing to enter fully into the *way* which facilitates spiritual growth.

2. Yoga (samadhi) is the (result of) cessation or stopping of the transformations and modifications which ordinarily occur in the field of individualized awareness.

It is helpful to know that in this text the reader needs to understand the meaning of the words "consciousness" and "aware ness" as intended by the author of the *Yoga Sutras*. In secular usage they are sometimes considered to have the same meaning, but for practitioners of yoga their meanings are precisely defined. *Consciousness* is the essential nature of the One Life which is the basis of all expressions of life, and our essential nature. It can be self-knowing without having to have an object to support it. *Awareness* always has an object—it is always in relationship to something, whether objective circumstances or subjective thought processes and feelings. *The purpose of yoga practice is to remove awareness from its supporting objects so that consciousness can be experienced directly.* This being accomplished, one can then choose to live freely in the world with flawless knowledge of higher realities and mundane circumstances.

When identified with mental processes and impressions rooted in the unconscious, soul awareness becomes fragmented and confused. Memories (and conditionings caused by memories), tendencies, and instinctual drives, obscure the soul's awareness of its true nature. When, by self-discipline of sensory impulses and meditation practice, mental modifications become dormant, the soul is conscious of its innate beingness and luminosity. There are a variety of physical and mental techniques which can be used by the devotee to harmonize internal forces and clear the mental field. Mastery of the fluctuations and modifications of the mind is accomplished by first restricting their influences, and then by returning their forces to their origins. Right meditation practice does not suppress mental activity; it refines and calms it. Proficiency in meditation practice regulates mental processes in a natural way and repeated superconscious experiences result in their dissolution.

Superconsciousness (samadhi) is the final result of practice and is referred to in this text as yoga. *Samadhi* means "to bring together." What is brought together? Soul awareness, identified with mental processes and thus experiencing a sense of separation from God, is again made conscious of its oneness in God as the result of right spiritual practice and surrendered meditation. The soul, being inwardly established in pure consciousness even when deluded, does not really become united with God because it has never been separated from God—a feeling of separation, along with mental confusion, prevails when soul awareness is overly extroverted. Union with God, then, only seems to occur when soul awareness is removed from identification with the restricting influences of the mental field and is restored to wholeness.

Samadhi, a superconscious state during which attention is removed from lower mind involvements, is not unconsciousness. In superconsciousness, luminosity is dominant; darkness and heaviness which accompany unconscious states is absent. Refined superconscious states result in pronounced soul awareness, God-consciousness, and transcendence.

3. **Established in pure consciousness, soul awareness remains steady in its own nature.**

During preliminary superconscious states which are qualified by thought processes and the influences of subtle cosmic forces (the gunas) operating in the mental field, the soul experiences being when transcendent and egoism when again identified with mental processes and sense perceptions. As the result of repeated unqualified superconscious states, one is able to remain established in being even while functioning through the mind and body. This occurs when all destructive mental modifications and tendencies have been dissolved and the brain and nervous system refined so that soul awareness can be processed without disturbance. Permanent awareness of our soul nature and the totality of cosmic consciousness is *sahaja samadhi*: "natural, spontaneous awareness of the truth at all times" whether meditating or not meditating.

4. **When not established in pure consciousness, soul awareness identifies with the mental field and its transformations.**

The mental field is the medium through which the embodied soul relates to objective realms: the field of nature. Because of the soul's *pervading awareness*, it is conscious at all levels of the mental field. Because of temporary delusion, the soul may mistakenly assume itself to be the mental field. This is *egoism*, resulting in the sense of independent selfhood—the root cause of all of our problems. The *mind* (*manas*, "to think") aspect of the mental field responds and reacts to perceptions and processes information. Information filtered through the mind is presented to the *intellect* which determines its validity. Pervading soul awareness, ego-sense, mind, and intellect, are the four component aspects of the mental field.

Seers teach that soul light "shines in the organ of intelligence" of the mental field and assumes identification with it. This identification is an appearance only, because soul awareness does not become matter. When mental modifications are settled during meditation or during spontaneous episodes of transcendence, only the light of the soul remains. When we are not established in Self-awareness we tend to identify with modifications and transformations persistently occurring in the mental field.

Let us assume that we have before us a calm pond of water, into which we look and see, deep down, an electric light shining. Let us stir the water until sediment from the bottom of the pond begins to circulate, mixing with the gentle waves. At first the light will be somewhat distorted and may seem to be dispersed throughout the pond. Eventually it may be completely removed from our sight. We know the light is there but we cannot see it. The more frantically we stir the water in an effort to reveal the light, the more our perception of it is obscured. If we remain quiet, doing nothing but observing, in time the waves will calm and the sediment will settle to the bottom of the pond. Soon, behold!, the light is self-revealed.

Right meditation, while involving concentration, does not require frantic activity or emotion-supported endeavor. It does require alertness and an exercise of will or focused intent. Passivity can result in awareness becoming involved with subconscious and unconscious states which do not include samadhi, superconscious states.

Superconsciousness may also be experienced at moments other than during occasions of formal meditation practice. It is possible to be still and practice detachment to the point of experiencing pure being. When we exclude from our awareness everything that we are not—feelings, thoughts, objects perceived, body, the mental field—all that remains to our perception is awareness of being. Sitting in meditation is usually more effective because the process affords the opportunity to arrange circumstances so the body can be relaxed, the nervous system unstressed, and thought processes settled. Meditative contemplation can then proceed without distractions.

We can experience superconsciousness by devotion to the form or aspect of God that most appeals to us. By surrendering completely in God all other perceptions are renounced. Another way, is that of selfless service in cooperation with the trend of evolution. The way of abstraction is Jnana Yoga (wisdom Yoga); the way of surrender to God is Bhakti Yoga (the Yoga of love and devotion); and the way of selfless service is Karma Yoga (dissolving ego-sense by doing God's will). These approaches are suited to different temperaments, although it is well for devotees to include them all according to their capacity to do so. The most direct way to experience God-realization is the eightfold way of Raja Yoga because its processes remove awareness from involvement with outer sources of possible distraction and from inner conflicts.

Illumination of consciousness can be experienced by intentional practice and dedicated resolve, or it can spontaneously unfold. Simple faith and surrender in God can result in spontaneous soul awakening and enlightenment. Available to every rational person is the way of intentional practice supported by right understanding and firm resolve. In this course of action the devotee decides to take a stand against prevailing inner conflicts and do something to arrange conditions in his life so that restricting influences are weakened and dissolved. While adhering to useful routines the devotee practices meditation, using proven techniques so that superconscious states can be experienced. What is needed on this path is the will to persist in the right way and the willingness to surrender to the activity of grace as it becomes increasingly evident and influential. There must be no deluded thinking such as, "I do not need God—I can liberate myself now that I know the process." While functioning from ego-consciousness we cannot remove ourselves from it. Egoism is inclined toward preserving itself. Only direct experience of Reality can free the soul from bondage due to delusion.

Some beginners on the enlightenment path, under the spell of egoism, think, "I don't want to dissolve in the ocean of cosmic consciousness and no longer be me" or "I want to be a saint or a master. I want to be like a god or goddess." Delusion contributes to such vain ideas and prevents our complete surrender. There is nothing to fear on the enlightenment path. Just as life is better for us now that we have a degree of understanding, so it will continue to become better as our understanding improves and our realization of God becomes more complete. Do not be afraid of God, nor be reluctant to experience God as you continue on the discipleship path. Get the *little you* out of the way and let the *cosmic you* prevail.

5. **There are five classifications of mental modifications. They can be afflicted, painful, impure, and imbued with restricting influences; or not afflicted, not painful, not pure, and not imbued with restricting influences.**

States of consciousness, thoughts, sense perceptions, and inner drives and tendencies, can influence the mental field, causing changes and modifications. These modifications can be neutral if dormant or weak, or painful or pleasurable depending upon prevailing circumstances. Casual thoughts and feelings may arouse no specific response. We may, while calm, observe our thoughts and environmental circumstances with detachment. If emotionally involved, we may make judgments or have responses which causes us to feel either hurt or happy. Even pleasurable response can cause of future pain if we are dependent upon moods and outer circumstances for happiness, and our moods and circumstances change. Attachments which give us pleasure can contribute to pain when the object of pleasure is removed. Therefore, a person who is reliant upon moods and circumstances for happiness is a possible victim of such conditions.

We may feel strong and vital and be able to confront inner changes and outer circumstances of any kind with understanding. We feel ourselves to be in control. At other times, when tired or confused, even little disturbances may cause us serious emotional upset. Early in the morning, after refreshing rest, we may be extremely self-confident and capable of easily handling our thoughts, feelings, and relationships. Later in the day, when weary or overburdened with sensory input, we may become impatient, and react unwisely to circumstances. Even the memory of a past failure or hurt may trigger a painful emotional response.

The solution is not to withdraw from life but to see it in a new light: to experience the moment without being dependent upon circumstances for our peace of mind. We successfully renounce the world by seeing it correctly and relating to it intelligently. We disarm potentially pain-causing mental conditionings by objectively analyzing them, and weakening and dissolving them by meditation and living always in a superconscious state.

6. **There are five classifications of mental modifications: perception based on valid knowledge which has been learned, misinterpretation (illusion), hallucination, sleep, and memory.**

Mental images and transformations of the mental field can be based on knowledge or on illusion, because of accurate or inaccurate perceptions. The remaining three kinds of mental modifications are purely subjective and occur only in the mind itself.

7. **Valid knowledge can be acquired by direct perception, inference, induction, deduction, and the testimony of a knowledgeable person.**

Accurate perception is discernment without error. Inference is the process of determining conclusions from assumed premises based on probabilities. Starting with a reasonable theory, we can arrive at a probable conclusion. Inference is not always infallible because it is dependent upon sense testimony and the faculty of intelligence, both of which are material faculties. Example: when hearing an automobile entering your driveway and knowing that a specific friend is due to arrive, you assume the driver of the vehicle to be your friend even before you look to confirm the facts. A more obvious example: when you see smoke, you conclude that there must be a fire.

Inductive reasoning is the process of logical thinking, using known data. Deduction is the process of arriving at a conclusion by subtracting or taking away those parts of the problem which cannot be part of the solution. Vedic seers taught their students to look upon the world of multiplicity and inwardly say, "Reality is not this. Reality is not that." We may infer the existence of a creator by observing its creation. We may, by induction, determine that a creator exists, but if our data is not accurate or complete, we will not be able to comprehend the total nature of the creator. Deduction, removing from our sphere of observation all that the creator cannot be, can enable us to know what the creator is.

Whether by inference, induction, or deduction as the beginning mode of inquiry, if the devotee persists with intention to know, sooner or later unveiled intellectual abilities and awakened intuition will enable the truth to be discerned. The use of intelligence can enable us to understand almost everything about the realm of nature, including inner plane conditions and circumstances which are also of material substance. However, to know that which transcends nature, intuition, the soul's capacity to directly perceive, must be used.

Another source of valid knowledge is the testimony of a knowledgeable person. If we are informed by such, we can take his or her word about the matter and proceed. Trusting in such knowledge is but the beginning. We must then engage in study and careful examination of the evidence if we are to know the truth for ourselves. To take on faith the teachings of the masters is the right beginning on the spiritual path and we are indeed fortunate if we have a relationship with someone who can declare the truth as well as show the way to the realization of it. Paramahansaji used to say to disciples, "If you will allow me, I will introduce you to God." The guru-relationship is extolled above all others because the guru works with the disciple to show the way to soul freedom.

8. Illusion (false knowledge) results when the reality of an examined object is misinterpreted.

Illusion is misperception. Because of errors in perception, we may not accurately see what is before us. One might be walking at dusk, for instance, and mistake a bush to be a threatening animal or person. One might see a mirage reflected above the desert sands or above hot pavement on the road ahead.

Assuming the world of appearances to have independent existence is based upon lack of true knowledge and the inability to discern subjective levels of supporting influences. The world is not an illusion, but our misunderstanding of it creates the sense of illusion. The universe is real because it is a manifestation of cosmic forces. The universe is illusory because it is subject to change.

Illusions can also result when we hear someone speak, or when we read a book. What is actually articulated or intended may not be what we hear or apprehend. Illusion always has to do with our misinterpretation of the true character or essence of the object examined. The author of a book may understand the subject but be inadequate in the use of words to explain what is known. Or the explanation may be clear but we may not be able to get behind the words to the message. There is a way to discern the intent of a speaker or an author. It is to attune ourselves to the state of consciousness of the person initiating the communication, thus accessing the same field of knowledge. Friends and lovers frequently do this with each other. Sometimes the attunement is so harmonious that words are not necessary. When reading these sutras, it is helpful to go beyond the words of the original text to the field of consciousness and its knowledge which inspired the words. We can then have access to the entire range of knowledge of that field.

9. Hallucination results when the mind projects a false image which is not based on fact.

Hallucination is a psychological perception having no corresponding object. It is distinguished from an illusion which does have an object but is misinterpreted. There can be a variety of causes for hallucinations. If one has a desire or wish, and suppresses or represses it, the force of desire may manifest itself as mental images as a way of finding expression. One may, for instance, desire to experience communication with a recently deceased friend. Later, a vivid mental image, manifesting as a vision or conscious mental projection, may suddenly appear. This would be a form of wish-fulfillment which may satisfy emotional needs but would not be an instance of clairvoyance. It would be an hallucination.

Illusions and hallucinations may have psychophysiological contributing causes. Chemical, hormonal, and biological disturbances may cause hallucinations which manifest through hearing, sight, smell, taste, and touch. Disordered mental contents can produce delusion and false beliefs. Delusions of persecution, delusions of grandeur, delusions about one's station in life whether high or low, are hallucinations. *Perceptual disorders* produce illusions and hallucinations. *Thinking disorders* produce delusions (erroneous beliefs or convictions).

10. Sleep is a modification of cognitive powers of awareness.

That we remain somewhat aware when we sleep is indicated by our memory of the experience. During sleep, tamasic influences prevail, clouding our field of awareness. Since superconsciousness (samadhi) is negated when any mental modification is a controlling factor, even sleep should be acknowledged as a condition to be overcome. This is not to say that we should avoid sleep—we should learn to be inwardly conscious and beyond the influences of unregulated mental transformations when the body is at rest.

Three states of consciousness are ordinarily common. The waking state is evidenced by awareness of internal and external phenomena. The dream state is evidenced by the effects of subconscious mental modifications. Unconsciousness, during sleep or at any time for whatever cause, is characterized by the absence of wakefulness. A fourth state is superconsciousness.

One of the first procedures sometimes taught to students new on the spiritual path is to learn to intentionally regulate states of consciousness—to sleep at will, awaken at will, be aware of dream activity, be aware while seeming to be unconscious, and to experience superconsciousness. Initial success in mastering states of consciousness increases the practitioner's self-confidence and provides skills needed to regulate them whenever desired. The untrained person sleeps when tired and awakens when rested, is seldom conscious of dream activity, and is almost never aware of the possibility of superconscious experience.

Here are procedures to use for the purpose of acquiring control over states of consciousness. As you proceed, be inwardly centered and confident of your ability:

Sleep and Awaken at Will – When you retire for the night, or anytime you want to practice this procedure, relax in a quiet place and close your eyes. Withdraw attention from externals and from thought processes, and surrender to sleep. Before sleep, decide to awaken at a definite time. You will sleep restfully and awaken promptly at the chosen time. You have an inner time-sense and always know the time of day and your location in space. You can regulate your sleep pattern this way during normal occasions of sleep and when you want to nap for a few minutes, or for an hour or two. A downcast gaze often accompanies drowsiness as a prelude to sleep. With practice it is possible to look into the spiritual eye when entering the sleep phase and experience superconscious sleep.

Superconscious Sleep – Instead of surrendering to subconscious sleep, keep your awareness centered, with attention focused at the spiritual eye and upper brain centers. Feel the presence of God. Observe the process of relaxation and inward turning, remaining as the observer. You will experience deep rest while remaining in a meditative state. In the early stages, remain as long as you can at the doorway between wakefulness and sleep, then learn to move through the spiritual eye to superconscious awareness.

Lucid Dreaming – Whether going to sleep the ordinary way, or the superconscious way, choose to be conscious during the dream state. You may observe dreams emerging onto the screen of your inner vision. You may become aware that you are experiencing and observing the dream. You may choose to let the dream run its course, or with gentle will influence the dream to the extent that you can modify the sequence of events, dream in bright color or black and white, or awaken from the dream and return to it. While consciously dreaming you can walk through walls, levitate, expand your consciousness, communicate telepathically with people in this and other realms, and exercise all of the abilities you would have were you in the astral world unencumbered by the body and the laws of the physical universe.

Experience Superconsciousness at Will – Sit in an upright, relaxed meditation posture. Look into the spiritual eye and let your awareness pervade the crown chakra. Internalize attention. Experience calm, thoughtless awareness. Contemplate your consciousness to be as vast and clear as a cloudless sky. Do this when you start your regular meditation practice and learn to flow easily into the silence. Remember how it feels to experience superconsciousness and adjust your states of consciousness anytime during the day when you want to be soul-centered and peaceful. Repeated superconscious episodes will purify the mind.

11. Memory is mental representation of prior perceptions.

Memory always relates to an object. We can recall perceptions of our private thoughts, feelings, and perceptions and experiences we have had in relationship to others and our environment. Information presented to the mind is stored as an impression, a memory which can be accessed or recollected.

Ordinary operation of memory is selective: we recall impressions by choice or memories surface when they relate to present circumstances. It would be cause for confusion if the conscious mind were to be flooded with all of the memories stored in the subconscious. By training ourselves to think in an orderly manner and to perceive without error, we can avoid accumulating misinformation which might further confuse the mind and contribute to disordered thinking. Memories are as real as the objects they represent, but they are more subtle. They exist in the subconscious as images, sometimes holding emotional energy. Memories, along with the psychic force they retain, can be the cause of compulsions and destructive behavior. Even to recall an unpleasant memory may trigger an upsurge of painful emotion which causes fear, anger, resentment, guilt, and a host of similar feelings. Such memories, if repressed, can block the flows of psychic (soul) forces, create emotional and mental conflicts, and interfere with endeavors to function creatively in everyday circumstances. They should be acknowledged, processed as information only, and their forces released and directed for constructive purposes.

By intentional use of creative imagination we can visualize ideal circumstances and experiences with such vividness that memories of imaginal creations are retained in the subconscious. This is one way to reorganize the contents of the mind, as well as to work creatively in cooperation with Cosmic Mind to improve our relationship with the outer world. During meditative contemplation, it is sometimes possible to recall memories of former incarnations and of subtle realms between earth-sojourns. A constructive practice is to contemplate the first moment when you came into contact with space-time: when you assumed the false sense of independent self-identity. Then recall how it was with you just before that moment, when you were fully conscious and still aware in the field of God.

12. Mental modifications can be weakened and dissolved by meditation practice and by detachment.

The mental field can be purified by meditation practice and by calm self-analysis. You are not your thoughts or fluctuating mental states—you are pure consciousness. By becoming aware of destructive and nonuseful mental drives we can renounce them. By releasing our attachment to them, their influential power is effectively neutralized. Or they can be resisted in constructive ways and their forces transformed for higher purposes. For instance, when inclined to behave unwisely we can intentionally behave in a constructive manner, redirecting the driving forces of bad habits into positive actions. By successfully resisting and overcoming destructive drives we acquire their power for constructive ends. Mental modifications can also be weakened and dissolved by the superior force of superconscious realization. To meditate for a few minutes a day until superconsciousness is experienced will result in mental cleansing over a period of time. Superconscious forces, being superior to those which are modified by mental transformations, overcome destructive forces flowing through the mental field.

Now and then we may hear of a person who is believed to be demon-possessed, or otherwise controlled by dark forces. In such instances, the characteristics and behaviors of the afflicted person are due to neurotic or psychotic conflicts. All that needs to be done is to restore a reasonable degree of physical and emotional health, and the problem will be resolved. If one expresses multiple personality characteristics, the cause is deep-seated psychological conflict and not the manifestation of distinct entities. Some people "hear" voices which tease, speak about gross subjects, or tell them to behave in erratic ways. This phenomenon of mental hallucination is caused by psychological disturbances because of conflicts between conscious and unconscious levels of mind. The symptoms indicate auditory hallucinations. Not all of these "voices" urge the person to do self-destructive things. Sometimes they provoke in altruistic but impractical ways.

13. Of the two (meditation and detachment), concentrated flowing of attention to the field of pure consciousness is referred to as intentional practice.

For practical purposes we examine the relative world in order to acquire knowledge and to function with a degree of ease. To experience higher superconscious states and liberation of consciousness, the most useful spiritual practice is to contemplate the unmanifest field of pure consciousness during meditation, then maintain awareness of it while involved in daily routines. By becoming increasingly aware of the full range of consciousness, from the realm of nature to the unmanifest field, we not only acquire knowledge of the totality of life and its processes, we become increasingly cosmic conscious.

Aspire to know God and that which is beyond the field of God. Expand your awareness. Be surrendered in God and live as a true disciple on the enlightenment path. Attend to all matters which can contribute to inner peace and outer harmony. Meditate deeply, rising above all mental restrictions and exploring the inner realms. Practice meditation with diligence. Become proficient in superconscious experience. This is the way of highest spiritual practice.

As a result of right practice, sense urges will no longer be dominant and "the ways of the world" will no longer be attractive to you. This does not mean that you will withdraw from the world, or deny friends and family your friendship. You will see the world in a different way and you will live in it from soul awareness, not from ego-needs. You will be an emotionally mature and responsible person. Your motives will be pure and everything you do will be constructive and life-enhancing.

14. That practice becomes firm and steady as a result of devoted, persistent endeavor.

Because of focused endeavor we become grounded in the practice of spiritual disciplines, strong sensory urges are neutralized, the mind is illumined, and the body's forces are harmonized. Increasing satisfaction with successful meditation practice inspires us to continue on a steady course. Temptations are more easily resisted; restlessness and laziness are replaced by enthusiasm and God-inspired dedication to further practice.

There can be no success on this enlightenment path without intentional practice. Even if it requires of us an exercise of will, we must practice if we are to fulfill our purposes in this incarnation. The easiest way to proceed is to surrender to the processes and attend to all duties with a cheerful attitude. As a responsible person, it is my duty to do all things necessary to help myself. As a responsible person, it is your duty to do all things necessary to help yourself. There is evidence of grace as we proceed, which removes many of our burdens and carries us through difficult times. While doing our very best to help ourselves we are to renounce the results of our efforts. In this way we avoid anxiety, and experience soul contentment.

15. One becomes established in dispassionate detachment by mastering compulsions and instinctual urges.

Learn to discern the difference between wisdom-guided will and whim-guided will: the inclination to act based on intelligence versus the inclination to be responsive to moods. Memories of previous pleasurable experiences may be so attractive to us that we may be inclined to repeat them even if by so doing no useful ends are served. In this way we may tend to remain involved in behaviors and relationships which, while not harmful, are not useful or necessary. We may hear of possible experiences from friends, or through the media, and be tempted to have them. We may be restless and allow ourselves to behave in sense-oriented ways which prove to be mere diversions. We should, of course, enjoy life and be happy, flowing with constructive circumstances which are appropriate to our lifestyle and purposes.

Compulsive behavior is restrictive even if it is not always destructive. Although intentional cultivation of good habits is a useful way to overcome bad habits, even good habits can be binding if they result in unconscious, programmed behaviors. After good habits have served their usefulness by enabling us to live in constructive ways, we should continue them consciously and spontaneously. Subconscious conditioning techniques can often interfere with endeavors to facilitate spiritual growth by causing us to be compulsive instead of being freely responsive. If affirmations are used, they should be used superconsciously to awaken and clear awareness. Hypnosis should never be resorted to by a devotee on the enlightenment path, as its practice may further condition the mind and modify awareness.

Ask yourself, "Why do I do what I do?" Be knowledgeable about your motives and drives. Decide what is important to your continued spiritual growth and overall success in life, then realistically proceed. *It is by focusing on essentials and eliminating nonessentials that we condense experiences by concentrated endeavor and accelerate our progress.*

Establish a limit on your desires, and on the expenditure of energy and resources for egocentric needs. Use energies and resources to satisfy necessary needs and accomplish worthwhile purposes. Self-mastery should be the guiding rule of our lives. Modify behavior in all aspects of your life so that everything that is done supports your intention to be Self-realized. Choose a pure food diet, keep your personal environment clean and orderly, select your friends and social activities wisely. Be prudent in the manner in which you spend money and use available resources. Further your education, as needed, to acquire useful knowledge and improve skills helpful to your purposes.

Many truth seekers read metaphysical literature and meditate on a regular schedule, then allow themselves to be dominated by restlessness, moods, or purposeless involvements at other times. Their social interactions are not always wholesome. They waste time in idle daydreaming, worry, or gossip. They may then wonder why they are not experiencing satisfactory spiritual progress.

16. The highest renunciation is the result of Self-realization which enables the devotee to disregard and transcend all cosmic forces.

Cosmic forces are regulated by the gunas, the influential, attributes of nature present in the mental field which contribute to changes and transformations. An exercise of will may be necessary in the early stages of meditation to enable you to remain free of restlessness and overcome heaviness or drowsiness. If you are alert, you may be able to meditate easily without distractions caused by the influences of cosmic forces in the mental field.

An easier way to be removed from such influences is to be dispassionate—to be inwardly centered and not involved with them because of being focused on the field of pure consciousness. In this way, you experience soul awareness and are no longer attracted to the attributes of nature. To merely resist mental influences will not in itself result in Self-realization. The meditator should contemplate the idealized object of his meditative concentration and experience superconsciousness and higher superconscious states.

In the *Bhagavad Gita* (2:59) information is given regarding how the highest renunciation occurs:

> Sensual enjoyments cease for the soul which abstains from them, but the urge for sensual experience remains. Even this urge is dissolved when the Supreme is realized.

Sensual enjoyments are experienced in the mind, the senses being but the channels through which perception is communicated. Habits and tendencies of any kind can be resisted by use of will, then neutralized as the result of transcendence. Even though mental impressions which support habits and tendencies may remain after we have withdrawn from active involvement with them, they will eventually be dissolved as a result of the purifying fires of superconscious realizations. When the gunas are transcended and they subside, they no longer stir mental impressions which can cause restlessness or fluctuations of thought patterns. When the impressions are dormant and the gunas are in motion, they can influence our states of consciousness. Tamas guna contributes to dullness and lethargy. Rajas guna contributes to difficulty in concentrating. Sattva guna contributes to ease in concentration and luminous inner perceptions. Even sattva guna influences must be transcended if soul awareness is not to be disturbed.

By regular practice of superconscious meditation, superior habits of God-contemplation become established so that meditation becomes easy and enjoyable.

17. The superconscious (samadhi) state of wisdom is accompanied by thinking, tranquility, and the realization of unity with universal consciousness.

The superconscious state during which the meditator experiences oneness with universal consciousness and its manifestations, is named the "samadhi of wisdom." As soul awareness stops moving toward material attraction it turns progressively in the direction of its source and begins to reflect the pure light of God. While there is a possibility that soul awareness can immediately transcend identification with all relative manifestations, it is common for initial superconscious states to precede transcendence. As consciousness becomes progressively more clear, the meditator may experience superconscious states accompanied by reasoning, philosophical discrimination, clear perceptions of the totality of life, and a sense of oneness with God and the universe.

In reverse order, when one becomes progressively involved with matter and forgetful of the true nature of the soul, one loses awareness of God, identifies more with the realm of nature, loses the ability to discriminate, experiences diminishment of reasoning powers, and finally assumes ego-consciousness. This is how it is with souls when they first come into involvement with matter, and with devotees who progress on the spiritual path only to fall back because of inattention to their practices or involvement with inner and outer distracting influences.

The experience of preliminary superconscious states may persist for a relatively brief duration, for many years, or for centuries. If one becomes enchanted by the variety of inner perceptions which are possible to experience in meditation, the desire to go beyond them may diminish. Thus, many saints remain involved in beatific states of consciousness and fail to continue with practices which could result in final liberation.

I was once walking with my guru at his desert retreat in southern California and asked, "How many of the masters mentioned in *Autobiography of a Yogi* are fully liberated?" His reply was instant: "Not many. Some saints are so content to roam in the bliss of God-perception that they remain involved at that level, sometimes for millions of years."

As a result of experiencing the Samadhi of Wisdom all categories of cosmic manifestation are effortlessly comprehended and complete knowledge of life processes is revealed.

During early episodes of superconsciousness we may know we are experiencing a higher state of consciousness while thinking, "Is this really superconsciousness?" We are examining the experience and our relationship to it. Then, our intelligence enables us to know that we are indeed experiencing superconsciousness. Next, we no longer reason or analyze. We experience the experience. Finally, our awareness includes the perception of God along with perceptions of bliss consciousness.

18. When the mental field is clear, and its modifications are no longer influential, transcendental superconsciousness is experienced.

Lower and preliminary superconscious states are modified by the influences of mental impressions and the actions of the gunas. Because of this, an almost infinite variety of meditative perceptions and experiences can prevail. The meditator may experience visions, some of which may be routine and others chaotic. Some may be beatific and others may be transcendent in character. Visions can be understood as "superconscious dreams" in that while one is superconscious, mental influences are still present. While visions may be informative and sometimes revealing, the meditator should understand that they are products of the mind.

Failure to understand the causes and meanings of visions can result in illusion due to misperception. The meditator may experience astral-like perceptions and assume them to be celestial visitations, or experience a degree of expansion of awareness and mistake it for cosmic consciousness. All perceptions this side of transcendence are transitory. As we renounce the influences of habits and disturbing mental tendencies, so we should renounce their products—visions and various transitory perceptions.

You may, in the early stages of meditation, perceive flashing lights in the spiritual eye, clear sky, beautiful nature scenes, luminous dots of light, or changing, colorful geometrical patterns. These might be indications of awareness extending into unconscious levels of the mind and can indicate progress in clearing the mental field.

Lacking firm determination to rise free from the influences of the mind, and being neglectful of the advice of seers, some meditators remain enchanted by superconscious perceptions. They may become focused at lower astral levels of perception, thinking themselves to be in communication with beings from those realms. They may fantasize that they have been given a special revelation or have been chosen by God to be a messiah. They may become preoccupied with the temptation to use their newly acquired "revealed" understanding to satisfy their ego-needs or to help humanity before they are wise enough and strong enough to be of help to anyone. They may feel themselves to be fully enlightened, no longer in need of guidance. They may be satisfied with being somewhat godlike instead of experiencing God and That which is beyond the field of God. They can even become "fallen saints" and again become involved with the forces of nature, resuming a self-centered lifestyle or having to return to their spiritual practices with true humility and surrendered dedication.

Lower superconscious states are supported by the influences in nature: one's own mental impressions and the cosmic forces. Higher superconsciousness is pure awareness without support.

19. Superconsciousness devoid of true knowledge may be temporary. From this state one may continue to higher realizations or again become involved with the relative spheres, the realm of manifest nature.

Superconsciousness, as a *state* of consciousness, is not of itself, knowledge. A state of consciousness enables us to comprehend what is possible to know at that level but is not itself that which is examined. Superconsciousness in relationship to an object contemplated results in knowledge of that object. Higher superconsciousness is not permanent until we are fully aware that we are pure consciousness.

Beyond the state of "free while living" is the permanent state of "supremely free." From this level there is no possibility of falling into blind involvement with matter. When a supremely free soul becomes involved with causal, astral, or physical realms to assist the trend of evolution, that embodiment is referred to as an avatar incarnation: a descent of divine light and power into the realm of nature.

Lahiri Mahasaya wrote the following advice to a disciple:

> All meditative perceptions and visions are secondary. Whatever appears must disappear; hence, it cannot be permanent. Truth is eternal realization.
>
> Removing ignorance by dissolving ego is the only way to absolute knowledge. The aim of practicing yoga is to dissolve the ego, removing the cause of ignorance.
>
> When the seeker returns the mind to its source he attains inner realization. When he attains the state wherein everything is realized as one, the seeker is then attuned with eternal realization.
>
> When the seeker is established in samadhi, his practice becomes natural and spontaneous. In that state he does not have to practice with effort. Effort is shed, and without even practicing meditation he enjoys its benefits.
>
> Listening to the inner sound, the seeker actually sees gods, seers, and sages of the past in the spiritual eye.
>
> When the seeker transcends awareness of meditation and is stable in inner awareness, which is similar to the void but full of bliss, he has reached the true state of samadhi.
>
> There is absolutely one Self which is the ultimate existence. The seen is nothing but the reflection of the seer. The ultimate Self is the source of all.

20. Preceded by Self-knowledge, firm self-confidence, self-discipline, enthusiasm, and attentiveness, one can practice meditation and attain final liberation of consciousness.

Fully attentive practice means that, not only during meditation, but at all times—during occasions of spiritual study and inquiry, when involved in daily relationships and duties, during interludes of leisure—the devotee constantly thinks of God and exercises discernment in order to see through appearances to That which is permanently real. The ideal is to live so that every moment is used with benefit to increase higher knowledge and realization. In this way, regardless of our station in life or present circumstances, inner states of consciousness can be regulated and our relationship with the Eternal maintained.

In the Kriya Yoga tradition, two classifications of knowledge are defined. *Lower knowledge* is that of relative spheres which enables us to function in the world with understanding. Our efforts to acquire lower knowledge can be valuable training for later study of *higher knowledge*. By learning how to function in the relative world we have an opportunity to unfold and use our innate abilities. However, an accumulation of lower knowledge does not necessarily mean that one has the ability to comprehend higher matters. Higher knowledge is of the subjective realms and of God.

To progress on the spiritual path, remain focused on practice and loyal to the way best suited for soul growth, always supported by inner guidance and faith—avoiding moods, indecision, doubt, and superficial speculation. Once resolved on the right path, adhere to it with self-confidence, self-discipline, enthusiasm, and attentiveness. This is the way of discipleship.

21. Such devotees, intent upon meditation practice, soon experience superconsciousness.

We identify with that which fascinates our attention. If our attention is extroverted most of the time, we will remain involved with externals. If we remain at the level of lower superconscious perceptions—unless we resolve to move to higher states, or grace becomes influential—we will continue in illusion and fantasy. After preliminary superconscious experience the devotee should engage in surrendered meditation in order to move from lower to higher states.

Our involvement with the physical body and circumstances

in life is due to our identification with them. It is convenient for living in this world to relate to the mind and body, but when our identification becomes compulsive we forget our divine nature. Many people are strongly identified with their body and personality: proud of their appearance, proud of their accomplishments, proud of what they have been and what they intend to accomplish. This is vanity and a waste of precious opportunity for spiritual growth. From a more cosmic perspective we can see that the One Life is identified with all bodies and personalities for the purpose of relative expression. We are not then vain about such involvement because there is no importance to it except that the purposes of creation be fulfilled. We should be like this. We should identify with mind and body sufficiently to accomplish our purposes, while inwardly knowing our changeless nature as pure consciousness.

Superconsciousness can be experienced quickly by that devotee who is willing to devote time and attention to meditation practice and contemplation of higher realities.

22. Devotees who are more focused attain superior results in meditation practice.

Results are in relationship to our right endeavors. Some devotees are mild in their approach to spiritual practices, some are moderate, a few are intentional and concentrated. For those who are mild in interest and involvement, progress may be extremely slow, mildly slow, or moderately slow. If one's approach is slightly more focused, progress may be extremely moderate, mildly moderate, or steadily progressive. For one who is intentional and concentrated, progress may be mildly intensive, moderately intensive, or extremely intensive.

To maintain extremely focused involvement, cultivate devotion, be attentive to all disciplines and duties, and meditate more deeply each day than you did the day before. Even if pressed for time because of unexpected intrusions into your schedule, meditate for at least several minutes at the predetermined time. Practice the presence of God at all times. No matter what you are doing, be aware of your relationship with God and feel that the power of God is expressing through you. After acquiring a degree of proficiency in the practice of preliminary meditation techniques, learn and practice more advanced techniques. Be initiated into Kriya pranayama and engage in regular practice according to instructions given at the time of initiation. In these ways your spiritual evolution will be rapidly accelerated and you will experience obvious advancement on the path.

23. Samadhi can be realized quickly by surrendering in God.

The perfect realization of the heart (the soul) is consummated by surrender in God. Ask yourself: Are all of my thoughts, feelings, and actions God-surrendered? When I meditate, am I God-surrendered? Am I prepared to see God face to face? Am I prepared to accept the completion of my destiny? Let us clearly understand this great essential—*surrender in God is the way to perfect realization.*

You may ask, "How can I surrender in God if I do not know what and who God is, and if I do not know how to surrender?" If you will study this text, if you will pray to God, if you will yearn to know God, everything you need to know and everything you need to do will be revealed to you. Helpful information will come your way, daily experiences will afford you the opportunity of learning, your innate knowledge of God will unfold.

God can be worshipped with form and without form. If you have difficulty in contemplating God as Spirit without form or attributes, then contemplate God in the way which satisfies your mind and your devotional nature. Know that behind the form of God you worship is the field of pure consciousness. Be willing to let go of your concepts of God as higher understanding unfolds. If God, to you, is like an omnipresent, loving father, then cultivate awareness of father God as being with you and caring for you at all times. If you see God as nature, as a universal mother, then live with that understanding, knowing that God is expressing around you and providing for you. Your form of worship is personal. If you are surrendered in that mode of worship you will know the all-ness of God in the present incarnation.

Many saints, who no longer need a personal form of God to contemplate when they meditate, often sing devotional songs for enjoyment and celebration and to inspire others on the path. They may even perform meaningful rituals before an altar. Some establish temples of worship and places of pilgrimage to provide encouragement to devotees still in early stages of spiritual growth. Devotional chanting, prayer, ritual worship, and visits to temples and shrines, can be helpful in awakening soul forces as well as in releasing divine forces into planetary consciousness.

If we no longer need to contemplate God with form, we will neither feel a need to defend our understanding nor to find fault with the practices of others. If we are self-righteous because of our presumed knowledge of God, we need to rid ourselves of that attitude by surrendering more in God.

24. God is the initial expansion from within the field of pure consciousness, with attributes and characteristics, transcending all dualities.

I once visited a spiritual master in India. We were sitting with a few people. He asked me, "Is God pure, or impure?" Knowing the philosophical basis from which the question was asked I responded, "Impure." Several who were present seemed somewhat confused by my answer. In some cultures the general belief is that God is pure and the world is impure. But that was not the real question. The question was about the characteristics of God in relationship to the field of pure consciousness, not about a comparison between God and nature.

That *God is the initial expansion from the field of pure consciousness* means that the Godhead is not the field of pure consciousness. It is the outward expression of supreme consciousness endowed with cosmic forces. The mixture of cosmic forces in the Godhead results in God being impure in relationship to the unmanifest field of consciousness. Sattva guna prevails in the Godhead while the other two gunas are present and subordinate. If they were not, further expansion resulting in world manifestation would not be possible.

God has transcendent and manifest aspects. The transcendent aspect is forever the same, as Being. The manifesting aspect shines on the field of primal nature endowed with cosmic forces from the field of God, and the universes emerge into manifestation. In religious terms, God involved as the director and producer of the cosmic drama is referred to as the lord or ruler of creation. The Sanskrit word for this aspect is *Ishwara*, "God as the governing or regulating power." God as power orders the activities of cosmic forces which further express as varied forces in nature. When we pray to this aspect of God we pray that God's will be done through us. We do not have to instruct God to do anything or tell God how to run cosmic affairs. We have but to surrender and let the controlling influence of the Higher Power express through us, while learning to understand its purposes and inclinations.

25. God is transcendent, containing the innate potentiality of omniscience, omnipotence, and omnipresence.

Each soul—you, me, everyone—contains the innate potentiality of omniscience, omnipotence, and omnipresence because God *is us*: specialized as units of consciousness. When our awareness is contracted because of identification with matter, mind, the conditionings of the mind, and prevailing innate cosmic forces, we feel ourselves to be restricted; we are not then aware of being omniscient, omnipotent, and omnipresent. We feel ourselves to be human, limited, and in need of help. By cultivating devotion to God, surrendering in God, meditation practice, and progressive superconscious experiences, we are released from restricting influences, enabled to express unbounded awareness.

Temporary perceptions of transcendence can occur spontaneously and people whose lives are otherwise ordinary sometimes report such incidents. Many people believe in the possibility of such perceptions because of their innate soul knowledge. Spiritually awakened souls experience and sometimes demonstrate their knowing, power, and freedom. When innate knowledge unfolds, soul powers become expressive, cosmic consciousness is experienced, and soul potential can be actualized.

26. That Supreme Being, beyond the limitation of space, time, and causation, is the true guru, the teacher of even the ancient teachers.

Knowers of knowledge come and go; knowledge itself remains

accessible to anyone who becomes receptive to it. Truth teachers come and go; truth remains what it is. Appearances in the relative spheres come and go; God remains. Hence, God is referred to as the teacher of even the ancient teachers. Truth teachers do not invent God; they only discover and reveal the nature of God. All enlightened teachers emphasize that what they know, all can know, and what they teach has been taught in times past and will be taught in the future by knowers of truth.

In the *Bhagavad Gita* (4:1-4) Krishna's words explain the process of the transmission of truth through the Ages:

> I proclaimed this imperishable yoga to ancient wise men and makers of the laws by which men are governed. They handed it down from one to another, through a line of royal sages, until this truth was lost to the world through a long lapse of time. The same ancient science has been today declared to you by me, for you are my disciple and friend and this is the supreme secret.

Seekers in whom the light of knowledge has yet to dawn and blossom must take recourse to the teachings of the seers in order to learn of the nature of Reality and engage in the practices of righteous living. All fully enlightened souls know God as God is—and know cosmic processes as they are. Only partially enlightened people speak of special knowledge and unique revelations, or claim their understanding to be superior. Higher knowledge is incomprehensible to the average person because of unawakened soul capacities, thus the common admission: "I do not understand. I cannot understand. I do not see how anyone can understand." Yet, we are advised by the masters that, as they have understood, so can we understand.

Do what you can to unveil your understanding. Instead of identifying with others who may be mired in delusive states of consciousness, wandering through this world in a confused condition, in your mind and heart honor the saints and inwardly say, "I want to be like that. I want to know God. I want to be surrendered in God." According to your aspiration, and your responsible behavior and surrender, it will be done unto you.

27. The manifesting symbol (evidential aspect) of God is Om.

The Gospel According to Saint John 1:1-5:

> In the beginning was the Word, and the Word was with God. The same was in the beginning with God. All things were made by Him; and without Him was not any thing made that was made. In Him was life; and the life was the light of men. And the light shineth in darkness; and the darkness comprehended it not.

When the triple aspects of cosmic force become unbalanced in the field of God, the creation process begins. The outflowing force results in a sound-frequency, Om, the Word. This is why it is referred to as God's manifesting symbol. It is evidence of the existence of God, as any sound-frequency is evidence of that which produced it.

God, through the Word, framed the worlds. God caused all things to manifest. There is nothing in manifestation that is not comprised of fine cosmic forces and their further transformations. When we see the field of nature we know that something caused it to manifest. The existence of an outer expression is proof of its underlying cause.

God's life is the life of every person and every creature. God's energy is the energy of the atoms. God's light shines upon the realm of nature but because of deluded consciousness some souls cannot comprehend the existence of the light.

The Sanskrit word representing Om consists of three letters spelled as AUM. "A" represents manifestation; "U" represents maintenance; "M" represents dissolution. This primordial sound current makes possible manifestation, preservation of that which is manifested, and the dissolution of manifestation. The universe is forever undergoing change due to transformations.

28. One should meditate on this Word, analyzing it, surrendering to it, and being conscious of its real nature.

Om is the highest mantra to contemplate in meditation. By merging in Om we can flow attention back to the field of God.

Om can be heard as the background sound of nature. It is the sound from which all other sound-frequencies emerge and into which they return. It can more easily be heard when we are meditating because we have withdrawn attention from sensory perceptions. An easy way to proceed is to look into the spiritual eye and listen within, imagining the sound to be present. When you do this, feel that you are immersed in Om and be gently attentive to it. Behind preliminary sounds is Om. When you are calm and creative forces begin to move upward through the spinal pathway to the brain centers, discernible sounds may be heard emanating from the chakras. Soul force, prana, when involved with body functions, manifests as different frequencies to perform various operations. From the base chakra upward to the throat chakra the sound-frequencies are of the five primal element-influences: earth, water, fire, air, and ether. At the spiritual eye, which transcends the element-influences as well as regulates them, the sound is Om. Listening to Om removes attention from the lower chakras and allows it to be directed to the source of Om, God.

Listen to Om, merge in Om, dissolve in Om, be Om, go beyond Om to experience pure consciousness. Your attention will become so fascinated by the inner sound that you will meditate without effort. Om comforts the mind and allows soul awareness to be experienced. Merge in Om for relaxation purposes and to experience stress reduction during short meditation sessions. Merge in Om to experience higher superconscious states during extended meditation sessions.

After preliminary meditation practices, after techniques have been used with benefit, meditation on Om remains the final focus and will lead your attention through levels of superconsciousness to God-realization. Om meditation can be used by devotees of any religious or philosophical persuasion because it is beyond all contrived names or forms of God and beyond all concepts of God.

Om can be chanted aloud prior to internal listening. The way to chant Om is to inhale and let the sound flow out with natural exhalation—OOOOMMMMmmmnnn—concluding with a nasalized humming sound. Breathe in easily and repeat. Do it slowly and naturally, with no attempt to force or sing it. Chanting in this way regulates breathing rhythms and results in natural pranayama, balancing of life forces in the body, and coordination of the brain hemispheres.

Chant audibly for a while, then quietly, then a whispering chant, then mental chanting. Be still and listen to Om internally, surrendering to it. Gaze into the spiritual eye as you do this, looking into the distance of inner space, feeling your awareness expand in Om and beyond, to the field of pure consciousness.

29. Contemplation of Om results in cosmic consciousness and the removal of mental and physical obstacles to success on the spiritual path.

The harmonizing influence of Om contributes to mental tranquility and coordinated functioning of subordinate life forces in the body. Contemplation on Om expands awareness and frees us from mental restrictions and distractions. Being attentive to Om, the manifesting symbol of God, and by actualizing the qualities of God, psychological transformation occurs and destructive behaviors are modified and eliminated.

As the mental field is cleansed and the brain and nervous system are refined, cosmic consciousness will be expressed through the body, resulting in a glorified body and literally heaven on earth for much of the global population.

Soul awareness awakens from unconsciousness to subconsciousness, to conscious awareness, and superconsciousness. From superconsciousness the soul awakens to cosmic consciousness, to God-consciousness, and transcendence. Contemplation of Om will lead your attention progressively through these states of soul unfoldment as the field of God like a magnet attracts your attention back to the Source.

30. Obstacles to success on the enlightenment path are disease, laziness, doubt, negligence, procrastination, philosophical confusion, failure to make progress, attachment to sense pleasures, misperception, and mental distractions.

All problems have delusion as their basis. The first step for any person who wants to overcome all obstacles, regardless of their manifesting symptoms, is to turn to God. If this is not done all attempts to solve problems at a superficial level will only result in temporary relief.

One may successfully eliminate disease symptoms but not their causes. Relief will be experienced but not total wellness. If underlying causes are present but dormant, there will remain the possibility of future illness. To accomplish our purposes we have an advantage if we are healthy and vital so that productive, long life is assured. For this reason, enlightenment masters prescribe routines and procedures for the purpose of enabling devotees to be healthy, fulfill their obligations, and realize God.

There is always hope for people who sincerely endeavor to help themselves but there is little hope for a lazy person. Fortunate are you if you know the usefulness of accomplishing your worthy goals and are enthusiastic about doing so. Laziness may be merely a bad habit due to lack of any sense of purpose in life. It may be due to a predominance of tamas guna or to a biological or chemical imbalance. It is frequently the result of self-centeredness and emotional immaturity. Banish laziness by surrendering in God while doing constructive things to enable you to successfully play your role in life.

Occasional doubts can be useful if they cause us to examine our thoughts and come to terms with life. Persistent doubt is a destructive habit, a form of preoccupation with mental processes which enables us to justify our avoidance of responsible behavior. In philosophical matters, take the word of enlightened teachers on faith, then practice recommended procedures to discover for yourself what is true. Do not doubt the testimony of a knowledgeable person. Do not doubt the existence of God. Do not doubt your inner reality and your God-endowed capacities. Proceed with faith and confidence and prove in your life the principles you learn. Avoid prolonged philosophical speculation about matters which are not relevant to your spiritual growth. Direct your attention to the essentials.

Negligence is due to disordered thinking and lack of interest. Paramahansaji told a story about himself as a new disciple with his guru, Sri Yukteswar. A transient visitor to the ashram told Paramahansaji that it was not important whether or not one worked in this world because it, being illusory, would pass away, leaving no trace. Pondering this information, the new disciple neglected his ashram chores. One day, Sri Yukteswar asked him why he was behaving so inappropriately. Paramahansaji "instructed" him as he had been instructed. Sri Yukteswar retorted, "As long as you breathe the free air of this world you are obligated to render some service in return!"

31. Some effects which might accompany distractions may be grief, anxiety, unsteadiness of the body during meditation, and irregular breathing.

To merely advise a person that he is a spiritual being—a perfect expression of pure consciousness—and that he need not have problems, is seldom sufficient to solve his problems. Sometimes such advice does cut to the core and causes an immediate adjustment in perspective and attitude. More usually, when one is firmly rooted in disturbances a sense of helplessness prevails. Arjuna, in the *Bhagavad Gita* narration (2:7–9) at the beginning of his instruction by Krishna, exclaims:

> My very being is stricken with the weakness of pity. With my mind bewildered about my duty, I ask; tell me, for certain, which is better. I am your disciple; teach me, as I seek refuge in your guidance. I do not see what will drive away my sorrow which dulls my senses; even if I should win the battle and emerge victorious. I will not fight.

When we are receptive to instruction, the help we need is readily forthcoming, for life always provides what we need when we need it, if we are receptive to it.

Often, we but dramatize grief and anxiety because we are playing a role, pretending to be helpless when we really could do better if we tried. We sometimes become so confused that we feel like giving up, but we cannot. During occasions of severe challenge it can be useful to pull back, to rest, to be refreshed spiritually. Even oppressive circumstances seem less formidable to us when we are rested and in a more positive frame of mind.

We may grieve because of our weaknesses, or because of the pain experienced by others. We may grieve when we experience

a loss of some kind: when we are rejected, when we experience
failure, or when a cherished object or person is taken from us for
one reason or another. Grief always has attachment along with
misunderstanding as its basis.

Inability to sit still during meditation can be overcome by
adhering to prescribed meditation procedures. When sitting to
meditate, resolve not to move during the practice session unless
for the purpose of adapting to a more comfortable position. Let
the muscles relax, look into the spiritual eye, pray or use a meditation technique to internalize attention. Be so involved inwardly
that the body is forgotten. If mild energy flows cause the body to
move, do not encourage this or allow it to persist. Relax, and
take the processes more deeply within. Some beginning meditators assert that sitting for ten or fifteen minutes is their limit—
and that sitting for an hour or more is beyond their capacity!
They say this because they are restless and have not given themselves the opportunity to experience relaxed meditation. In deep
meditation our time-sense is transcended and we remain rapt in
superconsciousness, oblivious of time.

A novice meditator might ask, "How can anyone sit for two or
three hours, or more, in meditation without becoming bored?"
Successful meditation practice is not sleep; nor is it an occasion
for indulging in reverie or persistent thinking. Meditation is yoga
and yoga is samadhi, superconsciousness: a state of awareness
outside of the field of time.

Irregular breathing patterns accompany mental and emotional unrest. By regulating the breathing pattern, thought
activity and moods are regulated. This is the psychophysiological way to intentional participation in the process of stopping
and dissolving the fluctuations of the mind.

**32. To control and eliminate these mental distractions one
should practice meditation and contemplate Om, the manifesting creative force of God.**

Listening to Om and being absorbed in it will result in overcoming all mental distractions. First, the meditator's attention
is withdrawn from restless mental processes because of being
elevated to superconscious levels of awareness. Second, the har-

monizing influence of internal sound—and with it an infusion of superconscious force—dominates the mental field and restrains and calms the mind, causing the tendencies which contribute to restlessness to become dormant.

Do not be overly thrilled when you first perceive inner light and sound manifestations. In the early stages these may be neurological phenomena caused by concentration and the pressure of flows of life force in the body. There are certain techniques which can be used—and which are sometimes used by yogis, as preliminary practice—which stimulate the optic and auditory centers in the brain, causing inner light manifestation and inner sound perception. Such induced lights and sounds are not the spontaneously manifested lights and sounds perceived as a result of deep inward contemplation.

33. The mental field is calmed and purified by the cultivation of feelings of friendship, compassion, joy, and neutrality; and by analyzing ideal possibilities.

By analyzing the range of possible states of consciousness and mental-emotional states common to the human condition, we can experiment by adjusting our attitudes and moods to discover that we have a considerable degree of control over them. With practice, we can choose to be friendly, compassionate, joyful, and even-minded instead of allowing ourselves to be victimized by shifting moods and mental states. When feeling unfriendly and perhaps at odds with others, imagine yourself as being friendly and that the whole world is friendly. Affirm, "I am on friendly terms with a friendly universe." Continue in this way until you feel love and compassion and are secure in the knowledge that the universe is supportive of you. Cultivate inner joy: not emotional excitement, but the joy of the soul.

Cultivate understanding, relate to the world while inwardly being somewhat detached, viewing the unfolding drama of passing events as incidents occurring in the field of space-time. They are only relatively real. You will be able to master states of consciousness and see the world as you choose to see it.

Rabindranath Tagore, noted poet and novelist of India, wrote a collection of prose offerings entitled *Gitanjali*. In one of them he wrote:

> When thou commandest me to sing it seems that my
> heart would break with pride; and I look to thy face,
> and tears come to my eyes.
> All that is harsh and dissonant in my life melts
> into one sweet harmony—and my adoration spreads on
> wings like a glad bird on its flight across the sea.
> I know thou takest pleasure in my singing. I know
> that only as a singer I come before thy presence.
> I touch by the edge of the far spreading wing
> of my song thy feet which I could never aspire to reach.
> Drunk with the joy of singing I forget myself
> and call thee friend who art my lord.

**34. One may definitely overcome all such obstacles by practice
of pranayama.**

"Mind is nothing more than restless breath," say yogis. By
this, they mean that the movements and transformations occurring in the mental field are driven by cosmic forces, which in
turn are driven by the forces of prana in the body. Mental processes interact with body forces and can be trained by attitude
and behavioral adjustments. Just as mental conflict can contribute to physical imbalance, so physical harmony can contribute
to mental peace. When we are happy and optimistic, biological
processes are inclined to be orderly. When we are unhappy and
pessimistic, biological processes are inclined to be disordered.
By regulating breathing rhythms we can regulate body functions
as well as mental processes.

One who can control life force can control body functions, emotional states, and mental processes. Mastery can even extend to
the environment, when accomplished devotees know how to
attune their consciousness and life force with the life forces which
maintain and regulate processes occurring in the field of nature.

When restless or emotionally disturbed, breathe deeply and
slowly for a minute or two and notice how your mind becomes
more calm and emotions subside. Before meditating, sit in the
prescribed posture, inhale rather deeply, pause, exhale easily and
almost completely. Do not force the process but merely breathe

more slowly and deeply than usual. Do this a few times. Breathe in peace and joy, relax when you breathe out. Your attention will be easily internalized. Proceed immediately with meditation.

Intentional pranayama is experienced by breath regulation and by surrendered meditation practice. Spontaneous pranayama occurs when superconscious states are experienced and when soul force moves upward through the chakras into the spiritual eye and crown chakra. Notice how your breathing pattern is regulated when you are concentrating.

35. Inner perception and experience of subtle cosmic forces and their manifestations cause a change in the mental field and enable the devotee to be stable in meditation practice.

When fascinated by inner perceptions during meditation, we have the opportunity to examine them and the subtle forces which contribute to their manifestation. When we are absorbed in contemplation, mental fluctuations become orderly and settle into a dormant state, allowing perfect concentration.

Fluctuating cosmic forces in the mental field contribute to various perceptions. When the mind is calm the meditator may see in the spiritual eye a brilliant white light like a clear moon against a background of dark infinite space. The ball of light may be dark blue; dark blue with a golden halo; or dark blue with a golden halo centered by a point of sparkling white light.

By steadily looking into the spiritual eye, gently endeavoring to see through and beyond initial light perceptions, pranic effulgence will be seen. Life force frequencies of the chakras may be seen reflected in the spiritual eye, accompanied by their corresponding sound frequencies heard in the inner ear or vibrating inside the skull.

When the spiritual eye is seen with a gold halo around a blue orb centered with brilliant white light, know this to be the reflection of cosmic forces emanating from the medulla oblongata at the base of the brain. Soul force flows into the body through the medulla to the brain, then throughout the body. By withdrawing prana from the senses and directing it back to the brain we are able to inwardly see the cosmic forces at the spiritual eye. Gold is the prana-frequency of Om. Blue is the prana-frequency of God involved with creation. The white light is the prana-frequency of consciousness beyond primal nature.

When you see the light of the spiritual eye, surrender to it while listening to Om. *Feel yourself merging into the gold light,* becoming one with all-pervading Om, with the universe floating within your consciousness, including the subtle realms behind the screen of gross matter. *Contemplate the blue light and merge into it,* feeling yourself to be one with omnipresent, omnipotent, omniscient intelligence-consciousness. Let your thoughts and feelings be in accord with your religious considerations. If your approach is more impersonal, feel yourself to be one with the mighty cosmic power of the universe. *Contemplate the white light and merge into it,* feeling yourself to be pure Spirit.

In the beginning you may be conscious that your involvement with the light is due to your intentional visualization. Eventually, you will have actual experience and your inner transformations will bear witness to this. If you do not see the light of the spiritual eye after a few meditation sessions, or after many, do not despair. Even without light perception you can still experience higher superconscious states. Your path may be the way of knowledge rather than the way of vivid light perception.

Meditation perceptions vary according to the influences of the cosmic forces active in the mental field and consciousness of the meditator. If tamas is dominant, awareness may be unclear and perceptual abilities somewhat obscured. If rajas is dominant, awareness may be more clear but illusory perceptions may result. One may be overly fascinated with visions, the possibility of astral projection, or of exploring the celestial realms. One may also be attracted to the experience of ecstatic states and preoccupied with unfolding and demonstrating soul abilities. When sattva is dominant, meditation perceptions will be more refined, elevating, and transcendent. In all instances our discernment should be our guide, enabling us to perceive and enjoy while moving through the planes of phenomena which come within range of our inner vision. Whatever we are attracted to will only be appealing so long as we have corresponding psychological needs.

36. When the light of Reality is experienced, the mental field becomes tranquil and supreme Self-confidence results.

The light of pure consciousness constructively influences the mind and body and further awakens soul consciousness, resulting in beneficial changes and personality transformations. It is redemptive, displacing everything unlike itself. The more this light is evidential, the more transformative is its influence. The mental field is cleansed, subtle sheaths are refined, and the body becomes a responsive conduit through which Spirit expresses in the realm of matter.

Self-confidence, soul conviction, becomes pronounced and all doubts and fears are banished. The devotee thereafter lives with perfect faith in the goodness of God and has the assurance of conscious immortality this side of the unmanifest field and eventual transcendence when involvement with the universe ends.

37. By actualizing the virtues and states of consciousness of role models, saints, and seers, the devotee's mental field becomes harmonized.

If we do not know how to solve problems or behave appropriately in this world, we can look to the example of others who are successful in their relationship with the universe and learn from them. Because we are states of consciousness expressing through mind and personality, we can learn to adjust our attitudes and apply ourselves to manifest desirable qualities.

What has been known by one person can be known by another. What has been done by one person can be done by another. If only one other soul in this world has awakened from the dream of mortality, we can also do it.

Who are your role models? Whom do you most admire and want to be like? What are the attitudes, states of consciousness, and modes of behavior you most admire and want to emulate? To be successful, observe others who are already successful and find out how they function—then apply what you learn. To be successful on the spiritual path, observe enlightened men and women or read about them, then emulate and actualize the virtues and states of consciousness you deem most desirable or useful to your purposes. The procedure is simple—find out how to do what you want or need to do, and do it.

Attune your mind to the highest possible levels of awareness and function from those levels. Associate with saints by thinking about them and aspiring to be like them. Avoid eccentric or inappropriate behaviors, choosing to embody the desirable characteristics. If you are an initiated disciple, stay in tune with your guru and the guru line, and receive through this attunement the waves of grace which are constantly flowing through the gurus from God. When you meditate, invoke awareness of God's presence and visualize your guru line in the spiritual eye until you feel the overshadowing presence of God. If thoughts persist as you move through higher superconscious states when meditating, let them be thoughts of God and the gurus. Hold fast to that which will carry your attention to its final resting place.

38. By analyzing knowledge of dreams and dreamless sleep states, understanding of states of consciousness is acquired.

Our awareness is operative on four levels: superconscious, conscious, subconscious, and unconscious. With practice it is possible to be aware during sleep states and to analyze them. During dreamless sleep, latent tendencies are dormant and we are unconsciously nearest to soul awareness. Learn to be aware during interludes of dreamless sleep and transform unconsciousness into superconsciousness. In this way, use the hours of sleep as an opportunity for exploring the possibilities of soul unfoldment.

While dreaming, learn to observe dreams and connect dream happenings with subconscious causes, or intrude upon the dream and modify it to suit your fancy. In this way you will learn how to consciously regulate intention and mental imagery instead of being subject to uncontrolled subconscious drives and desires.

By becoming proficient in such practices, the yogi learns how mental processes operate and understands that the mind is subject to intentional influences. It is then possible to become aware of individualized mind as a portion of Cosmic Mind, the Mind with which we cooperate when we exercise creative abilities for the purpose of achieving goals and accomplishing purposes. We discover that as mental impressions in our mind result in thought activity, mood changes, and alterations in the physical body, so our desires and intentions find expression in the outer realm through the medium of Cosmic Mind.

39. By meditating according to one's inspired choice, the mental field becomes harmonized, tranquil, and disciplined.

When inwardly surrendered and in a devotional mood, one may spontaneously be inclined to contemplate according to the desire of the heart (soul). On such occasions without any prior plan, thoughts turn Godward. This can occur when the soul urge to know God is pronounced, when self-sense is diminished, when prana flows upward, and when grace is influential.

We may use any formula or technique for meditation which we have found to be helpful. When we are surrendered in God, meditation proceeds naturally, directed by the soul's innate intelligence.

40. The devotee, by contemplative meditation, can experience mastery from minute aspects of matter to infinity.

The soul, as a unit of consciousness, can assume a relationship with whatever it contemplates. Identified with the physical body, the soul assumes itself to be the size of the body. In like manner, if an atom (or any aspect of matter) is contemplated, soul awareness can identify with it, assuming the size of the object contemplated, or can enter into it and observe its characteristics. The soul can expand awareness to include the gross, subtle, and fine universe. It can include in its field of awareness universes in other space-time dimensions unrelated to the universe we know through our senses. Myriads of universes are in the process of manifesting and dissolving, expanding out of the field of pure consciousness and flowing back into it. When consciousness transcends the universe to embrace the unmanifested field, all aspects of that field and its emanations can be known.

41. When the mental field is purified, it can accurately reflect whatever is presented to it.

When the mental field is purified, only soul awareness remains. Just as our mind reflects thoughts and images presented to it during ordinary sense-perceived relationships, so the purified mind reflects the light of pure consciousness during higher superconscious states. Any object that comes within the range of our mind can be reflected therein. Directing attention to gross or subtle aspects of nature, the meditator can so identify with them that accurate information will be reflected in the mind. In this way, abilities usually thought of as supernatural can be demonstrated.

42. At this level, while thought transformations persist and the mind is not yet perfectly tranquil, contents of the mental field are intermingled.

In lower superconscious states there can be confusion due to subtle, continuing thought processes which are driven by the force of unconscious impressions or the actions of the gunas. For instance, because of confusion we may observe an object but not fully understand its characteristics, or we may have partial understanding of an object but not know words to describe our understanding. In the former instance we may know what God is like but are unable to understand the nature of God. In the latter instance we may have partial understanding of God but be unable to put our understanding into words. We may be able to experience the results of conviction and faith in God, but not be able to fully understand how the process works. We may know the process of how faith works, but not be able to exercise pure faith in order to manifest the results. While the mind remains unsettled, only partial knowledge can be demonstrated.

43. When samadhi (superconsciousness) without gross thought processes is established, the mental field reflects the light of pure consciousness.

By contemplation of God, gross mental processes are rendered inoperative and God-realization unfolds. So long as the waves of the mind are agitated, only glimpses of God can be experienced. One may experience cosmic states but this is not yet the final realization. How long this takes depends on the power of concentration and residual karmic impressions which are yet to be cleansed from the mental field.

44. During higher superconscious states, transformations of mental states continue.

Initial superconscious states may be accompanied by philosophical speculation, or attempts to understand various aspects of the mind or nature. One may be reflecting upon how knowledge can be used in everyday experience, or how to improve understanding of the processes of life. During higher superconscious states one is inclined to contemplate subtle matters—the categories of cosmic manifestation and the true nature of God—and in this way progress on the enlightenment path.

What is perceived during meditation can be analyzed after meditation to allow inner realizations to be comprehended. The process of mental transformation is constant during meditation, during normal waking hours, and during interludes of sleep.

45. Contemplation of subtle aspects of matter ends with awareness of the field of primal nature.

Primal nature (Om, space-time, cosmic particles), from which the universe came into manifestation and by which it is supported, is the primary aspect of consciousness in manifestation to be contemplated. It is from this level of awareness that seers can demonstrate mastery over nature and perform what unenlightened people refer to as miracles. These events unfold either by an act of will or by allowing the creative force to flow to fulfill needs. In the former instances, the superior intention of a clear-minded person causes a movement in the primal field of nature which reflects in the field of outer manifestation. In the latter instance, when one has a need, the soul's equilibrium is disturbed and the universe moves to meet the need in order to restore soul consciousness to a condition of harmony.

Through successive superconscious states the meditator progresses from knowledge and mastery over the body, knowledge and mastery over the senses, knowledge and mastery over mental processes, knowledge of subtle aspects of nature, to knowledge of the field of primal nature.

46. The four states of superconscious thought transformation are "with support."

This refers to the four states of mental transformation earlier mentioned in sutra 17—thinking about what is contemplated in a deliberate manner, philosophical speculation, occasional or frequent perceptions of higher superconscious states, and initial experiences of God-realization. This level of superconsciousness is therefore supported by mental concepts and impressions.

During this level the meditator may also experience oneness with Om, with light, or with whatever is contemplated. This is lower samadhi—a bringing together of awareness with the object contemplated.

47. When consciousness is pure and flows without disturbance, the luminosity of the true Self is manifested.

Prior to this, the light of God is received fully into the mental field instead of being received through the screen of impressions. Yogis refer to the direct shining of the light of God into the mental field as "the path of the sun." The distorted reflection of the light of God, because mental impressions yet remain, is referred to as "the path of the moon." In the first instance, one knows the reality of God by direct experience. In the second instance, one knows the reality of God but realization is not complete because of the disturbing influences of mental conditionings.

48. In higher superconsciousness, direct intuitive knowledge of truth is known.

By using the faculty of intelligence, the material medium of discernment, everything this side of the field of God can be objectively examined. To clearly know God, however, the operant mode of knowledge is intuition: the soul's ability to directly perceive. The state of superconsciousness with knowledge is referred to as truth-bearing, truth-in-Itself. In this state we do not merely know about God, we know God. We can also know about that which is "beyond God," the unmanifest field.

Knowledge may fade if the mental field is not completely

cleansed. The devotee should continue to be inspired on the spiritual path by reading from authoritative sources, and by philosophical reflection and deep meditation.

49. Knowledge acquired by conversation, reading of books, usual modes of learning, and preliminary superconscious states, is different from intuitive knowledge.

Knowledge received from others may be partial: mixed with their opinions, or not fully comprehended by us. Such knowledge requires analysis, just as superconscious knowledge requires analysis. Truth has to be known by direct perception. Devotees who are well-educated and endowed with superior intellectual powers may mistakenly assume that because they are capable of understanding relative matters they are equally capable of understanding transcendental matters.

50. Mental impressions of the samadhi-of-wisdom inhibits other mental impressions, producing permanent beneficial changes.

Impressions resulting from ordinary sense experiences—thinking, desiring, reacting to circumstances, observation of the environment—may condition the mental field and interfere with self-determined thinking and spontaneous behavior. This accumulation of impressions with possible influence to cause effects is our karmic condition. Deep-seated impressions in the unconscious may, when circumstances cause them to be aroused or are ideal for their actualization, result in events and experiences. These may be pleasant, painful, or neither pleasant nor painful. Because they contain the seeds of possible future effects, they should be eliminated.

We can manage the influences of impressions which are known by being conscious of them and by either agreeing to allow them expression or refusing to allow them expression. Mere refusal to allow them expression may not eliminate them. They may return to dormancy only to be restimulated later. They should be weakened by the use of will and discernment, conscious implementation of constructive patterns, and cultivation of desirable states of consciousness, attitudes, feelings, and behaviors.

When pleasurable experiences unfold as a result of the manifestation of karmic influences, we can accept them and let the force of karma be expended or we can modify the effects by transforming them into more useful outcomes.

When pain-causing circumstances unfold, we can train ourselves to discern their causes and cultivate patience until the causes are removed or transcended. Frequently, all that is required is to shift awareness to a higher plane of consciousness so that karmic impressions which are operational at a lower level are rendered ineffectual. What bothers us when we are in lower states of consciousness may not even faze us when we are in higher states. Failure to dissolve these impressions can result in difficulties later in life—when one becomes older, tired, experiences an episode of minor illness, or when spiritual practices are neglected.

Higher superconscious states leave impressions in the mental field which are entirely constructive and effect personality changes which prevent accumulated mental patterns from actualizing. In this way the seeds of karma are returned to their origins. They are restrained, resisted, and dissolved.

51. Upon the dissolution of gross mental impressions, super-conscious impressions also fade from the mind, resulting in permanent illumination of consciousness.

When gross mental modifications are dissolved, lower superconsciousness is transformed into higher superconsciousness and permanent identity with God is experienced. Impressions resulting from superconscious experiences are then dissolved and the soul is liberated while embodied.

Now supremely free, the soul's qualities, capacities, and powers are unrestricted. Living is untroubled, satisfying, and spontaneous. Whether meditating or involved with circumstances and relationships, awareness of the wholeness of life is undiminished. From this enlightened state there is no returning to blind involvement with matter.

CHAPTER TWO

The Practice
of Kriya Yoga

1. Intentional regulation of sensory and mental impulses, self-analysis, profound metaphysical study and meditation, and surrendering self-consciousness (egoism) in favor of God-consciousness, are the practical means of attaining perfect concentration. This is the path of Kriya Yoga.

Because of delusion and restrictive mental impressions acquired in present and former incarnations, the average person is unable to understand the nature of God, much less experience Self-realization. However, the sincere devotee who wants to know God can engage in intentional practices for the purpose of cleansing the inner faculties so that God can be known and experienced.

Concentrated desire to know God is a most powerful aid to realization. Yearning to know God results in the unfoldment of latent capacities, and the movement of inner grace which facilitates psychological and physical transformations. Helpful circumstances are also attracted to the devotee who sincerely desires to know God. Such a surrendered soul cry moves the universe to the extent that fine cosmic forces are called into involvement with the devotee's personal endeavors.

Since our often uncontrolled drive to be too externalized accompanies delusion and restlessness, we are encouraged to train sensory impulses by self-disciplined behavior. This is to be done in relationship to urges, thoughts and attitudes, feelings, habits, to others, and our environment. Discipleship is for that person willing to be completely self-responsible for everything thought, felt, or done.

We err if we assume that we can ignore obvious needs to further our education, learn appropriate behavior, and direct attention and energies for the purpose of fulfilling responsibilities and living in harmony with nature's laws. A dedicated disciple will be practical in all circumstances, attending to the basic requirements that ensure a firm foundation for higher spiritual practices. One will cultivate the virtues, attend to duties essential to wellness and personal security, relate to the world intelligently, and always keep God-realization as the primary goal. The enlightenment path is not compatible with egocentricity. The true devotee will open his heart to God and serve the needs of humanity and the planet. This becomes possible by adherence to the guidelines set forth in this first sutra. Contemplate its meaning, understanding that the path of Kriya Yoga is more than meditation practice—it includes everything to which we should attend if we are to be successful in life.

Study of principles of right living prepares us for study of metaphysics which provides a complete education and reasonable understanding as a basis for higher knowledge. When we were small children we learned from our parents, from others with whom we associated, and as a result of observation and experimentation. Later we went to school, adding to our acquired knowledge and continuing to experiment, adapt, and live in the world with a degree of success. Such knowledge is lower knowledge—knowledge of relative matters necessary to get along in this world. Metaphysics is higher knowledge—knowledge of inner causes which govern outer effects.

No matter how long one has been confused, no matter what the present condition or prevailing state of consciousness may be, when we come to the enlightenment path with high resolve and proceed in the right way surrendered in God, progressive spiritual growth is assured. In chapter six of the *Bhagavad Gita* (6:37,38) questions common to devotees new on the spiritual path are described. Arjuna inquires:

> What about the person who cannot control the mind even though he has faith (in the teaching and in the usefulness of

spiritual practices), and who fails in his attempt to attain Self-realization? What is his destiny? Does he perish like a cloud rent in the sky by the winds? Is he left in limbo, missing both this life and life eternal?

Krishna explains the process of unfoldment which occurs as a result of right practice. The *Bhagavad Gita* 6:40-46:

Arjuna, neither in this incarnation nor in the hereafter is there destruction for the person who is rightly resolved; for never does a person who endeavors to do good tread the path of woe. Having attained (in the astral sphere) the world of the righteous and having dwelt therein, the person who has fallen away from his spiritual practice is again incarnated in a desirable environment. He may be born into a family of spiritually aware people who are endowed with wisdom. There he regains the mental impressions of previous realizations and is impelled to strive again for perfection and full realization. As a result of his former practices he is carried irresistibly forward. Such a seeker of truth goes beyond the rule of scriptures (traditional understanding). The sincere truth seeker who strives without slackening, cleansed of all karma, perfecting himself through repeated incarnations, attains the highest goal. Such a Self-realized soul is considered to be greater than ascetics; he is greater than one who is bound by rituals; therefore, becomes Self-realized. And of all such Self-realized persons, that devotee who is full of faith and who is established in the realization of pure consciousness, I consider to be the most attuned to this teaching and anchored in the Divine.

Study and analysis of consciousness and life processes includes explorations of the inner realms during meditative superconscious states and meditation on Om. What is meant by study is not mere superficial reading of popular religious literature or naive involvement with shallow metaphysical teachings. It is essential that we avail ourselves of the most authoritative information available. We can attract to ourselves what we need by opening our mind and consciousness, inviting the universe to supply our needs. When we are truly prepared to learn and to grow, if we are faithful and discerning, life will meet us at our level of need, on time and in the most useful ways. Learning experiences will be presented, information will be made available, role models and teachers will come into our lives, and guidance from within will direct us. Be resolved to settle for nothing less than the best information and guidance on the path.

When you are led to your destined enlightenment tradition, be true to it. Honor all authentic traditions while being faithful to your own. Be selective in your reading and about whose words you take to heart. Learn to use intelligence to accurately discern the truth of what you study. A subtle fact, which is little known and seldom mentioned, is that the written and spoken word carries with it the influences of the state of consciousness of the person from whom it emanates. Therefore, through the written and spoken word we can receive information and subtle influences which may be constructive or destructive. Experience of God is only possible to the extent that identification with externals is renounced. Useful relationships need not be renounced, only our attachment to them which causes identification with externals and prevents awareness of God. Begin by feeling yourself to be immersed in God at all times. Follow through by doing all of the things you know to do to live a righteous life. We cannot be surrendered in God and involved in improper behavior at the same time. When we learn what we must do to avoid present and future pain and unknowingness, we should do it.

2. Kriya Yoga is practiced to weaken and eliminate all physical and mental obstacles, for the purpose of realizing God.

Everything intentionally done by a Kriya Yoga disciple is for the purpose of fulfilling all of the aims of life, including God-realization. Because devotees who are not yet enlightened have some obstacles to remove or transcend, procedures for this purpose are recommended which enable the dedicated disciple to succeed on the enlightenment path.

These procedures have been tested and demonstrated by seers of many enlightenment traditions. If one will do what is recommended, results will definitely follow. As we proceed, we need to remember that we are not *causing* the unfoldment of consciousness; we are learning to *allow* consciousness to unfold as restrictions are removed. If results are not experienced we should not find fault with the procedures; we should improve our understanding of the procedures and become more proficient in practice. *There can be no true understanding of Kriya Yoga or satisfying spiritual progress without practice.*

3. **Restricting influences which contribute to pain and suffering and interfere with God-realization are: illusions (misperceptions) about the nature of God and the nature and purpose of life, egoism, attachments, aversion, and conflicts about the processes of birth and death.**

Illusion, misperception, causes delusion—the primary cause of all other problems a devotee has. Caught in a web of misunderstanding, one is inclined to wander through space-time under its spell, creating new problems and adding to the accumulation of existing conflicts. In this way do souls continue in spiritual darkness until, because of God's grace or an intentional turning to a Higher Power, they begin their inward journey to transcendence.

When we are responsive—because of the force of constructive karma or because the brain and nervous system are sufficiently refined to allow more subtle perceptions to be experienced—soul capacities unfold, resulting in spontaneous spiritual growth. Or, when weary of living a meaningless, perhaps problem-centered life, we may actively seek for a higher way, the metaphysical law of causation is put into effect, and we become responsive to the currents of evolution which assist us in our new direction.

4. **Imperfect perception of the Real is the field of all restricting influences, whether these be dormant or active.**

Mental impressions may remain dormant until dissolved, or they may become expressive and influential. Some expressive influences of mental impressions provide minimal challenge because their drives are not strong or because we are able to restrain them by self-discipline. Others may become fully expressive, causing constant and perhaps extreme difficulties for the devotee. They are nurtured in ignorance: unknowingness, the condition known as delusion.

We may become aware of tendencies toward impatience, anger, greed, jealousy, or purposelessness. From a higher level of consciousness we can be self-determined and resist and overcome these tendencies by actively cultivating patience, calmness, generosity, understanding, and purpose in life. From a lower level of consciousness, being less in control, we may remain the effect of such tendencies, caught up in a confusing maze of uncontrollable behavior and the resulting circumstances. From a superconscious level we can see all restricting influences for what they are—mere products of ignorance which are not characteristics of our real nature—and live our lives with understanding.

We may remain for years at the level of struggle, seeking help from many sources and perhaps feeling ourselves to be hopelessly addicted to destructive behavior. There is no shame in seeking help when we need it, but to remain at the level of coping with problems instead of solving them and moving on to higher levels of understanding and performance, is to remain at the level of resisting the unwanted, instead of overcoming it. Addictive personalities behave like this. Lacking self-esteem, self-confidence, and a clear awareness of purpose in life, they spend time and resources resisting their problems instead of learning to be free and functional. No longer at the mercy of their former habits they identify with and remain addicted to the therapy process. Devotees sometimes do this with their spiritual practices. They may become so involved with their studies and practices that they persist for years—sometimes for incarnations—as seekers instead of knowers, avoiding their soul destiny.

We need to overcome destructive drives and proceed to higher levels of understanding and expression. Self-analysis and behavior modification is only the beginning on the enlightenment path. There must also be intentional cultivation of higher states of consciousness and the implementation of practices for the purpose of improving wellness and clearing the mind of the causes of problems. The brain and nervous system should be refined so that consciousness can be more easily processed. For this purpose the Kriya Yoga system includes procedures and meditation techniques which enable the devotee to clear the mental field and contribute to altering the structure of the brain and nervous system.

5. Ignorance is assuming the noneternal to be eternal, the impure to be pure, the painful to be pleasurable, and the ego as the real being.

This is a description of normal human consciousness. Many people erroneously think that their limited perception of the universe is accurate and have no clear understanding of *That* which produced it and makes possible its actions. They may say: "The world is real; there is no God; there is nothing other than this realm. This present life is the only one; to affirm otherwise is to be a dreamer of dreams, to be unrealistic about the facts of life." They say, "You only live once. You do your best, and then die." Such are those who are ignorant of higher realities even though reasonably wise in the ways of the world.

Lacking higher knowledge, many are content to live ordinary, unconscious lives and to continue to assume that sense pleasures are the highest ones: that living for personal gain, even at the expense of others, is the way life is meant to be. They do not know that continued outward seeking will never result in true, lasting happiness; that their outward drives will persist with them in the astral realms after departure from this world. They will never have peace until they turn from creation to the Creator, from appearances to the Cause of appearances.

Delusion results in egoism, the false sense of independent individuality. One might then say, "I am a person and perhaps God exists." Or, "I am an individual and I want to know about God and perhaps experience union with God to improve my personal circumstances." Usually, strong ego-identification results in self-centered thinking and behavior which adds to an already complicated and confused life. Egocentric people almost always want things their way regardless of the consequences. Under the spell of delusion a person might acquire enough understanding to use metaphysical laws of causation to somewhat master personal circumstances and falsely conclude that he now knows "God's laws" and is spiritually aware. He does not know that he is still but a child on the path and has yet to grow to maturity. Many at this level are more concerned with blessings than with knowing the source of blessings; more concerned with the miracle of causation than being a surrendered instrument of That which makes miracles possible. When influenced by sattvic qualities one's behavior will be constructive. When influenced by rajas qualities one will be motivated by a need for power. When influenced by tamas qualities one will be destructive.

6. **Egoism (the sense of independent existence) is the result of the soul's identification with mind and matter.**

Because the soul never becomes completely identified with mind and matter, its identification is but an appearance. A degree of "I-ness" always remains.

Cosmic egoism is the result of the blending of Spirit with matter. As God is ever conscious within the field of creation, so a Self-realized soul can be ever conscious of its involvement with matter. To a Self-realized soul, partial ego-consciousness is but a convenient viewpoint from which to perceive the world and the play of cosmic forces. While assuming this viewpoint the soul can know its omnipresence and reality in God.

7. **Dwelling on pleasure and objects of pleasure produces affection which results in attachments.**

Pleasant sensation can result in affection for that which produces the sensation. We often mistakenly refer to affection as love. We say, "I love my friends," or, "I love my job." We may even assume that we love our spouse or children because the relationship affords us a degree of pleasure. Real love for another is more than affection due to the pleasure we derive from the relationship, just as real love for God is more than the feeling of satisfaction we may derive from a partial relationship with God. There is no self-serving attitude when love is present. We are then inclined to sacrifice whatever might interfere with it.

We may derive pleasure from our successes when we accomplish purposes, achieve goals, acquire knowledge, or create something unique. The pleasure experienced in these ways is helpful reinforcement to productive behavior. What is to be avoided is dependence. Also to be avoided is compulsive, pleasure-motivated behavior which brings pain and failure in its wake.

The pleasure-seeking tendency of the mind is an instinct helpful to enabling us to satisfy legitimate desires. When not disciplined, the pleasure-seeking tendency of the mind can lead us off course, involving us in useless actions and relationships. It can even cause addictions to states of consciousness which provide a degree of emotional satisfaction, to mental attitudes which reinforce egoism, to behavior which is purposeless or harmful, and to relationships which are not useful to higher ends.

Knowing this about the mind we can, during meditation practice, introduce into the mental field the superior, constructive and permanent pleasure of superconscious experience. The mind then becomes attracted to this refined pleasure-producing experience and desires to again enjoy it. In this way affection for meditation is cultivated, attachments to outer circumstances and their possible harmful addictive influences are weakened, and spiritual practices become more appealing. This is the superior way of overcoming the passions of the mind which cause restlessness, and the way to enjoyably remove identification from egoism and become increasingly aware of our innate reality.

8. Being repulsed by that which may contribute to pain or discomfort produces aversion.

Aversion is the opposite of attachment. We naturally do not like, and want to withdraw from, that which may cause unpleasant consequences. On the enlightenment path the devotee who is God-centered is averse to everything which is not conducive to continued soul unfoldment. One who enjoys sense indulgence might be averse to philosophical speculation and practices, and to behaviors which might interfere with what is considered to be present happiness. There are those who love the light and avoid darkness, and there are some who love the darkness and avoid light. Between these extremes are those who are confused about their priorities.

To vigorously resist that which is undesirable may result in preoccupation with it. The higher way is to renounce involvement with the undesirable and put more attention on the desirable. To see the good is a practical way to expand consciousness.

9. The urge toward death exists along with the inclination

toward life, even in the wise. These urges are propelled by their own innate drives.

The urge toward death is common for persons who are tired, world-weary, and overcome with a sense of futility. Here, *death* refers to unconsciousness; ceasing to be aware of life and its processes. There is an instinctual awareness of the inevitability of physical death because of dim memories of past incidents of transition from previous physical bodies and transitions experienced in other realms. We are also reminded of death because the event is so common in nature. We may not clearly remember prior transitional episodes but we can imagine what it would be like to die. Along with the intimation of death is the drive to live, and the inner conviction that life is more than physical; that the beingness of us existed prior to embodiment and will continue after the body ceases to function.

Some fear life because they do not know how to live. Some fear death because their understanding of the continuity of life is not clear. Even the wise who are not fully enlightened are perplexed by the paradox of life and death. Many highly advanced souls become comfortable with life in the body and are reluctant to leave it when their moment for departure draws near. Some even attempt to accomplish a condition of physical immortality, not understanding that even the universe will eventually dissolve into the formless field of pure consciousness. Long life in the body has value because it affords the soul opportunity for continued spiritual growth and world service. To this end there are ways to ensure wellness and life extension.

A few illumined masters on the planet have maintained their bodies for hundreds or thousands of years. They are sometimes referred to as mortal-immortals. Having utilized their knowledge of vitalizing regimens, and by superior realization, they retain the body while remaining cosmic conscious in order to work with evolutionary trends which contribute to planetary transformations and the spiritual growth of its inhabitants. Certain limitations are imposed on the average person by cosmic forces operating in the present cycle. The more illumined a soul is, the less it is influenced by these forces and the more it is able to express the divine nature which is superior to them.

God-realization is the certain way to overcome the idea of death and to remove the fear of after-death states, for it results in the understanding that both physical birth and death are but incidents in the soul's extended journey through space-time.

Self-realized souls are able to intuitively determine the time of transition from the body and to depart easily and consciously. Meditation is the best preparation for conscious transition because when we meditate we "die to the world." Having become proficient in higher meditation practices we already know how to shift attention from the outer to the inner, from the lower to the higher. Surrendered in God at the moment of transition, the soul slips free of the body and moves into subtle realms or the field of God, depending upon its state of consciousness and prevailing karmic conditions. If we can experience God we can transcend body, mind, and subtle sheaths. If our awareness of God is only partial, and some identification with mental processes continues, these will determine our experiences in the inner realms. The *Bhagavad Gita* 8:3-10:

> Transcendental Consciousness is indestructible and supreme; individualized Spirit is referred to as the soul. Karma is the name given to the creative force that brings all manifestations into expression. The basis of all manifest forms is the combinations of tendencies in nature; the basis of all transmutation [from lower to higher] is inherent in Spirit. And whoever, at the time of departure from the body, contemplates Spirit alone, he experiences absolute freedom. According to what one contemplates at the moment of leaving the body, he experiences upon moving into the astral, causal, or celestial realms. Therefore, at all times contemplate pure being and persist. When attention and insight are firmly set on Supreme Consciousness you will realize It without doubt. He who contemplates Reality as a result of constant practice, who does not think of anything else, realizes the truth. He who contemplates the pure Light which is behind darkness [the primal field of nature] at the time of departure from the body, centering his attention and life force at the spiritual eye, attains enlightenment.

Yogis recommend that Om be contemplated at the time of departure from the body. By contemplating Om, bringing the life force up through the chakras into the spiritual eye, and surrendering in God, soul awareness is withdrawn from the body and mind, leaving behind all that formerly restricted awareness. One who is proficient in higher meditation procedures undoubtedly makes an easier transition, but even if one has not acquired proficiency, the possibility of merging in God still exists. We are not the body or the mind, nor are we the karmic patterns impressed in the mind. Cleansing the mental field of restricting influences enables us to function more freely. The ordinary, functional mental aspects are no longer needed when we awaken to levels of awareness which transcend the field of mind. Then, just as the body is returned to the elements of nature, so individualized mind dissolves into Cosmic Mind.

10. These restricting influences should be overcome by resolving them into their subtle origins.

Misperception, egoism, attachments, aversions, and conflicts about birth and death remain dormant, somewhat influential, or fully operational until they are resolved. So long as they remain in the field of the mind their influential force can, in varying degrees, affect awareness and behavior. They should be resisted, restrained, and dissolved. Misperception is eliminated by learning to perceive and comprehend without error. Egoism is eliminated by surrendering in God and experiencing cosmic consciousness. Attachments are eliminated by renunciation. Aversions are eliminated by understanding and dispassion. Fear of death and thirst for embodied life are eliminated by superior realization. The origin of all restricting influences is delusion: unknowingness, a deficiency of higher knowledge. Enlightenment eliminates delusion.

11. The gross modifications of pain-causing influences are to be overcome by calm, introspective self-analysis and superconscious meditation.

A disciple once said to Paramahansaji, "Sir, I find it almost impossible to control my thoughts and habits. You have to understand that I'm not perfect yet. You can do the things you say I should do because you are a master." Paramahansaji replied, "How do you think I became what I am? It was by doing what I had to do. You can do it, too, if you want to."

While self-analysis is helpful, more helpful is superconscious meditation experience. A degree of functional freedom can be experienced by ordering thoughts and coming to terms with inner drives and tendencies. Complete freedom results from higher superconscious experiences because we are then able to function with understanding. Superconscious forces introduced into the mental field weaken and dissolve mental impressions which are basic causes of psychological unrest.

12. **Unconscious and subconscious impressions may result in the manifestation of unplanned experiences in this and other life cycles.**

Until we are spiritually aware, we only believe we know why we behave as we do and why circumstances unfold as they do. We may not be aware of the fact that, for the most part, we are driven by inner forces over which we have no control because they are unknown to us. Until the mental field is cleared, an ordinary human being is driven through life instead of being self-determined; the unwitting effect of causes which determine sequential experiences. According to what our state of consciousness is, so will be our perceptions, motivations, behavior, and experience. Our consciousness can also be influenced by inherited tendencies. When we are born into a body we assume many of the karmic influences transmitted through our genetic line.

Just as mental conditionings determine the general pattern of experiences in this incarnation, so they can determine future ones. Our circumstances have been somewhat determined by experiences in previous incarnations. What the remainder of this incarnation and possible future ones may be, can be known by correctly assessing present states of consciousness and the contents of unconscious and subconscious levels of the mind. Unless involved in transformative spiritual practices, one's future can be predicted with a fair degree of accuracy by examining present conditions which are contributing causes to future unfoldments.

Engage in honest self-inquiry and find out why you were born into the world and what you must do to allow yourself to be soul-directed and focused on your destiny. Merely to persist as the effect of prior causes will maintain the sequence of causation, because without spiritual awareness, reactions to present and future circumstances will create more mental impressions which may cause future unplanned behavior. Caught in a web of causation, souls may continue for countless incarnations, unaware of their innate reality and unable to resist the forces which determine their lives. See the world without illusions, living from a higher level of understanding. If you have present challenges, imagine higher possibilities while engaging in practices which can contribute to spiritual awakening and growth.

13. As long as the causes of effects reside in the unconscious, their influences can manifest according to species and span of life, and in relationship to perceptions of pleasure or pain.

In lower life forms, instinctual urges primarily determine behavior. In higher life forms, in which mental capacities exist along with karmic impressions, these impressions determine behavior according to their drives. In human beings—the most evolved of life forms—the mental field is complex, with a vast accumulation of impressions and inherited traits. These represent probable causes of near or future effects according to species, span of life, and their relationship to pleasure or pain experienced by resulting circumstances.

Both the righteous and the unrighteous can die early or later, depending upon inner causes or outer circumstances. *All effects due to causes are fated; unfoldments due to the impulse of Spirit comprise one's pattern of destiny.* Some people are predestined to die at an early age because of karmic conditions, lack of need to remain in the body, or because of circumstances beyond their control: being born into a condition of extreme poverty, being born into a family whose karma is destructive, being unknowingly in a life-threatening situation, being born into a defective body. Some souls survive almost impossible odds, and not only prevail, but excel. Grace also plays a role in our lives, for even with many challenges and in difficult circumstances, and in spite of what we do or do not do, the supportive influence of evolution often puts aside relative conditions in order to express its inclinations.

14. Pleasure or pain, joy or sorrow, can be the result of maturing mental impressions, according to whether their character is constructive or destructive.

Ends follow origins; effects follow causes. The way to escape from the wheel of causation is to transcend it. The way out of darkness is to become conscious of light. How do we do this? We repent; we turn away from that which is binding and embrace that which is liberating. We turn away from deluded thinking and destructive behavior in favor of clear thinking and constructive behavior. We stop doing the things which contribute to difficulties and do those things which contribute to emotional maturity and soul growth. We stop being self-conscious and become superconscious. We stop being small-minded and become cosmic conscious. This is the only way out of the maze of mental confusion.

Be inspired by the masters. What do they do when in need of spiritual refreshment? They withdraw from outer involvements to pray and meditate, commune with God, and be restored to understanding. We should do this.

15. Wise people know that the possibility of pain exists even in the midst of pleasurable circumstances, because of the existence of latent impressions yet to be influential and because of the actions of cosmic forces.

Pleasurable circumstances presently manifesting because of the influences of constructive causes are not lasting. When causes are weakened or exhausted, their effects fade. So long as latent impressions remain in the mental field we are subject to their possible influences, according to their nature and character. A wise person will enjoy good times but will not be deceived by circumstances.

When the mental field is relatively pure or devoid of latent impressions, the presence and actions of cosmic forces regulated by the gunas may yet be influential. When tamasic influences prevail, there may be occasions of dullness. When rajasic influ-

ences prevail, there may be occasions of restlessness. When sattvic influences prevail, there may be occasions of clarity and soul
happiness. After karmic patterns have been rendered ineffectual,
the devotee must then rise free from the influences of the cosmic
forces which pervade the mental field. We are not only to transcend mental conditionings, we are also to transcend the forces
of nature. With an advanced level of Self-realization, but without karmic influences, so long as the cosmic forces operate in the
mental field we can be somewhat influenced. Tamasic influences
are overcome by purposeful action. Rajasic influences are overcome by cultivating soul peace. Sattvic influences are overcome
by transcendental realizations.

**16. Pain and suffering which has not yet manifested can be
avoided.**

Difficulties which have passed can be forgotten. Present challenges can be managed by corrective procedures and meditation.
A wise person does what is possible to prevent future troubles.
People lacking knowledge are not always concerned with the
possibility of future troubles or their avoidance.

It is helpful for one to understand the means by which problems occur and by which they can be avoided. Four things should
be known by a devotee—*the realm of nature and its modes of
operation; the causes of the nature-realm and its processes; the
way to experience liberation of consciousness; and the procedures
which make soul liberation possible.*

By examining how we presently think and behave, we can
know what our near and distant future experiences will be. By
knowing our past and present, we can know our future. If there
are deep-seated causes of which we are presently unaware, these
can be known through self-reflection, meditation, and further
study and learning. Signs and symptoms can be observed which
enable one to use objective means to determine subjective conditions. By these means the basic physical constitution can be
understood, as well as deeper psychological patterns. Vedic
astrological calculations can also provide an understanding of
the soul's relationship with earth's magnetic field and the influences of planetary emanations. Once conditions are known,

remedial actions can be taken to improve them, and to modify and eliminate undesirable influences.

Sri Yukteswar, while an accomplished master of yoga, was knowledgeable in practical matters—Ayurveda, psychology, and astrology. He told Paramahansaji, "It is only when the traveler has reached his goal that he is justified in discarding his maps. During the journey, he takes advantage of any convenient short-cut. There are certain features in the law of karma that can be skillfully adjusted by the fingers of wisdom."

Sri Yukteswar would, at times, after intuitive analysis of a disciple, consult the disciple's horoscope and prescribe behavioral changes, as well as the wearing of specific gems for the purpose of balancing the disciple's pranas and introducing subtle cosmic influences. The gemstone, worn as recommended, proved helpful. Also helpful was Sri Yukteswar's blessing.

17. Suffering is due to the soul's identification with nature.

All remedial actions taken to neutralize the causes of pain are limited in their effects because they exist in the realm of matter. Because the basic cause of suffering is delusion, the only certain solution is enlightenment. With inner restricting characteristics dissolved, the Self-realized soul expresses with complete understanding, under grace.

18. The objective realms, consisting of elements and powers of sensation, thought, and action, and influenced by cosmic forces, are for the purpose of providing consciousness with the means for personal expression and liberation.

Human consciousness is a blend of soul awareness and egoism, allowing for occasional awareness of Self and an almost constant feeling of being limited. The universe contains all that is necessary for our nourishment and overall well-being. The purpose of the universe is to allow cosmic forces a field in which to operate and to provide consciousness the means to express. Because of organs of action the soul can function through a body; because of organs of senses the soul can perceive its environment; because of mind the soul can process information received through the senses; because of intelligence the soul can exercise discernment in the relative spheres. Right use of these faculties makes possible freedom of expression. Right use of intuition makes possible Self-realization, knowledge of God, and cosmic consciousness. Seers remind devotees that they are fortunate to be functional in the world because here one has the opportunity to fulfill desires and comprehend truth.

19. The cosmic forces have four aspects according to their gross or subtle manifestations: the specialized, the unspecialized, the indicated, and that which is devoid of characteristics.

The *specialized* manifestations of cosmic forces are earth, water, fire, air, and ethereal states in subtle form; the five sensory organs, the five organs of action, and mind. These are the sixteen *specialized* manifestations of cosmic forces.

The six *unspecialized* manifestations of cosmic forces are the corresponding five subtle states preceding gross manifestation of the above mentioned specialized manifestations, plus egoism.

The *indicated*, known by its presence but without outer manifestation, is the faculty of intelligence by which the soul can examine nature and exercise knowledge.

The fine manifestations of cosmic forces which are devoid of characteristics reside in the primal field of nature and make possible the unfoldment of the worlds.

To understand more fully these modifications of cosmic forces, study the explanation of categories of world manifestation in the first section of this book.

20. The soul is pure consciousness only, even though it perceives through the veil of mind and senses.

Regardless of the extent of your involvement with mental processes and sensory perceptions, inwardly know, "I am pure consciousness. I am Spirit." Physical identification is only relatively true—it is a fact but it is temporary. Perceptions of the world are screened through the filter of the mind. When the mind is devoid of delusions and illusions, perception is accurate.

When identified with the body we may say we are deluded,

tired, or confused. We do not know delusion, tiredness, or confusion during deep sleep, which is the unconscious way of withdrawing from sensory contacts. Likewise, when superconscious, we cannot know delusion, tiredness, or confusion. When the body requires rest, know that *you* are never tired. When thought processes are disorderly, know that *you* are never disorganized. When you feel somewhat deluded, know that *you* are a bright, pure soul, a perfect ray of God.

Shankara wrote, in his book, *Self-Knowledge*:

> Realize individualized Supreme Consciousness to be distinct from the body, sense organs, mind, intelligence, and nondifferentiated primordial nature; it is the witness of their functions and the ruler of them. As the moon appears to be moving when clouds move in the sky, so also, to the nondiscriminating, individualized Supreme Consciousness appears to be active when in reality only the senses are active. As the movement that belongs to water is [sometimes] attributed, through ignorance, to the moon which is reflected in it, so also, enjoyment and other limitations which belong to the mind are falsely attributed to Supreme Consciousness. The nature of Supreme Consciousness is eternity, purity, reality, awareness, and bliss, just as luminosity is the nature of the sun, coolness of water, and heat of fire.

21. The purpose of the manifest universe is to serve God's will.

Here, we have it—the answer to the question we seem never to tire of asking: What is the purpose of this world? Manifested by God's will and formed of God's creative force, the universe can have no other purpose than to serve God's will. Vain people say, "Isn't God wonderful? Look at all the things he's done for us—by creating us and providing us with so many blessings." From a relative perspective, to acknowledge God and be thankful for our blessings is useful. From a higher perspective it is clear that the universe and everything expressing in it, including us, is an activity of God, and that the universe and every part of it is not for us alone, but for a divine purpose. We are to learn what God's will for the universe is, and cooperate with it if we want to be happy and spiritually fulfilled.

22. Although the universe is no longer perceived by one who has transcended it, it continues to exist for those identified with it.

Knowledgeable people do not waste time debating whether or not the universe exists if there is no one to perceive it. We perceive it when identified with it and do not perceive it when not identified. The universe remains in operation even if we are not present to observe it. It is always experienced and observed within the field of God's consciousness. Cosmic forces extending from the field of God maintain the worlds until they are dissolved. Souls, units of consciousness, are not the cause of the existence of the worlds, and the worlds do not cease to be when souls no longer observe them.

23. Cosmic forces emanating from the field of God mix with the field of primordial nature, causing identification with it.

The field of primordial nature, the manifesting creative force of God with attributes of space-time and fine particles, is influenced by cosmic forces emanating from the field of God which regulate nature's processes. Primordial nature, without the active influences of cosmic forces, is void and without form. It is only when cosmic forces are influential in that field that the dance of creation begins. A portion of God's involved awareness becomes self-veiled, making possible the appearance of cosmic individuality. Neither the transcendent aspect of God nor of the soul is involved with matter. Such seeming involvement, while illusory; is necessary if the drama of relative life is to occur.

24. Imperfect awareness of its own nature is the cause of the soul's identification with matter.

Incidents of spontaneous transcendence prove that imperfect awareness of our real nature is the cause of our identification with mind and matter. If we were mind or matter we would not be able to experience release from it. Knowing this, a devotee's focus in meditation is to withdraw from involvement with the senses and mental processes, and from cosmic forces operating in the mental field. Recommended spiritual practices and Kriya Yoga meditation techniques are for the purpose of enabling the devotee to disconnect awareness from body, mind, and cosmic forces. After initial awakening experiences, one is encouraged to continue on the enlightenment path. As a result of practice, all doubts are dispelled because of progressive realizations.

25. **By the final removal of the sense of identification of the soul with matter, unknowingness is banished and the seer (the soul) experiences absolute freedom.**

As preliminary experiences of transcendence afford insight and accelerate spiritual evolution, so final withdrawal from identification with matter eliminates all unknowingness. One may have difficulty maintaining steady progress because of occasional distractions and the influences of cosmic forces yet operational in the mental field. This is why the final stages of liberation may require a duration of time to complete. During this phase, degrees of ignorance alternate with knowledge. Eventually, perfect knowledge, complete freedom, and permanent transcendence is experienced. The final stages of withdrawal from identification with matter occur because of God's grace.

26. **Unwavering intuitive knowledge of God and nature is the means of removing suffering caused by delusion.**

False identity with matter and its consequences—delusion, illusion, birth, death, alternating between sickness and health, and all of the ills an unaware soul is heir to—are eliminated when delusion is banished by understanding. For this, unwavering intuitive knowledge of God and nature should be maintained; we should remain conscious of the reality of God and understand that the field of nature is but an aspect of God's manifesting power. Intuitive knowledge is experienced during higher superconscious states when attention is withdrawn from the senses and mental processes, and afterwards when the soul is able to function through mind and senses without losing awareness of the inner, pure state.

27. For the insightful devotee, intuitive knowledge unfolds through seven successive stages.

Years ago, Paramahansaji wrote of the yogic way to spiritual mastership and Self-knowledge:

> First, by discrimination the yogi detaches himself from his little circle of friends. This he does, not to be exclusive and negative, but to be all-inclusive. The yogi first excludes all attachments so that they may not stand in the way of perception of omnipresence. After achieving omnipresence, he includes in his love his family, friends, everything. Ordinary man is the loser by his attachment to a few paltry things which he must forsake in the end. The yogi reclaims his divine birthright first by all necessary efforts and includes afterwards all things he desires to have.
>
> Second, the yogi finds his consciousness, although freed from possessions which relate to the body, still tenaciously remaining imprisoned in the body and human consciousness.
>
> Third, the yogi by deep concentration silences the internal and external sensations which invade his body.
>
> Fourth, the yogi learns to quiet his breath and heart and to withdraw attention and energy into the spine.
>
> Fifth, when the yogi can quiet his heart at will, he passes psychologically beyond the subconscious state. The ego experiences joy and elation when it functions through the subconscious mind in sleep. In sleep the heart still works, pumping blood through the body while the senses are at rest. When attention and energy are withdrawn from them, the muscles and the senses are consciously put to sleep; then a joy greater than a thousand dreamless sleeps [during superconscious states] is experienced.

After becoming settled in meditation one can proceed for the purpose of experiencing superconscious states and higher knowledge. During the first stage of awakening to intuitive knowledge, one understands the restrictions which have to be removed if further unfoldment is to be experienced. This insight makes possible concentrated effort in positive ways.

The second stage is experienced when the restrictions which formerly caused pain have actually been neutralized to the extent they can never cause unwanted problems in the future.

The third stage is higher superconsciousness which makes possible investigation of subtle and fine levels of consciousness.

The fourth stage is experienced when the meditator clearly comprehends the relationship of soul to mind, and to internal and external phenomena.

At the fifth stage, influences from the mental field can no longer in any way contribute to changes in one's consciousness.

The sixth stage is God-realization, and the cosmic forces cease to be influential.

At the seventh stage, the soul, free from all influences of nature, rests in pure being.

28. The practice of Kriya Yoga results in complete mental purity, and enlightenment is definitely experienced.

Kriyas are cleansing actions. Knowing that the soul is inclined to express through the nervous system and mind due to the existence of restricting influences, the devotee engages in practices for the specific purpose of removing these restrictions. Enlightenment is experienced, expressed as radiance, inward joy, compassion, selflessness, and compliant surrender to God's will. The devotee then lives always in awareness of being a specialized viewpoint of the ocean of Infinite Consciousness, omnipresently aware, and outside of the influences of forces which operate in the field of space-time. In this state there is nothing more to be known or attained (awakened to). Any work performed is for the purpose of fulfilling obligations which relate to being in the world: to nurture societal well-being and contribute to the spiritual awakening and enlightenment of others.

29. Refraining from destructive behaviors, actualizing constructive behaviors, steadiness of meditation posture, regulation and transformation of vital forces, internalization of attention to flow it back to the source, concentration, meditation, and superconsciousness (samadhi), are the eight stages of yogic practice leading to realization of God and liberation of consciousness.

Proficiency in practice of recommended procedures for the

first stage will result in a moral life, psychological and physical health, and social harmony. Proficiency at the second stage will result in dedicated spiritual practice. Proficiency in meditation posture will free the devotee's attention for inner work. Proficiency at the fourth stage will result in balanced circulation of life forces and awakening of vital energies. Proficiency at the fifth and sixth stages will result in flawless concentration. Proficiency at the seventh stage will result in surrendered meditation and preliminary superconscious states. Proficiency at the eighth stage will result in refined superconscious perceptions.

Coordinated practice of these procedures will facilitate superior results. We do not have to be entirely skillful at lower stages in order to contemplate higher ones; we should engage in practices which simultaneously result in improvement at all stages. Degrees of success at lower stages helps us to be proficient at higher ones, and degrees of success at higher stages will beneficially effect our practices at lower stages. We are to do the best we can at each level, coordinating all of the procedures as personal aptitude and capacity allows. Even a little practice of the basic procedures will aid our meditation endeavors and even marginal success in meditation will contribute to improvement of performance of basic procedures.

The ideal is to be totally involved, doing everything we can to help ourselves. We should not be content to merely involve ourselves at the lower stages, neglecting the higher ones. Some devotees do this. They observe some guidelines and practice a few yoga routines, and believe themselves to be practicing yoga. Pure yoga is superconsciousness: the various procedures, if attended to, lead to this. Do not be self-deceived into believing that because you try to live a moral life and attend to a few other practices that you are on the spiritual path. Only when involvement is focused on enlightenment are you truly on the spiritual path.

The behavior advised is that which naturally occurs when enlightened understanding regulates our actions. By emulating behavior which is natural to an enlightened person, we can learn by experience how to live effectively, how to meditate, and how to experience God.

30. The five restraints to be observed are harmlessness, truthfulness, nonstealing, firm resolve on the enlightenment path along with right use and transmutation of vital forces, and nonpossessiveness.

These are basic requirements to the practice of yoga, as well as to almost all religious practices the world over. For a God-surrendered disciple they are not mere recommendations to be considered and perhaps observed (or ignored); they are admonishments for intentional living. To neglect preliminary practices, falsely assuming them to be unimportant, is a mistake that can have far-reaching, unpleasant consequences. There are many spiritually advanced souls yet to become proficient in the practice of these fundamental procedures and it is for this reason that their further unfoldment is delayed.

31. These practices are universally applicable and not limited by social status, place, or time.

Regardless of our circumstances, these teachings apply to every person who desires to live righteously. Anywhere in the world, in the midst of social intercourse or in remote circumstances, no matter the political or religious climate, the guidelines used for psychological wellness, social harmony, and the unfoldment of soul capacities are the same.

32. The intentional practices to be observed are purity and cleanliness, contentment, self-discipline of mental and sensory impulses, right study and analysis of the Self and of the nature of consciousness, and surrender in God.

Preliminary procedures for purity and cleanliness include personal hygiene, natural diet, cleansing of the body's internal systems, the cultivation of pure thoughts, and speaking kind words. Further procedures include exercises and techniques to refine the nervous system and cleanse the channels through which life force flows. The ideal is to provide the most suitable environment, external and internal, for wellness and function so that major purposes can be fulfilled.

Contentment results from desirelessness—by providing for

one's essentials but not longing for more than is needed to maintain one's lifestyle and achieve goals, and by cultivating patience at all times, under all circumstances.

Self-discipline of the senses consists of proper use of the senses while regulating impulses and responses to stimuli.

Right study is for the purpose of acquiring knowledge to live successfully, and to learn about God and how to know God.

Surrender in God begins with attitude adjustment, followed by practice, and by having God-relationship and God-realization the underlying motive for all actions.

33. To overcome and neutralize destructive, instinctual drives and tendencies, one should cultivate the opposite qualities and habits.

Whenever inclined to misbehave in thought, word, or deed, immediately choose to behave appropriately. Even if such actions result in temporary frustration, at least the impulses will be restrained until appropriate behavior can be implemented.

34. Instinctual drives and tendencies may be mild, moderate, or intense. Because they can cause pain and suffering, they should be removed by cultivating the virtues.

One reason for lack of success in endeavors, relationships, and spiritual practices, is that heaviness and confusion at deeper levels of the mind are influential even when we are not aware of their effects. If instinctual drives are mild, they do not influence us very much. If they are moderate, their influence is more evident. If they are intense, they can challenge us. Because these drives and tendencies interfere with self-determination, they should be recognized and eliminated by all practical means.

35. When one is established in harmlessness, all living things are devoid of enmity (hatred, dislike) in one's presence.

We injure ourselves and others by acts, words, and thoughts when our mental waves and behaviors are impure. What we give out to the world influences it. All living things respond more kindly to us when we are established in harmlessness. The universe is supportive of us when we are open to its inclinations to provide for us when we are on friendly terms with it.

The universe is alive, and the presence of different forms does not result in separateness. The outer surface of our bodies is not the limit of our consciousness or our vital forces. We live in a sea of pulsating, circulating cosmic energy. Our feelings mingle with the feelings of others and our thoughts flow into the collective mental atmosphere of the planet. Our realization of harmlessness flows out to the world to contribute to universal harmony. When we are centered in God-awareness and living by grace, only good fortune can be our experience. Obstacles and occasions of personal challenge will later be acknowledged, as opportunities for growth and life-enhancement. Accidents will be rare or nonexistent. Even if we are temporarily experiencing imbalance and misfortune, we will not be injured. If an occasion should arise during which we are threatened by circumstances, the power of the universe will come to our aid and establish harmony.

There are numerous instances of which I am aware when devotees were saved from harm by the intervention of divine grace. Paramahansaji once told disciples about a time in his life when he was concerned about their welfare. He prayed about the matter and received the revelation, as though spoken in his mind: "Those whom you love, I love, and no harm can befall them!" He always told us, when faced with challenge to do our best, to help ourselves and turn more completely to the protecting influence of God and gurus.

The Sanskrit word for harmlessness is *ahimsa*. It means more than avoidance of violence or killing. It means to be so inwardly settled in harmlessness that no impulse or thought of performing an injurious act will arise in the mind.

36. When one is firmly established in truthfulness, immediate and specific results of actions are experienced.

To be established in truthfulness is to be anchored in awareness of God. Thus being "of the truth" our thoughts are no longer in conflict. Our actions are precise and intentional. In this state of consciousness, our unspoken intentions are effortlessly manifested. This is what it means to have implicit faith. With pure faith, there are no doubts or resistance.

Enlightened teachers say that when one is established in truth consciousness one has the power to instantaneously manifest thoughts and words. Whatever we declare to happen from this state of consciousness, must happen because the power of the universe is behind our thoughts and intentions.

The realm of nature is responsive to causes introduced into it from subtle and fine levels of mind and consciousness. If we want to accomplish something worthwhile, if it is entirely within the range of possibility in the field of nature and we are not successful in our efforts, it may be because we do not believe with pure faith. It may be that, at deeper levels, we have conflicts or that our timing is not in harmony with unfolding events.

In cultures where these teachings are known, devotees with special needs may go to a saint and ask for a blessing. If the saint affirms that the desires of the devotee will be fulfilled, they must manifest.

37. When one is established in nonstealing, permanent prosperity results.

People steal because they are insecure, self-centered, greedy, meanspirited, or desperate. Economic hardship, or personal need of any kind, are not the causes of crime—these are only the outer circumstances which provide the opportunity for the mental tendencies to be expressed. One of the basic lessons we must learn is to be self-responsible for our food, shelter, and whatever else is required or desired, for ourselves and for others with whom we have a relationship or for whom we are responsible. Because the universe provides what is needed, we have but to learn to honestly appropriate it in adequate proportion.

A consciousness of lack is at the root of the tendency to steal. A consciousness of abundance, on the other hand, results in our being able to receive freely from the universal bounty, to see virtually unlimited opportunity for expression, and to experience true and lasting prosperity. We actually attract to ourselves everything that we need—opportunity, supportive friends, food, shelter, transportation, instruction—when we are open to the universe and surrendered in God. *When we are God-attuned, if there is any disturbance in our consciousness because of a need presented to the mind, the universe will move to arrange conditions so that this disturbance is removed and balance is restored.*

When we deny fair payment to another, or the universe, for services rendered, we steal just as obviously as though our withholding were an overt act. Many devotees do this in relationship to their teacher or the institution through which they are provided instruction. They want to receive but they do not want to give; this is not a fair way to relate to others and the universe.

When Lahiri Mahasaya asked Mahavatar Babaji for permission to initiate people, Babaji said, "Before you initiate, ask a disciple to give you his money and his family." That was his way of saying, "Ask disciples to be a good stewards of the resources at their disposal, and to treat family members with love and respect, understanding that everything belongs to God." He also said, "Before initiating a disciple, be sure that person is honest."

In the yogic traditions, students are taught to be responsible for the support of others and for helping to provide resources needed for the spread of the teaching. In this way they learn to open themselves to the universe. Lahiri used to request a modest donation from disciples he initiated. He worked to support his family, and had no organized institution. He sent the donations to Babaji in the Himalayas, who used them for charitable purposes—to build temples and educational facilities for village people and to feed and clothe the needy.

Paramahansaji said, "Prosperity is not always having what you want when you want it; it is having what you need when you need it."

38. When vital forces are conserved and transmuted, physical, mental, and spiritual strength is experienced.

Continence means "self-restraint" and regulation of sensory impulses, a necessity for conserving and transmuting vital forces. Without control and right use of vital forces, they tend to be wasted in compulsive, unnecessary actions, thus weakening the nervous system and eroding will power. Vital forces can also be wasted through excessive talking, mental restlessness, frantic behavior, excessive sensory stimulation of any kind, overeating, insufficient sleep, and by being continually overstressed. Worry, anxiety, grief, and persistent destructive emotional involvements of any kind also weaken the systems. Improper eating habits impose a hardship on the body, as does an accumulation of waste matters which are not regularly eliminated.

In this sutra, the word used to describe the processes of conservation and transmutation of vital forces is *brahmacharya* (*brahma,* divine, and *acharya,* going). One who goes the divine way as a disciple is practicing self-restraint.

Conserved vital forces are used to maintain health and growth. Gross vital forces are transmuted into finer forces. The end result is an accumulation of the pure essence of life force which imparts radiance to the mind and body, contributing to superior powers of concentration, intellectual ability, and radiant physical health. This refined essence, which contributes to strengthening of the body's immune system and nourishes nerve and brain tissues, is also increased by mental calm and superconscious meditation practice.

Without right use of vital forces, concentration is difficult. Without concentration, meditation will not produce satisfying results. The practical way to conserve and transmute vital forces is to live a balanced, purposeful life, practice meditation, and apply other helpful procedures to encourage soul unfoldment.

39. When established in nonattachment, ability to know the processes of birth and death is acquired.

Relationships depend upon interaction and exchange. We are constantly experiencing a flow of forces and thought processes between ourselves and the realm of nature. In our dealings with others we exchange ideas, energies, emotions, and resources. All things in the universe are interdependent. Therefore, to withhold from the universe what we should release to it is to block the flow of life. To be nonattached is to be in the flow, grasping at nothing. Selfish attachments contribute to narrow-mindedness and isolation.

We may try to cling to our thoughts and our knowledge. We may try to cling to our awareness of emotional peace. We may more obviously hoard by accumulating material possessions. Prudent care and use of material things is a sign of wisdom. We are responsible for helping to maintain the culture which nourishes us. We are responsible for contributing to research, education, the arts and sciences, and for providing a spiritual education to seeking souls. We are responsible for helping others in our society, at whatever their level of need for support and encouragement. The universe gives freely and we, like it, should be selfless conduits through which cosmic forces can express in practical ways.

Understanding these matters enables us to comprehend the larger field of relationships which extends beyond regional, national, and international boundaries, to the subtle realms and the field of God. We are then enabled to understand the laws of causation which uphold the universe and to know causes and their effects, beginnings and endings (births and deaths), and how life's processes function.

Be responsible for the right use of resources, managing your affairs so that you fulfill your own purposes in life while helping others to fulfill theirs. Until you are in the flow and perform spontaneously and righteously, establish a planned program of giving in ways which will result in benefits to society.

40. As a result of ensuring purity and cleanliness, one experiences wellness and immunity from sources of contagion.

The physical body is cleansed by natural means, the subtle body by the cultivation of self-discipline and patience, and the mind by meditation and contemplation of Om.

Natural diet, exercise, rest, and, if necessary, the use of specific body cleansing procedures, contribute to physical purity and radiant health. The most suitable diet for a human being is comprised of grains, vegetables, fruits, and herbs. Choosing a vegetarian food plan should be considered as righteous behavior, as essential spiritual practice.

While it is useful to attend to matters of personal hygiene and diet, it is likewise important that the inner life be pure. Self-discipline of sensory impulses and cultivation of patience which results in soul contentment are the ways to cleanse the subtle body, the seat of feeling and emotions. There is no value in being an angry vegetarian or emotionally upset even in righteous causes. Mental and emotional unrest poisons the body as definitely as does impure food and unfriendly bacteria.

The above practices are outer: meditative contemplation is inner. A balanced program which attends to all levels is the best, for each level supports the others. When the body's immune system is strong, when emotional peace is established and spiritual awareness is steady, it is impossible to be influenced by any external substance or force. When the body's immune system is weak, the body is subject to disease. When inner peace is not established, we are subject to emotional disturbance due to outer conditions. When we are not settled in spiritual understanding, we are subject to delusion and further confusion. Only a little examination of these guidelines reveals their practical usefulness in providing a firm basis for actualizing our soul capacities.

41. As a result of mental purity, one experiences serenity, cheerfulness, power of concentration, control of the senses, and fitness for direct perception of God.

The mental field is purified when *rajas* and *tamas* are no longer dominant and luminosity prevails. We then naturally experience peace of mind, are cheerful, and able to concentrate easily and effectively. The senses are easily regulated, vital forces are conserved, the intellectual faculty is unveiled, and Self-realization blossoms.

Just as the body can be rendered unwell because of coming into contact with sources of contamination, so the mind can be contaminated by coming into contact with "mental poison." Until you are naturally flowing with relationships and are centered in God, be attentive to the relationships you cultivate or allow to be formed. We can easily know our sense of self-worth and self-esteem by examining our relationships of choice. If we choose to regularly associate with negative, self-serving people, or those who are provincial and grounded in conditioned states of consciousness, it reveals our own lack of self-worth and self-esteem. If we choose to frequent places where discordant and destructive influences prevail, it reveals our uncaring attitude about the usefulness of purity. When it is necessary to mingle with people who are self-centered and self-defeating in their attitudes and behavior, remain inwardly established in soul awareness and depart from them at the earliest convenient moment. If temporarily in an environment which does not support your chosen lifestyle, conclude your business and remove yourself from that environment. *The Book of Psalms* 1:1-3:

> Blessed is the man that walketh not in the counsel of the ungodly, nor standeth in the way of sinners, nor sitteth in the seat of the scornful. But his delight is in the law of the Lord; and in his law doth he meditate day and night. And he shall be like a tree planted by the rivers of water, that bringeth forth his fruit in his season; his leaf also shall not wither; and whatsoever he doeth will prosper.

While choosing to live righteously, renounce inclinations to fault others for their behavior. Just as you, until enlightened, are subject to your mental conditionings and the influences of the *gunas*, so are others. Silently love and bless everyone while maintaining your own integrity.

Paramahansaji advised disciples to monitor their conversations, avoid too much idle talk, and refrain from unnecessary association with others who were not interested in the higher life. He advised us to always be courteous and respectful while remaining calm and inwardly God-centered. We were not to gossip or excessively indulge in frivolous conversation. He said, "Do not allow your mind to be poisoned by the mental venom of others, and do not poison their minds by verbalizing negative thoughts and opinions."

42. As a result of contentment, supreme peace and happiness are experienced.

When our emotions are calm, instinctual drives are under control, and thoughts are well-ordered, then peace of soul, the highest happiness, reigns. How can we be content in a sometimes chaotic world? We can do it by viewing the passing scene with subjective understanding; by seeing through surface appearances to their underlying causes. In this way we can attend to our duties and remain informed of community and world events without becoming upset. In today's world, with dramatically transformative and sometimes explosive events reported with the speed of light by radio and television, millions of people, feeling themselves unable to do anything about conditions, are overstressed and confused. They worry or attempt to escape by losing themselves in relationships, work, chemical dependency, or neurotic behavior.

To be supremely peaceful and happy, cultivate contentment by attending to spiritual practices and maintaining a proper perspective in relationship to your environment.

43. As a result of purification and self-discipline, one experiences perfection of the body, mind, and senses.

When inner restrictions are removed and self-discipline is natural, nourishing influences of nature as well as supremely nurturing influences of superconscious forces strengthen body and mind and spontaneously regulate sensory impulses. The body becomes resistant to disease, a responsive organ for the expression of spiritual qualities. When superconscious forces are influential aging is slowed and vital capacities are enhanced.

Many people die too soon because of poor health, emotional distress, accidents, or boredom. They are unable to achieve their goals because of physical problems, neurosis, or knowledge of how to proceed. Good health, mental acuity, and regulation of sensory impulses provide us with the means to accomplish our mundane purposes as well as to further our spiritual unfoldment.

44. By right study and right application of spiritual practices, direct perception of God is realized.

We cannot progress in the direction of our goals if we are ignorant of the facts of life. I have counseled many devotees who have admitted dissatisfaction because of their lack of spiritual growth. They sometimes ask the most basic questions because they obviously have not availed themselves of the opportunity to learn by reading available books or attending classes. I once asked a woman—who had informed me she was a meditator but had many unanswered philosophical questions—if she had read the *Bhagavad Gita*. She said, "When I was initiated into meditation practice my teacher didn't recommend any study material." When I asked her why she didn't seek out such material on her own, she replied, " No one ever suggested it. Besides, I've never been much of a reader."

Study authoritative sources. Read them repeatedly until you understand what the author meant when the words were written. Go beyond words to the source from which knowledge is derived. Then, armed with valid knowledge, your understanding will improve. Grounded in essential understanding, contemplate Om during extended sessions of meditation. Follow the sound back to the Source, the field of God. This is the direct, meditative way to God-realization.

45. By surrender, one experiences God-realization.

Just as self-consciousness is superior to unconscious and sub-conscious states, and superconsciousness is superior to self-conscious states, so God-consciousness is superior to all modified states of consciousness.

A seeker asked Paramahansaji many questions about God and the spiritual path, seemingly more interested in talking about possibilities than doing anything about them. Paramahansaji said to him, "You remind me of a person who carefully examines an apple but never bites into one to experience what an apple is like. You are like this with God. Why don't you take a bite?"

46. The ideal meditation posture is firm and comfortable.

The *Bhagavad Gita* 6:1-15:

Let the practitioner of yoga constantly concentrate his mind on Supreme Reality, remaining in solitude and alone, self-con-trolled, free from desires and longings for sense experiences. Having the body positioned in a firm posture, let the devotee be one-pointed; controlling thoughts and senses, let that one practice pure contemplation in order to attain inward purity. Holding body, neck, and head erect and still, flowing attention to the spiritual eye without allowing attention to wander, serene and fearless, firm in the vow of self-control, subdued in mind, let the devotee sit, harmonized, with attention flowing to the Single Reality. The devotee of controlled mind, remaining harmonized, attains to peace, the supreme realization.

For meditation, one can sit in a comfortable, upright posture, in a chair, or in a cross-legged pose. It is important that one be poised, relaxed, alert, and attentive, so that contemplation can proceed without distraction. An upright seated position contributes to an alert mental attitude and allows full attention to be given to the purpose of meditation. Merely to sit in this manner for several minutes contributes to a degree of mental peace because body movements are stilled—the first step in the meditation process of inward turning. Control of physical impulses leads to control of mental and emotional processes. If you are a beginning meditator, unable to immediately calm thoughts and feelings, at least sit in the prescribed way.

47. As a result of deep relaxation, mental transformations make possible the release of awareness into God.

During meditation, as internal forces flow to the higher brain centers, attention is withdrawn from physical processes, and mental processes become progressively subtle and are finally transcended. This is a natural process and cannot be forced. As recommended procedures are followed, results unfold. Gross mental processes are transformed into subtle and fine processes. Finally, all mental processes cease and soul awareness is free in the field of God.

48. When restrictions are removed, freedom from involvement with body processes and mental influences allows one to experience transcendence.

Being internalized, the meditator is no longer influenced by physical sensations, emotions, mental fluctuations, or delusions or illusions about the true nature of the soul or the nature of higher Reality.

When strong flows of life force surge, it is not uncommon for physical movements to tend to occur and for emotional and mental processes to become agitated. If this happens, relax more and allow the flows to move through deeper levels while observing the process so that mental peace is not disturbed.

49. The meditation posture having become established, breathing rhythms become coordinated and refined, and internal flows of life forces become harmonized.

When concentrating, our breathing patterns are automatically regulated, becoming slower and sometimes suspended during episodes of concentration. This is natural pranayama: the regulation of life forces accompanied by controlled attention. A meditator experiences spontaneous inward turning and harmonizing of life forces as concentration becomes steady. Should concentration and surrender to meditation be difficult in the early stages of practice, there are procedures which can be used to afford the meditator a degree of conscious control. With practice, conscious control can extend to the involuntary systems, enabling one to slow the heartbeat, adjust body chemistry, and awaken healing energies. During deep meditation, breathing sometimes becomes so minimal that inspiration and expiration are unnoticed. In some instances, breathing may be suspended for a few moments while the body remains energized by cosmic forces. Breathlessness is not always accompanied by superconsciousness. If it were, we would only have to learn to suspend breathing to experience samadhi states and final liberation.

50. Modifications of pranayama are either external, internal, or motionless. They are long, short, or restrained, and modified according to space, time, and number.

Preliminary pranayamas, such as observing the flow of breathing rhythms, can assist in reducing physical stress and improve concentration. More advanced procedures can be used to cleanse the blood of carbon, freeing life forces from body and sensory involvements so they can be directed into the spinal pathway and brain. The *Bhagavad Gita* 4:29:

Others, devoted to life force control, having restrained the movements of alternating flows of prana in the body, neutralize these flows and rise beyond body and mind to awareness of Absolute-Existence-Being.

Prana is influenced by breathing patterns which may be suspended after exhalation (*external*) or after inhalation (*internal*), or during an interlude of intentional pause (*motionless*). *Time* relates to the duration of practice. *Number* refers to the repetitions practiced for specific purposes.

51. Another modification of pranayama is that of neutralizing inflowing and outflowing breaths, which balances flows of life forces in the body and mental field.

The practice of Kriya pranayama neutralizes alternating flows of breath by cleansing the blood of carbon and directing life forces from the body to the brain. When prana flows are completely neutralized, even subtle mental processes cease, allowing the meditator to more easily practice contemplative meditation. Before Kriya pranayama is learned, the meditator can progress to advanced superconscious states by devotion to God, surrendered contemplation, and the use of preliminary, preparatory meditation techniques. Restlessness and impatience may cause a devotee to think that "higher, more advanced" meditation techniques must immediately be learned and practiced if more rapid progress is to be accomplished.

Instead of being too anxious to learn advanced methods, first become proficient in basic how-to-live regimens, as well as fundamental meditation procedures. Techniques are but tools we use to accomplish our purposes.

52. The darkness which veils the light of the soul is removed by mastery of pranayama.

By the practice of Kriya pranayama the mental field is cleansed and the light of the soul is revealed. Pranayama is like a wish-fulfilling tree. Asian folklore has it that if one searches diligently, one will discover a magic tree in whose presence all wishes will come true. Pranayama is like this; its right practice allows the desire for God-realization to be satisfied.

53. By the practice of pranayama, mental processes are ordered and purified, making possible concentration on God.

So long as mental transformations continue, flawless concentration is not possible. Right practice of pranayama harmonizes prana flows in the body, calming and clearing the mind. Meditation can then proceed easily.

54. Internalization is accomplished when attention and vital forces are withdrawn and directed back to their source.

Internalization is accomplished when the meditator's attention is removed from the senses to flow to the higher brain centers. The Sanskrit word for this process is *pratyahara*, "the opposite attraction of psychic (soul) force." Instead of flowing outward, attention and vital forces flow inward, resulting in attention being displaced from distracting influences, to be used for meditative contemplation.

This process occurs partially during sleep. People who are by nature, or habit, compulsive in their outward involvements, may think it impossible to internalize attention during meditation. They may even think it strange for anyone to want to do it. Yet, when tired or overwhelmed by sensory input, the need to withdraw from outer involvements becomes pronounced, and they sleep. Meditation is the best conscious training for returning awareness to wholeness.

55. By internalization of attention and vital forces the yogi acquires supreme control of the senses.

By conscious exercise of will we can somewhat master sensory impulses. When awake and emotionally unsettled, tired, caught up in outer circumstances, or under the influence of alcohol or drugs, control is absent. When we are accomplished in the practice of meditative internalization, mental impulses and drives are spontaneously regulated by soul awareness. Self-control is then effortless.

CHAPTER THREE

Contemplation and Unfoldments of Unrestricted Soul Abilities

1. An undisturbed flow of attention is concentration.

When solely influenced by unconscious and subconscious drives, mental forces are dispersed and powers of concentration are impaired. By directing mental forces by an act of conscious will, the forces of the mind come under the volitional control of the devotee, contributing to success in planned ventures and realization of desired states of consciousness during meditation. Concentration requires mental training and skillful use of will power (intention). It occurs easily when attention is fascinated by an object which elicits curiosity, and is effortless when attention is absorbed in contemplation.

The mind is a material organ of perception. Do not say that you cannot control your mental processes; control your states of consciousness and mental attitudes, and orderly mental processes will naturally occur.

When meditating, sit in the prescribed posture and enter into the process with conscious intention. Assume an attitude of responsible command, knowing that you are but regulating body processes and mental forces to prepare for meditative contemplation and surrender in God. Flow attention to the highest ideal possible when you meditate. Acknowledge God and saints. Remind yourself that you are a ray of pure consciousness. Know that God's grace is expressive in and through you. The purpose of meditation is to experience superconscious states.

If the mind is restless during the early stages of meditation, pray for increased awareness of the presence of God. Use meditation techniques—pranayama, listening to Om, and contemplation of the boundless field of pure consciousness. Ignore all outer circumstances. You are meditating to experience Self-knowledge and to surrender in God. Forsake passions, needs, problems, and psychological conflicts. Everything will be harmoniously adjusted as a result of successful meditation practice. After meditation, you will be in a superior position to examine and relate to any personal challenges and environmental circumstances. Let God alone be your focus when you meditate.

When meditating, be involved with conscious intention to remove awareness from identification with relative matters for the purpose of experiencing superconscious states and exploring the inner realms. Until proficient in practice there may be a variety of preliminary perceptions to experience and transcend.

2. Unwavering, internalized concentration is meditation.

Some meditation teachers suggest that concentration is unnecessary for the practice of meditation; that attention can be attracted to the object of meditation without an exercise of will. Yet, resolve to meditate must be influential before the process can begin. While concentration need not be aggressive, it should be encouraged by providing something so attractive to the mind that attention is naturally inclined to flow to it. Effortless flowing of attention is pure concentration.

During preliminary stages of meditation practice, attention may be distracted. Do not struggle with feelings or thoughts. Think of God and engage in prayer and the practice of meditation techniques. When emotions settle and the mental field becomes calm, meditation will be spontaneously experienced. Superconscious influences will prevail over lower tendencies and you will enjoy deep meditation.

3. When the object concentrated upon is transcended and its reality is experienced, this is samadhi.

When preliminary perceptions and lower superconscious

states are transcended, higher superconscious states devoid of gross influences unfold. Mental forces are stilled and only the faculties of intelligence and intuition are operative. Intellectual examination of higher superconscious states may persist for a duration, then intuition will become more pronounced, making possible accurate knowledge of that which is being examined.

Contemplating the nature of God, may cause concepts about God to arise in the mind—as a benevolent father, a protective cosmic mother, a cosmic being, or as lord of the universe. This may be followed by contemplation of God as the consciousness-energy which makes possible the worlds, and by an examination of God as an unfoldment from the field of Supreme Consciousness. Probe ever more deeply into subtle and fine aspects of God until the final truth about God is known and experienced.

When thoughts subside and the object initially contemplated is no longer present to awareness and its essence is experienced, this is oneness or samadhi.

4. When concentration, meditation, and superconscious perception are simultaneous, this is perfect contemplation.

The Sanskrit word for this process is *samyama*, "the bringing together" of awareness with the object of concentration. The bringing together of the meditator's awareness with the object focused upon results in identification. The devotee can then know the object because of being one with it. Prior to this, the meditator could only know about the object. Perception was objective. Now perception is subjective. When one with the object of contemplation, the meditator knows its entirety.

When strongly attracted to an object of contemplation, identification with it can occur instantaneously. If attraction is not compelling and mental drives and cosmic forces are still influential, acquiring proficiency in the practice of samadhi states will require patient practice.

As preliminary training, it is recommended that one practice concentration at random times during the day. To do this, select something to look at and gaze steadily at it without analyzing the object or becoming involved in thinking about it. See how long you can "just look" without distraction. Practice for a minute or two at a time.

When you meditate, direct your attention to the spiritual eye. Look through it into the far distance of inner space. Doing this will improve concentration and facilitate meditation.

5. As a result of mastery of perfect contemplation, the light of direct knowledge dawns in one's field of awareness.

Direct knowledge is intuitive perception: actual realization of that which is contemplated. During preliminary stages of meditation, the meditator may experience attunement with inner light and Om; during advanced states one will experience identification with inner light and Om.

Prior to transcendent states there may be an almost endless variety of perceptions and experiences in relationship to aspects of physical realms, astral realms, fine causal realms, and celestial realms. These might be explored for years without contributing to God-realization. Paramahansaji was asked by a disciple, "If the possibilities of perception are endless, when does such involvement end?" He replied, "When you experience endlessness [transcendence]."

While observing—and even enjoying inner perceptions—be willing to go beyond them. Absorbed in Om, your attention it will be led through all subtle realms, to their source.

The Indian saint, Kabir, a weaver of cloth, wrote:

My dread of death and birth came to an end
when the Lord in his glorious hue
revealed himself to me
and darkness disappeared.
When I contemplated within I obtained
the rare gem of the Lord's name (inner sound).
In the wake of my bliss
all miseries fled away.
The jewel of my mind became absorbed
in the Lord's love within;
Whatever happens, O Lord,
I accept as Thy will.
One who lives in Thy will
merges in spontaneous God-consciousness.

(Says Kabir): My mistakes have become ineffective,
and my soul is suffused by the One
Who is the life of the entire creation.

6. **Perfect contemplation should be practiced progressively to experience higher states of consciousness.**

While valid knowledge of manifest realms is attainable, the dedicated devotee should remember that the highest application of perfect contemplation is for the purpose of transcending lower states of manifestation in order to experience higher ones. As soon as one level is mastered the devotee should immediately move to the higher ones. In this way, knowledge of all phases of manifestation and of That which is beyond manifestation is eventually experienced. It is by this process that the devotee becomes a perfected meditator.

7. **These three procedures are internal in comparison with the five procedures which preceded them.**

Concentration, meditation, and contemplation are internal procedures in comparison to the restraints, observances, posture, pranayama, and reversal of the flow of attention from the senses and the mind. As a result of success in practicing the five preliminary procedures, sensory impulses are regulated, behavior is modified for useful purposes, mastery of personal circumstances is acquired, vital forces are conserved and transmuted, and exploration of inner realms becomes easier.

8. **The three advanced internal procedures become external to the practice of higher superconscious states.**

Concentration, meditation, and preliminary superconscious states provide access to more refined levels of consciousness. They are therefore external to these higher states. Upon experiencing higher states of superconsciousness one's inner guidance becomes more pronounced and the influence of God's attracting power becomes more evidential. The meditator then surrenders to processes leading to final realization. Personal effort leaves off and grace determines the outcome. Higher states of consciousness cannot be comprehended without direct experience because they are beyond mental processes, Cosmic Mind, and the field of primordial nature. The meditator may become aware of a benevolent "presence" which assists unfoldment processes until awareness is merged in God.

9. **As a result of higher superconsciousness, superior influences permeate the mental field. Destructive tendencies are dissolved as constructive tendencies become actualized.**

When the mental field is entirely influenced by divine forces, all destructive impressions rooted in the mental field are dissolved. Only beneficial impressions result which enable the devotee to more easily live a well-ordered life. The personality becomes completely transformed and the light of God shines through it without disturbance or interference.

10. **Due to its inherent, pure nature, the flow of divine consciousness is serenely peaceful.**

As mental conditionings are weakened and cosmic forces in the mind become harmonized, flows of divine forces becomes steady and calm. Anger, frustration, boredom, compulsiveness, impatience, attachments, anxiety, and all other characteristics of mental conflict, cease. The essential quality of divine consciousness results in corresponding effects.

Until the mental field is calm, conflict persists because of the presence of opposing forces. Sensory impulses will be in conflict with higher aspirations, and life forces, being unbalanced and unstable, will contribute to unrest. The committed devotee should exercise intention to regulate sensory impulses, engage in specific practices to acquire mastery, and meditate to experience superconsciousness so that divine forces can become influential. For some, the growth process will be difficult. For others, it will be easier. For a few, it will be very easy. One who is devoted to practice will persist with unswerving confidence in the spiritual growth process and in God. In this way success is assured.

11. **Higher superconsciousness is experienced when mental modifications are stilled, distractions no longer prevail, and pure consciousness is spontaneously experienced.**

When mental obstacles are removed, superconscious states unfold spontaneously. When we hear someone speak of the true nature of the soul, or ponder the matter of our own volition, we feel a genuine inner response—proof of our innate condition. Most of us can remember our childhood years when we apprehended our divine nature, and of having awareness fade as we became more involved with outer circumstances and acquired traditional attitudes and opinions. Many people have turned to spiritual practices after an episode of spontaneous soul remembrance during which glimpses of higher possibilities were provided.

12. **During concentration, mental impressions (memories) of past events are perceived as being similar to recent ones.**

During meditation, thought streams project mental images on the screen of inner perception, causing a blending of similar images. Recent impressions in the mental field are not the same as older memories but there may be a continuity to their unfoldments in the mind due to their similarity. We may also recall memories of past superconscious perceptions because they also leave impressions.

13. **The preceding four verses explain the property, secondary qualities, and states of elements, the body, and the senses.**

The mental field constantly undergoes changes and transformations. These occur obviously when we implement intention and when superconscious influences prevail. An ordinary person can occasionally express unusual abilities and a aware person can at times manifest divine abilities. A confused mind can become orderly and an orderly mind can be concentrated and infused with superconsciousness. Properties of elements, material forms, and mind and senses, can exhibit the effects of transformations resulting in secondary qualities. Primordial nature under the influence of cosmic forces manifests secondary qualities which make possible the emanation of the universe. The essential property of nature remains the same but the secondary qualities provide possibilities for external changes.

14. A substratum is that in which latent, not yet manifested, or expressive properties are innate.

A substratum supports its manifested qualities. The existence of qualities implies that which supports those qualities. Things cannot appear out of nothing. Whatever appears must have an origin: something which is its support. The existence of thoughts proves the existence of a mind. The process of observation proves the existence of the observer. Manifest nature is possible because of the simultaneous existence of an observer (consciousness), the process of observation, and that which is observed. If I do not observe the field of nature, it continues to persist because it, being the substratum which supports objective manifestation, is self-referring.

Past, present, and probable futures simultaneously exist in the field of primal nature. What was, is impressed as memories on this field; what is, is presently manifesting; what will be, will express in the near or distant future.

The future is subject to modification. By altering present causes the future can be correspondingly altered. The facts of one's personal past experience cannot be changed but the effects (our reaction or response) of memory can be changed. We can vividly recall past circumstances, acquire liberating insight, and release trauma so that the force of karma (causation) is neutralized. Another way to disarm karmic impressions is to observe them with discernment. When we clear our consciousness, what was influential when our awareness was clouded or conflicted is no longer causative. In these ways, karmic patterns can be resisted, modified, and eliminated.

We may choose to ponder memories of past events. We may choose to live in the present, attempting to ignore the past and avoid the future. We may fantasize about the future and neglect present responsibilities. Or we may come to terms with the past, live responsibly in the present, and look to the future with optimism. We may even apprehend future possibilities for ourselves and choose to actualize them quickly.

In relationship to your future as an enlightened being, why not consider the possibility of being enlightened as soon as possible instead of hoping for it in the distant future? Why not do what you can now to actualize your soul capacities? To do this, move through time in your imagination and see yourself as you can be.

By using creative abilities through the agency of the mind we can introduce beneficial changes in our lives and the lives of others. We can implement constructive mental influences which will interact with the field of Universal Mind to contribute to harmonious relationships, health, prosperity, and spiritual progress. We can do this for ourselves and we can do it for others by seeing with faith what is desirable and calling it into manifestation.

15. The orders and arrangements of underlying influences are the causes of external transformations.

The arrangements and actions of subtle cosmic forces result in the manifestations of gross forces and forms in the field of nature. The orders and arrangements of mental causes result in the manifestations of experience in our lives.

Because cosmic forces are present in Cosmic Mind, and cosmic forces regulate nature's primal substance, we can introduce changes in the field of nature by thinking, intention, and adjustments of states of consciousness. To effect transformation of matter one has but to learn how to visualize end results. To a person who does not understand this process, its demonstration will seem magical. To one who understands, the process is known to be the effective outcome of natural law, though by some it may seem to be supernatural because laws other than those ordinarily known at the physical level are operational.

No matter how extensive are the transformations occurring in the field of nature, the energy of the universe remains constant. Unmanifested energy comes into manifestation and expressive energy flows back to the unmanifested state. The total energy remains the same. Everything comes out of the Source and flows back into the Source.

16. By perfect contemplation on the three kinds of transformation, knowledge of past and future is acquired.

A person who can exercise reason, can fairly accurately know his past and his probable future. Present circumstances are due to past and present causes. By evaluating present circumstances in the light of past and present thoughts and behaviors we can determine why circumstances are as they are. By knowing present influential causes, probable future circumstances can be known.

What our habitual states of consciousness and actions are, determines our future. We also tend to experience progressive improvement of circumstances because of the force of evolution. If your future as you see it is acceptable to you, flow with present trends. If your future is in need of modification, introduce constructive influences.

17. Words, meanings of words, and ideas about them, are often intermingled. By perfect contemplation on sounds one can comprehend the meanings of sounds uttered by all living creatures and things.

Nonverbal communication is common between people who are "of one mind." When we are with a person with whom we share an affinity we often know what they are thinking and can anticipate their actions. They also know our thoughts and can anticipate our behaviors. Mental and spiritual attunement is so complete that little effort to communicate is required.

By determining the causes of inarticulate, verbal sounds a person makes we can fairly accurately know that person's moods and desires. This can also be done with creatures. Plants and mechanical objects may also emit sounds which we can learn to understand, and the reason for them.

18. By perfect contemplation of the driving forces of mental impressions, knowledge of past life cycles is revealed.

Instinctual drives differ from karmic drives. Instinct impels curiosity and prompts desire to satisfy basic urges: to be secure, happy, functional, successful, and Self-realized. The driving forces of karma impel us to compulsive actions which may result in outcomes which are either constructive and life-enhancing, destructive and life-suppressing, or which serve no useful purpose because nothing worthwhile is accomplished. By analyzing the driving forces of mental impressions (conditionings or karmic patterns) we can understand their origins, interactions, and current or potential influences upon our personality, mental states, and behaviors.

Although our prior earth-life cycles may be many and varied, from a higher perspective they are as inconsequential as the dreams we have when we sleep. Attempts to remember prior incarnations almost always result in confusion and distract attention from more important life-purposes. It is of interest to note that enlightened teachers who have the ability to know past life cycles seldom mention such matters. If they considered the subject important they would emphasize it. Some masters know their past experiences on the planet as well as those in other spheres. They know the reason for their present sojourn here and what they will be doing when they depart. Some even predict their future returns and plan them so they can continue their destined work. Paramahansaji told disciples that, after leaving this world, he would spend some time resting, then be reborn and be with Mahavatar Babaji in the Himalayas and elsewhere. He also said that some of his disciples would be with him and Babaji during that phase of his next incarnation.

19. By perfect contemplation of the mental processes of others, knowledge of their mental states are known.

One who understands his own mental processes and is accustomed to observing other people can often discern their mental states by examining their behavior. It is also possible to see through superficial indications, acquire insight into the contents of the minds of others, and know their secret thoughts, motivations, and drives. In this way the observer's clear mental field accurately reflects the contents of those with whom it is attuned. We should not do this unless we have the other person's permission or we are responsible for their welfare and need information in order to help them.

20. Contemplation which reveals the contents of another's mental processes does not always reveal their causes and supporting influences.

Merely reading the content of a person's mind may not provide knowledge of the causes of memories, thoughts, or the objects of desire. One may discern current thought trends but not discern past circumstances which have contributed to them.

The way to scan the contents of another person's mind is to be mentally calm while desiring to know them. Impressions will stream into your mind, sometimes as clear mental pictures which can be observed and evaluated without judgment. To probe more deeply, attune yourself with the other person's mind until superconscious rapport is established. You will then know that person's feelings and thoughts, and their supporting influences. You may also have access to their memories and know past behaviors and experiences.

21. By perfect contemplation on body form, on suspension of the receptive power (contact between the eye of the observer due to reflected light from the body) one becomes invisible to others.

This method of vanishing from the sight of others is not the same as dematerialization of the body. Rather, the yogi prevents light from being reflected from his body so that he or she cannot be seen. We can do this in a less obvious way by attending to our own interests; thus, remaining unnoticed by others because of not radiating thoughts or feelings into the mental atmosphere.

22. By this process the disappearance of sound, taste, touch, smell, and hearing is explained.

We cannot be disturbed by that of which we are no longer aware because of having withdrawn our attention from it.

When absorbed in reading or observing something which attracts our attention, we might be oblivious of our environment. When absorbed in meditative contemplation, external circumstances cease to be a cause of distraction. Environmental perception can only occur when there is a connection between the perceiver and the perceived. During meditation we "reverse the searchlights of attention" and focus on God.

23. By perfect contemplation on karmic patterns which are fast or slow in manifesting, knowledge of death and other unusual happenings is known.

Some mental causes manifest their effects quickly; others manifest slowly, depending upon their force and the existence of prevailing circumstances suitable for their expression. By knowing inner causes we can know why outer happenings occur. We sometimes ask, "Why do good people suffer?" or, "Why do bad people experience good fortune?"

Good people can make mistakes because they are driven by inner forces of which they have little or no awareness. Misguided people can have some positive traits and occasionally be in the flow of grace. God does not reward good behavior or punish wrong behavior; universal laws work according to orderly principles. It may only be our simplistic beliefs about God that prompt us to draw unreasonable conclusions. If we believe we will be rewarded for certain behavior, we may be rewarded according to our belief, not because God is pleased with us. If we believe we will be punished for behaviors which we feel to be wrong but which in fact are not, we may experience hardship according to our belief, not because God is displeased with us. Attitudes and beliefs are also karmic influences: causes which can result in effects. It is not only the storehouse of mental impressions that represents the totality of the karmic condition. We often look to causes originated in the past when they are present as our existing attitudes, beliefs, and misguided behaviors.

Some karmic impressions which might cause us discomfort are slow to manifest because our awareness is clear and we are healthy and productive. Present states of consciousness and behavior then determine our experiences, and residual karma is restrained from expressing. In the near or distant future, when we are not so aware and purposeful, latent troublesome karmic impressions may become influential. Our current states of consciousness and constructive behaviors are more influential than what we thought or did in the past. People who are not willing or able to remain aware and responsible, almost always remain the effect of past causes and present transformative circumstances. They are almost always thinking, "Why is this happening to me?"

By understanding our motivations and states of consciousness we can know their effects. As when experiencing conscious dreams we can manipulate them by adjustments in attitude and conscious intention, we can manipulate circumstances by adjustments in attitude and exercise of conscious intention. We can be aware of causes and let them unfold or we can choose to be self-responsible.

24. **By perfect contemplation on friendliness, compassion, and other noble qualities, one experiences mental, moral, and spiritual strength.**

Because it is a characteristic of consciousness to identify with that with which it associates, by contemplating desirable qualities we can assume them. When higher superconscious states are regularly experienced, their qualities spontaneously manifest because they are innate to the soul.

Physical, moral, mental, and spiritual decline can result from unwise choices. For instance, choosing to associate with people who are negative and self-destructive, accepting our weaknesses and harmful habits as being our true nature, extreme enjoyment of sensory stimulation, being unhappy because of another's good fortune or happy because of their misfortune, are self-defeating behaviors. We may unwisely maintain and nurture self-defeating myths about ourselves. We may persist in feeling unworthy of being successful, believing that we are helpless, unwanted, and unloved. We may do little or nothing to adjust our states of consciousness, or to train ourselves to see the many life-enhancing possibilities available to us. We may neglect to cultivate elevating qualities, unwisely choosing to instead remain involved with restlessness and inertia.

The most obviously unrighteous person can become righteous by cultivating the qualities of righteousness. By being established in harmlessness and contemplating friendliness, compassion, and other noble qualities, you will definitely experience mental, moral, and spiritual strength. If you are reasonably intelligent, healthy, and functional, and are not growing spiritually, it is because you do not want to grow spiritually. It is because you have not chosen to unfold your innate soul qualities. I have known devotees who remained deluded for many years despite their regular meditation practices because they were not fully committed to the processes of psychological and spiritual transformation. If you sincerely want to be enlightened you can definitely experience transformative changes.

Train yourself to look upon the world with enlightened understanding. Especially after meditation, contemplate friendliness, compassion, and all noble qualities. Let intentional divine contemplation contribute to your spiritual growth.

25. By contemplation on various aspects of power, one becomes empowered.

God is the one manifesting power. Because all forces in the universe are but aspects of the power of God, it is to God we should turn when in need of strength to meet challenges and accomplish worthy purposes.

Do not think that mind or any other created thing has power. There is no power but of God. Clearly understand that God is the only power and that surrender in God is the certain way to have infinite power flow into expression.

The power cannot flow freely when we are not open to it, or when conflicted mental states restrict its inclination to express. To be open and responsive to the power of God, do this:

1. Meditate until established in superconsciousness.

2. After meditation, remain quiet and poised. Know your true relationship with God—that you are an individualized expression of God's consciousness, complete and perfect.

3. Know that through your mind you are in harmony with Universal Mind, God's mind.

4. Know for yourself: order, right action, and appropriate response to circumstances. Affirm:

"I am a perfect expression of divine qualities. I maintain rational thinking, appropriate behavior, and cosmic awareness. I live in the world in divine order, doing my responsible best while trusting in God completely. Friendly, compassionate, and expressively caring, I acknowledge the only power—the power of God. I am always conscious of its ever-present, ever-appropriate manifestations. I am happy. I am thankful."

26. By perfect contemplation on the light of consciousness one acquires knowledge of things which are veiled, subtle, and remote.

Being one with the all-pervading light of consciousness, we can know that which is hidden from ordinary people, see into the fine structure of matter and into subtle realms, and know what is happening at a distance.

By being receptive, we can have access to knowledge which is not ordinarily apprehended. Novice truth students sometimes ask, "Why, if the masters know things which would be helpful to the masses, do they not reveal what they know?" They do, to those who are able to comprehend and who will use knowledge wisely. If you want to know the "secrets" of God and the universe you have only to prepare yourself to be a trustworthy receptacle of knowledge, then ask for it. Knowledge will unfold from within, or you will be led to sources of valid information.

Do not desire too much higher knowledge until you have mastered what you already know by demonstrating it in your personal life. Become proficient in the basic procedures first. In this way prepare yourself for advanced training. Cultivate your interior life. Higher knowledge is not to be acquired in the chaos of the outer sense-stimulated world. If you want to know what the masters know, you must live like the masters live. You are now as knowledgeable as you are capable of being. Increase your capacity to know and you will know more.

Some seekers ask me to explain the reality of God and to show them how to be happy and productive. If they are ready to "know the truth" they can receive it. If they are grounded in ego-ism and living an undisciplined and directionless life, they cannot receive it. In this current Age, with many people becoming

more spiritually inclined, enlightenment teachers, out of compassion and a genuine willingness to be helpful, teach philosophical principles and meditation instruction more openly. They hope
that a few among the many who are thus informed will benefit.
This is "quantity" work: sharing useful information with many
people to help some to a better way of life. The "quality" work is
a private relationship between the guru and disciple, and this
relationship is often challenging to the disciple because the guru
will do everything possible to encourage psychological transformation and spiritual growth.

In the guru-disciple relationship no area of the disciple's life
remains hidden. While instructing in matters of higher metaphysics and spiritual practices, the guru may also inquire into
personal matters. He or she may ask, "How do you earn your
living? Is it honest work which benefits others and society, or
does some harm result?" Do you pay your bills on time? Are you
good to your wife (or husband) and children? Do you support community efforts, cultural activities, and spiritual institutions? Do
you read the scriptures every day? Are you becoming proficient
in preliminary practices—sense control, attitude adjustment,
right behavior, and other matters essential to psychological health
and moral living?" If the disciple's answers are affirmative,
instruction will continue. If they are not, the guru may say, "Go
home and get your personal life straightened out. When you have
done this, come back, and we will then continue our studies."

At preliminary levels of spiritual understanding one can know
of events transpiring at a distance by telepathic means. This is
possible because when operating at the level of mind, one can be
attuned to what is taking place in the collective mind. At a higher
level one can know whatever is desired to be known, merely by
knowing. At this level, because one's awareness is omnipresent,
there is no need for information to be transmitted.

**27. By perfect contemplation of the central sun one can have
knowledge of regions and planets, and of evolution and
operations of the universe.**

Knowledge of the operations of the universe can be had by
analysis and contemplation of it. This helps us to live harmoni-

ously in relationship to nature's processes. The inner meaning of *the central sun* is the inner light and the course it takes when moving from body confinement to explore the inner realms behind the field of gross universal manifestation. We are rapidly improving our knowledge of the physical universe, but may not be aware of subtle inner realms and their spheres and dimensions. Knowledge of outer phenomena is helpful to our continued development and well-being. Knowledge of inner planes contributes to our higher understanding and spiritual evolution.

To contemplate the central sun within, the meditator becomes established in Self-realization and diverts attention from the body to subjective levels. In doing this one follows *the path of the sun*, the way of illumination. One may immediately transcend all intermediate planes this side of the field of God, or may progressively experience and move through them, observing their characteristics. One may become aware of luminous astral spheres, some beautiful and harmonious and some dark and discordant. One may become aware of celestial realms wherein dwell highly realized souls which abide in superconscious states and continue to advance Godward in their understanding. In these regions the devotee may observe universes, with planets and galaxies. If focused, one will move through these spheres to the sphere of God, and beyond to the field of pure consciousness. Centered in Self-knowledge and God-realization, everything is viewed with calm detachment, in the knowledge that all phenomena is but the production of cosmic forces and that no permanent satisfaction can be derived from dependence upon it.

When an enlightened soul leaves the body it takes *the path of the sun* to the Source, to the field of pure consciousness. To go any other way is to remain involved with phenomena.

28. By perfect contemplation on the moon and star systems, one can have knowledge of their actions and relationships.

In this sutra the inner meaning of *moon* is the reflected light of the sun of pure consciousness. Contemplation on the inner sun results in knowledge of pure consciousness. Contemplation on the reflected light of consciousness results in knowledge *about* pure consciousness and its manifestations. When identified with reflected light, the soul does not have complete knowledge of its own reality but is aware as an individualized entity with some self-consciousness remaining. From this state of consciousness it can somewhat explore inner realms, but cannot have access to realms for which it is not prepared to comprehend. Even the realms perceived will not be fully comprehended. One may mistakenly assume that lower levels of astral, causal, or celestial manifestation are the highest ones and be content to reside there. Fundamentalists of various religious traditions often believe that the highest state to which the soul can attain is a heaven-like condition. Christians may believe the ultimate reward to be heaven with Jesus and saints, along with the company of other believers. A Hindu may believe the highest good to be heaven with Krishna or other adepts of traditional lore. Unenlightened people who think of the possibility of heaven almost always envision a glorified human condition. Some who cannot imagine even this, think that heaven for them would be to dwell in a beautiful astral realm with their friends and "loved ones." Those who cannot imagine heaven sometimes speculate about other possibilities. When they make their transition they may be pleasantly surprised to discover that circumstances are better than they had thought possible for them. Sometimes they are not surprised—because they mentally create a temporary condition which reflects their expectations.

29. By contemplation on the polestar, one can have knowledge of the motions and movements of celestial bodies.

By examining the placement and movements of stars, solar systems, and galaxies, knowledge of their movements and influences can be acquired. It is only during the past few hundred years that researchers in the West have become aware of planetary and galactic movements and relationships. It is only recently that scientists have been actively exploring the influences of the sun's radiation upon magnetic fields in the solar system and the effects of gravitation between planetary bodies. Electromagnetic forces affect the magnetic fields of living things, but the full implications are not yet generally known. Electromagnetism is the phenomena that occurs as a result of an electric charge in motion.

Creation theories are still being examined. How did the universe come into existence? Was there a "big bang" that resulted in what we now observe, or does the universe have a creator? If there was a creator, what was its purpose for initiating the process? If there was not a creator, how did the process get started? Was there really an initial explosion, or did the universe "emerge" and expand to its present state?

30. By contemplation on the chakras and nerves, one can have knowledge of the processes occurring in the body.

After preliminary study of anatomy and physiology and of the processes by which the body is formed and regulated, one can contemplate with inner vision to fully comprehend the workings of the subtle astral sheath and physical body. Absorbed in meditative contemplation it is possible to see the chakras, observe the nervous system, and know the locations and functions of the organs, circulation of blood and other fluids, and the changes and transformations occurring in the tissues.

31. By contemplation on the vital centers which regulate appetite and thirst, one can acquire control over these functions.

Thirst and hunger are natural, physical urges which can be regulated by intention and agreement. The urge to compulsively consume fluids and foods can be checked by overall regulation of sensory impulses. By learning to nourish the body with prana we can reduce the body's dependence upon the gross medium of food. Quite apart from the nutrients in food, we absorb solar radiation converted by plant life. A few spiritually advanced souls know how to perform an intricate kriya process, which involves the cervical chakra, by which the body can be nourished directly by an infusion of astral light and soul force flowing through the medulla oblongata at the base of the brain.

Paramahansaji wrote of a woman living in a remote village in India who had learned from a yogi at an early age how to practice this technique. She later married and assumed family and community responsibilities, living an otherwise normal life except for the fact that she did not eat because she had no desire to do so. She spent most nights in superconscious meditation, at times communing with saints on the inner planes. Theresa Neumann of Bavaria was known to live without liquids or food. A Catholic nun, she discovered, after an illness in 1923, that she did not desire to eat. When Paramahansaji met her, in 1935, he asked, "You do not eat food—but you do eat something, don't you?" She replied, "Yes, I live by God's light."

It is the experience of many meditators that, because of increased soul awareness and self-reliance, all sensory urges are minimized and food requirements are diminished.

32. By contemplation on the centers of equilibrium, one can experience steadiness of individual consciousness.

Being centered is a matter of discovering our beingness. As a result we can learn to remain poised and maintain our mental and emotional balance at all times. We may do this by collecting our thoughts and feelings so that we feel centered and poised. It may help to "feel around" inside the body and find a balance point in the chest, the heart chakra, or just below the solar plexus. Diaphragmatic breathing to induce relaxation of the abdominal muscles will help. Being centered is primarily a matter of feeling secure and comfortable where we are, in command of our states of consciousness, thoughts, feelings, and behavior. Exercise, purposeful living, and diet suited to our basic psychophysiological constitution can also be helpful.

33. By perfect contemplation on the light at the spiritual eye and crown chakra, souls liberated from restricting influences experience direct perception of Reality.

Contemplation at the higher centers enables mental faculties to be transcended and intuition to function. The meditator may then obtain glimpses of subtle spheres, as well as occasionally see beings of light, highly evolved souls, and illumined spiritual masters. These may appear before the inner vision during meditation or may sometimes be communed with during occasions of conscious sleep, during superconscious dreams. They may even be occasionally seen while the devotee is in a calm state during ordinary waking moments. If such perceptions are helpful, they can be allowed, but should not be sought. Devotees of God should avoid illusions and hallucinations of all kinds, as well as preoccupation with visions and the possibility of visitations by "angels" or other imaginary phenomena.

Several of my spiritually advanced brother and sister disciples reported that they had seen "bright beings" which would appear to them during meditation and at other times. One brother disciple told me that especially when he needed guidance he would occasionally see a radiant personage manifest before him. Guidance would be telepathically transmitted and the being would vanish. He said of such manifestations, "They're beautiful! The longer they have been liberated the more beautiful they are!"

Paramahansaji said that he frequently saw "gods" and "goddesses" on the grounds of his ashrams and in the lecture hall when he was speaking. On one occasion, during a gathering of devotees, he said, "Oh, if you could only see the saints who are here today! They have come to be with us and bless us."

During advanced superconscious meditation the devotee may see in the spiritual eye the guru, the guru line, or other bright souls. With practice one will be able to discern the difference between true perceptions of saints and illusory mental imagery.

Several of Lahiri Mahasaya's disciples saw Babaji in Lahiri's presence. Swami Pranabananda was once visiting Lahiri's home. Lahiri asked him to come with him to the outside entrance, and there made a gesture of greeting to an invisible guest. Pranabananda was perplexed, until Lahiri touched him at the spiritual eye to calm his mind. He then saw the bright form of a saint of youthful appearance. It was Mahavatar Babaji, who talked with them and answered many of Pranabananda's questions. He confirmed at that time that he had indeed retained his body for several hundred years by applied knowledge of ayurvedic procedures and the power of cosmic consciousness.

Illumined masters whose present work is to assist spiritually advanced souls rather than to be publicly active, are seldom seen by others who would not be able to comprehend their enlightened state or appreciate their influence. The devotee can only communicate with them when intuitive faculties are sufficiently cultivated. Masters such as Babaji can appear to a devotee's inner vision or manifest in more obvious ways when conditions are suitable.

The highest benefit of awakened spiritual consciousness is that of being enabled to apprehend Absolute Reality.

34. By perfect contemplation on the supreme light of Reality, all knowledge is revealed.

Like light before the dawn, awareness unfolds prior to discriminative perception as the intellectual faculty is transcended and intuition makes possible knowledge of higher realities. It is useful to examine the varied aspects of the manifest realm in order to acquire understanding and live effectively, but contemplation of the Light of lights should not be neglected. Always keep before you the true purpose for your being on the enlightenment path and persist in wanting to know the ultimate truth of life. Do not settle for anything less than complete understanding of universal processes and full realization of God.

35. By contemplation on the heart, one acquires knowledge of consciousness and of Cosmic Mind.

The "heart" of you is your beingness. When seers advise to search out the truth in our heart, they mean for us to contemplate *that* of us which is permanently real. When we are calm and introspective we can easily discern that we are not the body; we are not the mental waves; we are not the mind. We can know that we are an observer and experiencer.

When we observe the actions of our thoughts and our deeper mental processes we acquire knowledge of how the mind functions. We can then inquire into how our mental field is related to Cosmic Mind. By creatively experimenting with thought processes and mental imagery we can learn how our thoughts and mental images are impressed upon the field of Cosmic Mind to cause effects. We then learn that Cosmic Mind is the Mind common to us all; that our individualized mind is but a particularized unit of Cosmic Mind. What we put into the law of mental causation tends to be expressed in our environment. Thoughts, though subtle, have substance and can be given more obvious form when impressed upon Cosmic Mind through focused intention. In this way we can cause our worthy dreams to be outwardly manifested. When doing this, we must be honest and selfless in order to avoid creating complications for ourselves and others. We need not doubt our freedom to use our creative abilities. We have them for a purpose and they should be intelligently used.

Some devotees are reluctant to make decisions because they do not want to make mistakes or bind themselves to unwanted futures. Righteous desire is not wrong, nor is it harmful in its effects. Therefore, pray for guidance and learn to be self-responsible in the use of your creative mental abilities.

Out of the substance of Cosmic Mind all varieties of manifestation emerge into expression. With practice, you will only have to desire a useful outcome and cosmic forces will flow to fulfill your just desire. Mental causation, backed by enlightened will, is more result-producing than physical actions.

Blind desire is in conflict with the soul's innate urge to have awareness restored to wholeness because it can result in bondage to desire and its effects. Many people are caught in a web of circumstances of their own unconscious causing. Being unable to make right choices they act without wisdom. The mental laws of cause and effect function just as efficiently for the unwise as the wise.

Mental abilities wisely used contribute to the fulfillment of legitimate purposes and Self-realization. Unwisely used, soul abilities result in further problems. Superconscious abilities can also be used wisely or unwisely, to result in liberation of consciousness or in confusion. One saint said, "If you are conscious of using your powers you are in danger of misusing them. It is better to be led of the Spirit and to function without ego."

36. **By perfect contemplation on the true nature of the soul as being distinct from the faculty which makes possible experience of relative perceptions, one awakens to the knowledge of the True Self.**

The faculty which makes possible experience of relative perceptions is the intellect. Intellect determines the validity of sensory information. The faculty of intelligence stands between the field of nature and the field of pure consciousness. Looking outward through the faculty of intelligence and the mind, the soul views the realm of nature. Looking inward, the soul's awareness is removed from involvement with the senses and mental processes so that contemplation of subjective realities can easily proceed.

So long as one is embodied, life can be experienced as a drama of unfolding consciousness during which the devotee fulfills personal obligations and continues to facilitate spiritual growth. Mahavatar Babaji said, "Few people in mortal (conditioned) consciousness know that the reality of fulfillment includes this earth realm." The laws which make fulfillment possible are operational in all realms this side of the field of God, including the realm of physical matter. The devotee must learn to see with clear understanding from the level of soul identification before total fulfillment can be perceived and experienced.

We may find it difficult to remain inwardly poised in understanding because of imperfect perception which causes us to see problems and to believe in the reality of what our senses report to us. We then think that outer appearances are permanently real, forgetting that they are but effects of mental causes and of cosmic forces operating in the field of nature.

37. Some outcomes of perfect contemplation on God can be unfoldments of extrasensory perceptions in relationship to cognition: hearing, seeing, smelling, touching, and tasting.

By inner hearing we can discern astral sounds emanating from the chakras, and Om, and hear sound frequencies occurring in the various subtle spheres of which we may become aware.

With intuitive perception we can see what others cannot see, and discern inner causes of outer effects. Clairvoyance enables us to see light frequencies or auras, and light in the spiritual eye. It is estimated that the average person sees perhaps a billionth of the frequencies of the electromagnetic field, usually observing only the color ranges from red to violet. We commonly perceive only what is convenient to our purposes. Bees, for instance, are believed to be able to see ultraviolet light which attracts them to flowers.

Astral smell, touch, and taste can also be cultivated. A devotee may at times smell pleasant fragrances that others cannot detect, feel the presence of benevolent beings and forces, and experience during meditation unusual, delicate tastes which are the manifesting aspects of subtle element influences.

Extrasensory perceptions should be used to investigate the inner realms, leading to God-realization. Their unfoldments can be evidence of partial soul awakening but are not ultimate ends. The frequencies of astral, causal, and celestial realms coexist with frequencies of the gross cosmic field (the physical universe). By visualization and the use of mantra, energy frequencies of subtle spheres can be attracted into this realm. By these methods some yogis can cause subtle frequencies to be more influential and introduce beneficial changes into the environment. Knowledgeable use of mantra is effective because audibly or mentally chanted sounds correspond to those which exist in subtle spheres and invite them into one's environment. This is one reason why ashrams, spiritual retreats, and religious pilgrimage sites can have what is referred to as a sacred vibration which is felt by devotees.

38. These abilities, if allowed to flow mainly outward, are obstacles to the unfoldment of soul awareness. If used properly, they become supernatural abilities useful for regulating and neutralizing instinctual and conditioned destructive drives and tendencies.

Soul abilities can facilitate superconscious realizations when one's mind is purified, but are detrimental acquisitions for a mind in which thoughts and cosmic forces are fluctuating. The average person, becoming somewhat aware of unusual abilities, hastens to explore them further and to use them for self-serving purposes. For this reason, emphasis is given to the importance of morality and the cultivation of the virtues. A moral and virtuous person is not likely to misuse abilities. An immoral, egocentric person may misuse soul abilities.

There is value in legitimate research into the operations of soul abilities because understanding them can increase our knowledge and possibly improve our personal circumstances. It is enchantment as a result of preoccupation with phenomena which presents the major challenge, because such involvement prevents expansion of consciousness. Small-minded truth seekers often become involved with psychic unfoldment, engaging in hypnosis, mediumship, superficial endeavors to unfold powers of clairvoyance, mind reading, and healing with energy flows, forgetting to attend to their spiritual practices for the purpose of knowing God. They remain involved at the second level of soul unfoldment, often thinking themselves to be spiritually awakened when, in fact, they are functioning out of conditioned consciousness and actually preventing further spiritual growth. These are tamasic and rajasic activities which do not contribute to illumination of consciousness. When manifested spontaneously, soul powers are natural endowments.

39. By relaxing the causes of bondage and by penetrative flowing of attention, one's awareness can enter into the mind and body of another.

The restricting influences of all causes of bondage are relaxed or weakened by superconscious experience. By superconscious means we can remove and transcend restrictive physical, emotional, and mental conditions.

A guru may intentionally flow awareness into the mind of a disciple to change thought patterns and clear the disciple's consciousness. In this way the disciple's awareness is brought to the level the guru habitually experiences. The disciple can then be assisted through challenging circumstances and given genuine spiritual uplift which hastens spiritual evolution. A guru may say to a disciple, "Let us be attuned. Identify with my mind and consciousness and you will experience what I experience."

A brother disciple told me of his learning experience during a visit with our guru. After an interlude of pleasant conversation, Paramahansaji excused himself to attend to a personal matter. He told the disciple to meditate until later in the day when they would meet again. The disciple assumed that Paramahansaji was merely offering a suggestion rather that giving him specific instructions. When they again met, Paramahansaji said, "You didn't meditate. When I tell you to meditate, you should do it."

Later, when alone, the disciple meditated. After becoming calm and centered, he felt a force moving upward through the chakras to the brain. Deep meditation was spontaneously experienced. Later, Paramahansaji said, "Now, you understand why I asked you to meditate." By flowing his attention to the disciple Paramahansaji was able to direct the inner processes of life force and assist the disciple's meditation practice.

Our guru told us, "I go through your souls every day." At random times he would think of his disciples and accurately know their inner condition. He could then share his consciousness with them to assist their spiritual unfoldment, or later give them personal instruction that could be helpful.

In this way, too, an accomplished yogi can attune his mind with another person's mind to reduce the force of the latter's karma. Some masters transfer karmic conditions to their own astral body and dissolve it. They may do this when there is an emergency and the burden must be lifted immediately. A direct way to dissolve karma is to use superior powers of discernment to know the nothingness of it, dissolving it instantaneously.

Paramahansaji was once sitting with some disciples and suddenly asked them to leave the room for a while. When he summoned them later he told what had transpired. He had "received" a soul call from a disciple twenty-five miles distant who was in a hospital because of serious illness. He explained that he went there in his subtle form "to usher her into the Infinite." He said, "When I left her, she was happy. She had a body of light and no signs of the disease that had ravaged her physical form." Later that day the husband of the disciple called to report her transition. He described the final moments as Paramahansaji had recounted them. He said, "Just before she passed she opened her eyes and exclaimed, 'Yogananda is here! Yogananda is here!'"

40. As a result of mastery over the upward flowing prana in the body, one becomes invulnerable to various forces and manifestations of nature and experiences victory over death.

By regulating the upward flowing prana in the body one is able to move lightly and easily, avoiding rough or hard contact with the environment. A more obvious benefit is that one can, at the moment of conscious transition, cause upward flowing prana to move through sushumna and out of the body. Downward flowing prana helps the soul to remain attached to the body.

41. As a result of mastering the governing principles of fire influence, one manifests inner and outer radiance.

Inner "fire" transforms food to nourish the body and facilitates psychological transformation. At the physical level, contemplation of the inner fire influence and the aspect of prana it regulates, results in increased powers of digestion essential for good health and physical radiance. We say of people who enjoy vital health that they fairly glow with energy. By mastering this aspect of prana a yogi may cause an astral light to emanate from the body.

Paramahansaji once walked by the ocean near one of his ashrams. The night was cold. A young couple, who happened to be nearby, noticed a blue light emanating from Paramahansaji's body. It had manifested in response to the exercise of his will so that his body would be warmed. Some yogis who live at high mountain altitudes may practice pranayama and use visualization to generate bodily heat.

42. By perfect contemplation in Om, one experiences divine hearing.

By contemplating space while listening to inner sound the devotee learns to hear subtle sounds and Om. The mind becomes fascinated with the possibilities inherent in contemplating sound frequencies. Thus fascinated, attention is more easily withdrawn from sensory perceptions and thought streams. The way to enjoy steady inward turning when listening to internal sound is to listen for subtle sounds behind the sounds initially heard, continuing until soundlessness (transcendence or complete absorption) is experienced.

43. By perfect contemplation on the relationship between the body and space, and lightness, levitation can be experienced.

When upward flowing prana overcomes downward flowing prana, and when changes are made in the body's magnetic field in relationship with earth's magnetic field, the influence of gravity is somewhat neutralized. One's initial awareness is that thoughts are refined and superconscious states are more easily experienced. There may be a sense of levitation as one's astral body expands. In rare instances, actual levitation of the body may occur. This has been observed with yogis and mystics of various traditions. Rapt in ecstasy the meditator may not even be aware of the levitated condition. Or levitation may be accomplished by gentle intention to do so.

When you experience flying during occasions of lucid dreaming, this is what it feels like when the physical body levitates. More commonly, one acquires the ability to move through space through the spiritual eye, when upward flowing prana becomes pronounced.

While sitting quietly or practicing pranayamas, spontaneous energy movements may occur in the lower chakras, causing trembling of the body and thrusting movements of the lower limbs, resulting in peculiar hopping movements. Since this occurs without effort on the part of the meditator, brain-wave scans reveal the meditator to be experiencing calm superconsciousness while the body is reacting in this unusual way. Because this phenomenon can be easily produced, it is not an indication of advanced spiritual awareness.

The technique for using the sutras as themes for meditative contemplation is to first meditate to experience inner calm and tranquility, then contemplate the specific sutra to ponder and experience its meaning. In this way the results indicated in the sutras can unfold. Rather than to overly rejoice because you can perhaps demonstrate a few exceptional abilities, rejoice because you are surrendered in God.

44. By perfect contemplation on superconscious states, which are external to the gross modifications of the mental field, the coverings which conceal the true essence of Reality are banished.

When one becomes proficient in higher superconscious states, gross mental processes cease to influence soul awareness. Such superior realizations easily release from the mind the impressions which formerly limited consciousness. They are seen as mere material manifestations, and dissolve.

When we understand that higher laws govern lower laws, our universe no longer appears to us to be fixed or stable. The universe is formed of constantly flowing forces which can be manipulated by superior will and imagination. Merely to witness manifestations of soul abilities may not always result in a quickening of faith or strongly motivate the observer to unfold soul capacities. For some, seeing supernatural happenings strengthens their resolve. For others, it provides entertainment, or causes mental confusion.

If your innate soul abilities spontaneously express with useful results, allow them to do so without attracting attention to yourself. As you progress on the enlightenment path you will naturally experience manifestations of insight and grace and will not think them unusual.

45. By perfect contemplation on gross matter, its essential attributes and components, and their subtle parts and purposeful drives, one acquires mastery over matter and its energies and forces.

Scientists are advancing in their understanding of the inner side of nature and are learning to utilize heretofore hidden forces for the benefit of mankind. Matter is energy and behind energy are forces which regulate its manifestations. Behind these forces is consciousness. This is why a person who explores the fields of consciousness can, with practice, control the forces and energies which determine the manifestations of gross matter.

46. By mastery over the elements, one awakens siddhis (unfolded soul abilities and capacities), demonstrates perfection of body and mind, and realizes the indestructible qualities of energy and matter.

Some devotees, having no interest in cultivating soul powers, ignore them. If, as a result of their spiritual awareness unusual events occur in their presence, they will merely say that whatever happens is due to God's grace. Others become preoccupied with phenomena and slow their spiritual growth. A Self-realized person may demonstrate siddhis to accomplish purposes, minimizing their importance while emphasizing the importance of authentic spiritual growth. Soul abilities which can unfold are essentially those of perception, knowledge, and action.

1. *Smallness* – By perfect contemplation it is possible to assume a viewpoint comparable to the smallest unit of matter and to discern the inner aspects and workings of nature.

2. *Immensity* – The ability to expand awareness to include the universe, to extend awareness beyond the physical realm to apprehend the spheres of subtle and fine matter, Cosmic Mind, the field of primordial nature, and the realm of God.

3. *Heaviness* – The ability to so identify with the gravity force that the body is made heavy. A more useful result is to be "grounded" regardless of unsettled external circumstances. By identifying with any of the primal cosmic forces one can know their operations.

4. *Lightness* – The ability to experience transcendence, neutralize gravity and the influence of tamas guna, to move through inner spaces, and perhaps to levitate.

5. *Obtainment* – The ability to easily obtain whatever is desired, wherever and whatever it might be. By visualization, intention, or gentle inclination, one can attract whatever is needed or desired. If an object is not yet manifested, it will be created and made available. Supportive events and circumstances will unfold. For the spiritually advanced, objects and circumstances can be manifested instantaneously.

6. *Freedom in Space* – The ability to assume viewpoints in space—to be conscious at one place while simultaneously conscious and functional at another point in space.

7. *Dominion* – Control over the forces of nature, from influencing weather and plant life to transmuting energies from one form to another.

8. *Supreme Will* – Intentional right use of will to accomplish worthy purposes. Whatever is willed by a Self-realized person must occur.

If some enlightened souls on earth can do these things, why do they not put an end to poverty and use superior powers of will to manipulate the minds of people to create planetary harmony? They cannot, because they are limited in what they can do within the relative realm. They can help in many practical ways but they must still work with the trend of evolution and encourage individuals to unfold their own creative powers. To do otherwise would be to assume the role of God, a unwise action regardless of one's degree of spiritual awareness.

47. Perfection of the body consists of beauty, bright complexion, grace, strength, and adamantine hardness.

Adamantine ("hardness like a diamond") is the reference used to describe the physical condition of an illumined, Self-actualized person. An enlightened person does naturally whatever is most useful to maintain the physical constitution in a state of balance. The body is also nourished by soul forces. The mind is clear and psychological conflicts are absent.

With inner restrictions removed, with the constitution balanced, with pranas flowing in full force, the body of an illumined soul is maintained until its purpose has been served. There have been instances of bodily dematerialization at the time of a saint's departure from the world, but this is unnecessary. There have also been instances of bodies of saints remaining preserved for decades. This is a phenomenon which may inspire devotees but is unrelated for the soul's ultimate liberation.

48. One experiences mastery over the senses by perfect contemplation on their powers of cognition, inherent characteristics, pervasiveness, and influences.

To attempt to resist sensory impulses by will power alone may result in well-intentioned but crude endeavors to acquire self-mastery. It is better to study their inherent characteristics in order to understand how they function. Sensory impulses originate in the mind. Even the driving impulses of mental impressions are modified aspects of soul force. Memories are mental impressions with no life or intelligence of their own. The soul's outflowing tendency is the cause of sensory impulses. The origins of the organs of sense are the inner subtle organs of sense, formed of cosmic forces. These should by analyzed and understood. Study the information given in the discussion about the categories of cosmic manifestation in the first part of this book to understand the senses, their powers of cognition, inherent characteristics, pervasiveness, and influences. When you have understood these matters to your satisfaction, regularly review this text. Your knowledge will increase as your awareness clears and you apply what you learn.

49. As a result of mastering the senses, one has direct insight, can function independently of external sense organs, and has dominion over primordial causes.

The astral senses enable us to accomplish purposes unrestricted by gross forces. In this way we can regulate primordial causes which are responsible for outer effects. Whenever anything occurs in the physical world the manifestation has two aspects: the primary and the secondary. The primary aspect is subtle cause; the secondary aspect is the gross manifestation. It is by working at the level of primary cause that outer transformations are effected. A physical scientist does this by rearranging the components of matter to form different substances; this is chemistry, the child of alchemy. A spiritual scientist, a yogi or seer who understands the workings of fine forces which regulate the components of matter, influences fine forces by visualization, and perhaps by using mantra, to transform the energy of matter and produce desired substances and forms.

Everyone consciously or unconsciously modifies their environment by their thoughts and expectations. The mere presence of a person or creature has an effect upon the immediate environment. Without the presence of an observer, occurrences in nature continue in accord with influential cosmic forces. With the added presence of an observer, the actions of cosmic forces are somewhat modified because of the introduction into their processes of the cosmic forces present in the mind and body of the observer. This is why quantum physics is such an interesting field. The results of experiments may vary according to who or what is present, and in response to the expectations or mental attitude of the observer. In every relationship, with a person or with aspects of nature, we bring ourselves into the process of forces which are in operation. We influence our environment and our environment may influence us. All levels of creation interact when in proximity. Even when we are not actually in physical rapport with circumstances, our thoughts and states of consciousness can be influential to some degree because we are in relationship to the universal collective consciousness.

50. By perfect contemplation on the process of intellectual determination of what is observed and on the reality of Supreme Consciousness, one experiences omnipotence and omniscience.

The result of such contemplation is known as the state of consciousness is devoid of all sorrow. By understanding that the soul is individualized pure consciousness, the devotee experiences the omnipotence and omniscience of God.

During calm, deliberative contemplation of Absolute Reality, the soul acquires insight into it by using intelligence and intuition. By this, one can persist in contemplation to remove awareness from the error of independent selfhood. The final action is to remove awareness from even the process of determination in order to experience release, omnipotence, and omniscience.

51. By renouncing these powers [of omnipotence and omnipresence], one removes the causes of bondage and completely transcends the relative planes.

So long as we are conscious of experiencing omnipotence and omniscience, some sense of independent selfhood remains. By renouncing the awe and enjoyment of omnipotence and omniscience, the "seed of bondage"—egoism because of delusion—is removed. The devotee intent upon liberation of consciousness is advised to avoid attachments to any perception or experience; to observe and release them in order to experience higher states. When nothing remains except awareness of being, consciousness may again become somewhat involved with material manifestation without being deluded. With the dissolution of the illusion of independent selfhood, the soul, having transcended all possibilities of blind involvement with nature, is ever free.

52. There must not be any pride in the use of these abilities, or any attachment to them, as this can be the cause of reverting to lower or clouded states of awareness.

Most souls which depart from clear levels of realization, do so because of carelessness. By not remaining centered and focused, they become complacent or distracted. Many people drift through sequences of circumstances without any sense of direction or purpose. Even well-intentioned souls can become distracted from their spiritual goal because of pride or attachment. One may think, "Oh, it is wonderful that I can know these things and do marvelous works!" A partially awakened soul may have a degree of higher understanding, yet be influenced by the cosmic forces. If tamas and rajas predominate, the spiritually advanced soul may become a minor worker of wonders, a magician. If ego is pronounced and a drive for personal power is present, one may use soul powers for selfish or destructive purposes.

Preoccupation with preliminary and advanced processes used to facilitate Self-realization can also be self-defeating. One may become proud of yogic proficiency—skill in the performance of asanas, mudras, and pranayamas, and in the ability to adjust states of consciousness and regulate body functions. Procedures and techniques are helpful aids on the path; the final way to enlightenment is surrender, service, and reliance on God's grace.

53. By perfect contemplation on the moments of time and their sequential changes, one experiences true knowledge by the power of discernment.

The minimal unit of time is a moment, the duration required for the finest unit of matter to move from one point in space to another point in space. Movements of atoms were once the indicators of time, but now we know there are finer units. A continuous flow of moments is a sequence. Our awareness of sequential moment-events form our mental conception of time. Our sense of time is for our convenience in observing successions of moments. We compare the moment with memories of past moments and speculate about future moments in order to have a sense of time. There cannot be two simultaneous moments although there can be different observations of the moment. There is no actual blending of past, present, and future—there are only successions of moments. To attempt to identify something with thoughts or words is called "an indistinct notion of reality." We can only describe "what was" and not "what is."

The usual trend of personal growth is the result of successive changes and transformations. Could we but be removed from the sequence of successive moments we would experience timelessness. Our perception of time relates to the relative spheres in which movement occurs. During superconsciousness, when thought processes are dormant and mental processes are transcended, we are not aware of time because we have no awareness of successions of moments. This is why advanced meditators can experience superconsciousness for extended durations of relative time and not be bored. They are outside of time.

Because the soul only relates to matter and is not a material substance, the possibility of instantaneous enlightenment exists in the moment. This possibility is not acceptable to the average devotee because it can neither be understood or believed. Such a one thinks he has to "work out" his salvation by overcoming problems and struggling to remove himself from the tenacious grasp of restricting influences.

54. By perfect contemplation of moments and successions of moments, one obtains discernment of similar circumstances and events which cannot be recognized or measured by any outer signs.

Only intuitive perception can reveal subtle successions of moments of time and enable us to awaken to a realization of Great Time—the field in which relative space-time occurs. A siddha can know about past events, present occurrences, and of future unfoldments of events and circumstances based on knowledge of present causes. Future events are subject to modification as new causes are implemented. Outer indications of the times are not always reliable because their subjective causes may not be known without access to their realm.

55. Absolute knowledge includes comprehension of the entire universe, from the unmanifest field of pure consciousness to the material realms.

God knows everything. As rays of God's consciousness, all knowledge of God and of universal processes is innate to us. In *The Light of Asia*, Sir Edwin Arnold's story of Prince Siddartha who became known as the Buddha, "the Enlightened One," the poet's imagined view of the Buddha's experiences is described:

> And in the middle watch
> Our Lord attained *Abhidjna* (supernatural powers)—
>   insight vast
> Ranging beyond this sphere to spheres unnamed,
> System on system, countless worlds and suns
> Moving in splendid measures, band by band
> Linked in division, one, yet separate,
> The silver islands of a sapphire sea
> Shoreless, unfathomed, undiminished, stirred
> With waves which roll in restless tides of change.
> He saw those Lords of Light who hood their worlds
> By bonds invisible, how they themselves
> Circle obedient round mightier orbs
> Which serve profounder splendours, star to star
> Flashing the ceaseless radiance of life
> From centres ever shifting unto cirques
> Knowing no uttermost. These he beheld
> With unsealed vision, and of all those worlds,
> Cycle on epicycle, all their tale
> Of Kalpas, Mahakalpas—terms of time
> Which no man grasps...

Absolute knowledge includes knowledge of manifest realms and That from which they proceed. This is why a fully illumined soul is able to point the way to higher knowledge for sincere devotees. Having had the good fortune to be exposed to a teaching which reveals the way to us, we should honor it. Pure minded devotees do this willingly. Self-centered people tend to argue.

Dull-minded people either misperceive or ignore what is obvious to devotees of clear vision.

56. Liberation of consciousness is realized when the intellect is as pure and devoid of characteristics as is the soul.

The soul is pure. When the faculty of intelligence is similarly devoid of gross characteristics, it can be used to express knowledge. This is the state of soul liberation. So long as the soul is relating to relative spheres it requires a mental field through which to perceive and to determine what is perceived. Kriya Yoga processes are for the purpose of purifying the mental field, including the faculty of intelligence, so that soul freedom can be directly experienced and flawlessly expressed.

CHAPTER FOUR

Enlightenment and Liberation

1. **One can be born with awakened soul abilities, or they can be unfolded by the use of natural substances, the power of mantra, self-discipline, and practice of samadhi.**

One can be born with unusual abilities because of previous attainments. One can benefit from inherited characteristics—the general psychophysiological constitution provided by one's parents. Developmental forces which contribute to physiological and psychological growth can be determining influences. Supportive environmental circumstances can be helpful. Constructive prenatal influences can overcome challenging psychological, physical, and environmental influences to a considerable degree, as has been demonstrated by many people who have unfolded their capacities and accomplished much in spite of less than desirable beginnings. For a resolved devotee, memories of unfortunate early beginnings are no barrier to success. Even with natural endowments of physical health and mental acuity along with a supportive environment, many people ruin their lives because of their self-defeating attitudes and behaviors.

Mantra contributes to the unfoldment of superior degrees of self-mastery and refined levels of superconsciousness. With awakened awareness, capacities corresponding to levels of awareness spontaneously unfold. How we function is an indication of our habitual states of consciousness. How we live reveals the extent of our degree of authentic spiritual unfoldment.

The use of natural substances refers to foods and herbs used for nutritional and medicinal purposes, for strengthening and

enlivening the body's systems. Seers of many cultures researched
the uses and effects of natural substances for the purpose of cleansing the body and contributing to its vitality and long life. The
process used by yogis is Ayurveda, or "Life-Knowledge." Ayurvedic
texts comprise an almost encyclopedic range of knowledge from
Vedic traditions and other sources. Many Asian seers have been
known to make their abode in an area where the climate is good
and nutritious foods and beneficial herbs are abundant. Some
sages use a life-extension procedure known as *kaya-kalpa* which
enables the body to persist through time in order to complete
their spiritual practices and fulfill their divinely inspired purposes on the planet.

Disciplined regulation of sensory impulses and behaviors is
basic to the path of discipleship. Unwanted influences are banished and higher states of consciousness are encouraged to
unfold. From this, superconsciousness (samadhi) makes possible
all attainments and full realization.

2. **The transformation of senses, mind, and body is the result
of the natural flow of creative forces.**

Creative forces resulting in transformation of the senses, mind,
and body are of two kinds: our own awakened vital forces and the
creative influences of superconsciousness.

3. **The natural flow of creative forces occurs when obstacles to
their flow are removed.**

Material causes cannot cause spiritual effects, but material
actions can *allow* spiritual effects. For instance, good behavior
does not cause enlightenment, but good behavior can allow the
unfoldment of consciousness just as misbehavior can restrict spiritual growth.

A farmer or a gardener does not have to coax water to flow.
When obstacles to its flow are removed, it will stream forth naturally. Our intentional spiritual practices remove obstacles to the
flow of creative forces which naturally become expressive when
allowed to do so.

Constructive karma allows a constructive flow of soul force;

destructive karma impedes the natural flow. This is why we cultivate constructive qualities and minimize destructive ones. Virtue, as another instance, is not in itself purity, but allows purity to manifest.

By living a righteous life in harmony with nature's rhythms, creative forces inherent in nature then flow to result in constructive changes in body and mind. The body is maintained in a healthy condition and the mental field is strengthened and ordered. The nerves are refined and the brain transformed. The fine channels through which prana moves remain open and prana flows are balanced.

When dormant forces in the lower chakras are awakened, they move dynamically to bring about rapid transformation. They awaken because of our devotion to God, meditation and the practice of certain useful exercises, spontaneous actions of grace, and the guru's beneficial help. Kundalini becomes loosened and streams of force from it flow upward through the sushumna. Partial awakening results in powerful currents of life force being released to circulate through the body. Dynamic awakening results in accelerated transformation, surrendered meditation, and spontaneous unfoldments of superconscious states.

Shakti is the Sanskrit word for kundalini's manifesting creative forces in the body. *Shaktipat* is the "transmission" of shakti from guru to disciple, as well as its spontaneous awakening because of grace.

4. Individual minds are created by the power of Cosmic Mind.

The mind of every person and every creature is created from cosmic forces through the agency of Cosmic Mind. Cosmic creative force flowing through Cosmic Mind and influenced by the gunas results in mind-manifestation. Just as Cosmic Mind is a manifestation of the sense of Cosmic individuality, so individual minds are manifestations of the sense of soul individuality. Minds are also subject to transformation. When we acquire new understanding our mental field is transformed, otherwise, acquired knowledge would not be retained as memory.

5. The original mind is the director of all other expressions and modifications of conditioned mind.

The original mental field is the repository of all mental expressions and changes. From the moment we become involved with the realm of matter, through perhaps a long series of successive incarnations, we use the same mental field even though it undergoes a variety of changes. The mental field you had a million years ago, if you have been around that long, is the same one you have today. We hear people say, "My mind is not as good as it was," or, "My mind is better now than it has ever been." The soul is really the producer and director of the mental field; the mind itself is an assistant director.

A yogi can create other minds through which to work but they, too, are directed by his original mind. In instances of bilocation, when a yogi becomes aware several miles from where his body resides and at that distant place produces a body through which to function, the mind directing the body's activities is the original mind of the yogi. In this way it is possible for a yogi to simultaneously appear at several different places. But as his various viewpoints are his own, so various mind manifestations are related to his original mind.

From a higher level of observation, all seeming individualized minds are but expressions of the one Mind of God. Just as there is one Supreme Consciousness and many particularized expressions of it, so there is one Mind and many individualized expressions of it.

6. Of all classifications of mind, that which results from superconsciousness leaves no impressions of karma.

Superconscious experiences initially leave constructive impressions in the mental field but these do not cause harmful effects. They are not binding. They contribute to the ordering of thought processes and to transformation of the personality.

The use of soul abilities for constructive purposes does not result in an accumulation of binding mental impressions. Wrong use of soul abilities results in karmic impressions because of self-centeredness. Selfless service, performing work with righteous intent while surrendered in God, does not result in karmic impressions being stored in the mind. If good works are not selfless, then constructive karma results. The ideal is to rid the mind of karmic impressions in order to function freely according to need and inner guidance. In this way one can be creatively influential in the world while inwardly remaining a renunciate. The *Bhagavad Gita* 3:16-19:

> That one who does not, in this world, help to turn the wheel which has been set in motion (from the beginning) is dark in nature, sensual in enjoyments, and lives in vain. But the person whose enjoyment is in soul consciousness alone, who is in this wise content and satisfied, for that one there exists no work that needs to be done. Similarly, in this world the devotee has nothing whatever to gain by the actions performed and none to gain by the actions not yet performed. Therefore, without attachment, perform always the work that is before you, for one attains to the highest good by doing work without attachment.

Only an exceptional devotee can remain in seclusion, giving full attention to study and contemplation. Most people have desires and urges which can only be successfully transformed in the outer field of action. Our daily involvements provide an opportunity for the expression of desires and urges as well as opportunity to cultivate patience, love, even-mindedness, and surrender. Secluded without external relationships of any kind, the average person would remain in psychological conflict, unable to effectively concentrate because of unregulated drives from the unconscious.

7. **Actions of Self-realized souls are neither impelled by light (sattvic) nor dark (tamasic) influences. Actions of others are of three kinds.**

According to our modes of behavior and the drives of karmic impressions, so are our actions. Fully illumined souls function spontaneously, under grace. They are neither driven by karma nor willfully self-determined.

The actions of other people are of three kinds. A person who is deluded behaves destructively, harming himself and sometimes causing harm to others. A person who is somewhat conscious and whose drives are constructive, is impelled to constructive actions. He does good but acts under compulsion. A person who is no longer driven by unconscious conditionings, who is superconscious, is impelled by higher influences to be entirely constructive and selfless. His actions do not result in further karmic conditionings.

Constructive behavior neutralizes destructive drives; selfless behavior removes compulsive constructive drives; illumination removes one from the influences of all drives and causes, even from the influences of sattva guna.

8. **The forces and tendencies of mental impressions are manifested when prevailing circumstances are most suitable for their unfoldment.**

The deeper level of mind is like a vast reservoir containing myriad impressions, with forces and tendencies which await an opportunity to be actualized. They are more likely to manifest when environmental conditions are compatible for their expression. In an orderly environment it is more likely that constructive forces will surface. Similarly, a disordered environment will often stimulate baser urges and drives.

A person may appear to be almost saintly in an environment in which there is little or no temptation or challenge. However, given the opportunity, destructive drives may easily become pronounced. A saint can be soul-centered in all circumstances but a person whose mind is not yet purified should choose environmental circumstances and relationships with care.

General good health, happiness, and prosperity may be experienced by almost anyone when supportive circumstances prevail. When stressed or tired, or when good habits are neglected, one may experience sickness. Happiness may be replaced by unhappiness if expectations are not met. Economic hardship may be experienced if prosperity attitudes and behaviors are not maintained. If the seed-causes of possible effects remain in the mind, they may find expression in future-time unless they are resisted or neutralized. In this way people experience misfortune and good fortune in unexpected ways and at unexpected moments.

Karma can sometimes be worked out (and its force exhausted)

in dreams. It is also possible, by using advanced visualization processes, to work out the drives of karma during superconscious meditation. More usually, karma is effectively handled by processing thoughts and desires as they become apparent; by acknowledging them and choosing how to react to them. We can make wise choices, knowing that we are in command of the drives and forces in the mind because we are superior to it and its contents. Weak-willed people claim inability to resist their impulses or to curb the driving force of desire. They need to learn to resist, regulate, and transmute these forces into higher, more constructive channels of expression. This is where intentional behavior modification comes into play. By establishing guidelines and routines, and abiding by them, we consciously behave in constructive ways and destructive drives and tendencies, having no opportunity to manifest, must be transformed and eliminated. We actually assimilate the power of destructive drives when we master them. With every success we become stronger and more self-reliant. Success at minor stages of challenge provides us with knowledge and abilities to perform more effectively in the future.

9. **Because conscious thoughts and memory are similar, subconscious impressions of feelings arise simultaneously with memory even though they may be separated by birth, space, and time.**

Our thoughts are almost always attended by memories of past similar thoughts and by feelings associated with them. Thinking about something, or experiencing a certain circumstance, awakens memories and feelings of similar subjects and circumstances experienced before. Thus there is an uninterrupted sequence of flow of activities almost always occurring in the mind. Feelings associated with memory can arise simultaneously even though memory of a very recent experience, a few moments or a few days ago, is separated from the original cause of feeling by one or more incarnations, as well as place and time. Feelings impressed in the subconscious as a result of experiences which occurred in another part of the country or the world, can be as strong today as they were when originally experienced. We have memories which give rise to pleasurable feelings, which we may cherish, and we have memories which elicit unpleasant feelings, which we may wish to forget.

We often learn from experiences, attempting to duplicate actions which are pleasure-producing and to avoid actions which produce pain. If our lives are unsatisfactory we may tend to dwell upon memories of past pleasurable experiences or hope for similar future experiences. When depressed and dysfunctional, if things are not going well, we may become caught up in memories and feelings of discontent, frustration, failure, and pain to the extent that we feel hopeless and become even more depressed and incapable of self-responsible behavior. We cannot then cope with even small challenges because memories and feelings have overcome our ability to be rational.

Regardless of when memories were impressed in the mind, they are presently available to be recalled with total clarity. Their influence is not always recorded exclusively in the mental field; influences may also have impressed parts of the brain and body cells. Controlled electrical stimulation of different areas of the brain can cause us to "relive" past episodes with the full impact of earlier incidents.

Because feelings are usually associated with memories, mental impressions have inherent force to influence our consciousness and behavior. It is easy to say, "What is past is past, so forget it," but this is not always easily done. What is past is indeed no longer present, but memories are, often with a determining force which is as influential as the occasion which originated them.

Any self-observant person acknowledges the influence of memories acquired in the present incarnation but not everyone knows that prenatal memories of past life cycles, and of life in the womb before birth, may also be influential.

When aware of the processes of memory and feeling, what can we do to relate to them without being unwittingly controlled by them? The first step is to be self-directed, to live with purpose in present-time, supported in our efforts by worthwhile routines. Master environmental circumstances by regulating senses, thoughts, feelings, and actions to bring creative forces into focus. Spiritual practices and regular meditation are especially helpful. Consciously endeavor to unfold soul capacities and become more cosmic conscious, no longer fully identified with the mental field and its memories and stored feelings. From this elevated state of consciousness, be more objective when viewing the contents of the mind—experiencing the moment while clearly understanding that memories are of the past and possibilities are of the future. Only now is real, to be experienced however we choose to experience it.

We can choose to "replay" memories on the screen of the mind, with their associated feelings, and be dominated by them, or we can choose to recall them for useful purposes while remaining calm and objective. Useful purposes for recalling memories are: 1) to clear them by understanding them and their influences; 2) to use them to our advantage by duplicating or approximating past successful actions while avoiding actions which cannot result in desired outcomes.

Many people invest years in self-analysis for the purpose of trying to understand mental processes, hoping that when they finally understand them, and themselves, life will be better. Sometimes it does work out that way. More often, years are wasted roaming through the corridors of the mind—time which could have been better utilized in creative, productive behavior. With heightened awareness we can now be what we want to be and more effectively handle memories and feelings as they occasionally surface. We do not have to completely reorganize the contents of the mind before embarking upon an actualized life or beginning our spiritual practices. To live a balanced, purposeful life is the more effective way of organizing mental processes.

10. Because of the urge to life and expression which is innate to consciousness, there is no beginning to the flow of causes and their respective consequences.

Having an innate awareness of its immortality even when involved with mind and senses, the soul naturally desires to live forever. Hence, the thought of death is repulsive to the soul— although at times welcomed by the mind when mental conflicts and emotional distress become oppressive.

The soul unfettered by mental conflicts is naturally curious, happy, innovative, and possessed of a drive toward fulfillment. The mind of the average person, though in reality all-pervasive, expands and contracts according to the influences of the modifications presently influential. We feel expansive when mentally clear and confined when mentally confused.

Body and mind are of material substance; the soul is pure consciousness. Soul awareness does not evolve from matter. Soul awareness enlivens matter and expresses through material forms.

Involved in relative spheres, the soul's innate drive to express results in a chain of causes and their effects, but the original urge to awaken to Self-knowledge is without beginning, being inherent in consciousness. That which drives all of the life processes in nature is the urge of matter-involved consciousness to express.

We hear people say, "Life is meant to be lived, go for it!" At the root of possible problems inherent in this view of life is the tendency to focus attention entirely outward, neglecting one's inner life and ignoring the need for a more cosmic understanding. We then see examples of creatively functional men and women who demonstrate remarkable success in causing desirable effects while dedicated to a life of what has been called "spiritual materialism." There may be a degree of understanding of the laws of causation, used mainly for the purpose of improving the human condition, with little or no thought of actually knowing God and one's relationship with God. A religious philosophy which helps a person live a more functional life, but does not include an explanation of the true nature of God and the processes of cosmic manifestation and soul liberation, is incomplete. It serves human needs but does not satisfy the soul. What is needed is a philosophical understanding that will satisfy both immediate human needs and eternal soul needs. Human needs, when satisfied, provide security and supportive relationships. Soul needs, when satisfied, provide knowledge of God.

11. **All tendencies and karmic patterns are maintained by their causes and effects, the mind itself, and the support of objects of perception. When these are no longer present, tendencies and karmic patterns no longer exist for the soul.**

The initial tendency, present when the soul became involved with matter, is the will to live. From it all other tendencies and karmic patterns unfold, are impressed in the mind, maintained by the flow of causation, and supported by objects of perception.

Delusion, unknowingness, is the cause of all further tendencies and karmic patterns. Lacking knowledge, the soul performs unwisely, accumulating karmic impressions due to desire and reaction to circumstances. The driving tendencies and karmic patterns persist in the mind because of being involved in the continuing chain of causation, supported by circumstances perceived through the sense faculties.

Nothing that comes into manifestation can exist without having had a prior cause because modified tendencies in the mind are the result of the initial pure urge to live. Objective effects of causes are but gross reflections of their corresponding mental images. Outer effects existed as mental images prior to their actualization or embodiment. The universe existed as primal substance prior to objective manifestation, and primal substance existed prior to manifestation—as consciousness. Supreme Consciousness is Self-existent. It did not come into being; its reality supports the manifest realms.

When the drives of causes, the effects of causes, the mind itself, and supporting objects of perception are no longer cognized by the superconscious soul, influential tendencies and karmic patterns no longer exist for the soul. Being transcended they are not present to be perceived or experienced. This is why, when we meditate, we are lifted above involvements of the mind and karma does not influence higher superconscious states. Karma, mental impressions, influence lower superconscious states because the meditator has not yet removed his awareness from them. As a result of experiencing higher superconsciousness at will we can, when attending to daily duties, be detached from mental processes and emotional states and view them with understanding.

12. Past and future essentially exist due to the exchanges of cosmic forces.

Existing tendencies and mental impressions become transformed and are eventually resolved into their original condition of pure consciousness. As forces, they no longer manifest outwardly but remain as unmanifest potential force.

The past exists in the mind as memory. The possible future exists in the mind as impressions with potential to unfold. So long as cosmic forces, gunas, are involved with mental tendencies and karmic patterns, they persist while they undergo change, becoming more influential or becoming weakened.

As memory has prior perception as a supporting object, so future possibilities have present mental states as supporting objects. Our future unfolds from our states of consciousness and our mental states. Without memory and potential for future experience we would remain in our present condition. Memories of success-cycles—such as accomplishment of a purpose or positive results of meditation— can inspire and motivate us. The hope of future success can impel us to constructive action.

We are seldom aware of the entire contents of the mind and we do not always see ourselves in correct relationship to past and future. We may know our past better than we know our future because memories are more real to us than subtle causes of future circumstances. From a higher perspective we can learn to scan the contents of the mind and clearly see the stream of causation as well as possible futures. By doing this, instead of moving blindly through life taking each day as it comes and hoping for the best, we are able to plan more intelligently, go along with constructive circumstances and changes, or modify those which are not constructive.

13. The tendencies and karmic patterns, whether manifested or remaining in subtle form, are comprised of the three attributes or qualities of the cosmic forces.

Mental impressions exist because of the influences of the gunas. When these cosmic forces are in a state of equilibrium they are unmanifested: dormant and noninfluential. When they are unbalanced, subtle and gross states manifest.

The real character of these forces is never known by the senses because they are the causes of the senses and everything else in manifestation. Effects cannot know their causes because effects, being secondary manifestations, are results of influences. The primary manifestations of causes are cosmic forces.

Because conditioned tendencies and karmic patterns are the

effects of cosmic forces, they have no independent reality. They are subject to mutation, change, and transformation. This is why karmic patterns can be resisted, restrained, and their character changed by resolving them into their origins. Their forces remain, merged with cosmic forces. A person whose understanding is limited may think of karmic patterns as causative conditions which have to be worked out, allowed to express, or passed on to someone else. What becomes of our storehouse of karma when we withdraw from it? Do the various ingredients scatter to the psychic winds and float about waiting to be attracted to someone else? Of course not. They are resolved from gross to subtle states, then into nonmanifestation. In this way they are removed from relative involvements and restored to the field of cosmic forces.

14. Because of unified mutation of the cosmic forces (gunas) there is unity of things (objects).

Objects are as they are because of the present mutation of cosmic forces supporting their manifestation. When the supporting cosmic forces are rearranged, the appearance of the object changes. The bodies of humans, animals, plants, all forms in nature, are as they are because of the interplay of cosmic forces which maintain them. There is unity of manifestation because of coordinated mutation of these cosmic forces.

One aspect of force is not present without the others. Two aspects always support the predominate one. When they are in equilibrium there is nonmanifestation and they rest in their potential states.

Because we do not ordinarily apprehend transformations occurring at subtle levels, we perceive only the external result of transformations. We see an object, not its constituent parts, the cosmic forces.

From the field of primal nature through to its diverse expressions, there is but one thing manifesting. This is because everything in manifestation is made possible by the initial urge to express and the interplay of the three cosmic forces, which, in turn, are aspects of the single force with origins in the field of pure consciousness.

15. An object will be variously perceived according to the nature of the mind in relationship to the object.

Objects exist as manifestations of cosmic forces and are perceived differently according to the mental state of the observer. While we may agree on the common sameness of that which we observe, my perception of what I see will differ somewhat from what others perceive. According to our mental conditionings and our preconceptions, so do we perceive the world about us. We may view an object (a thing or circumstance) objectively or we may see its potentiality for pleasure or pain in relationship to us. We may judge what we see as good or bad, beautiful or not beautiful, according to how our minds are conditioned.

16. An object cannot be said to be dependent upon the perception of one mind, for what would happen to it in the absence of that mind?

We did not create the worlds. They exist independent of us. Some philosophers like to play mental games, suggesting that the universe does not exist if they are not observing it. It does not exist for them if they do not observe it, but it exists by itself as a play of cosmic forces. If what we observed only existed as the result of our observation, interior aspects of objects and those outside the range of our vision would not exist.

Undiscerning people may assert that the universe is but an illusion and does not exist. Yet, while saying this they use a "nonexistent" mind and body to convey their opinions about a "nonexistent" universe. They may say that, since they are, at the soul level, perfect, they do not need spiritual practices because they are already enlightened, but their enlightened state is not obvious by the way they live. They are only talking about knowledge; true knowledge is lacking.

17. Objects are known or unknown to a person according to how they influence the mind.

When our attention is attracted to an object, light and other characteristics emanating from the object are received through our sense organs and transmitted to the mind. What we then know about the object depends upon how our minds are influenced by it. Such influences can modify our mental processes. We may admire an object, or desire to possess it or use it in some way. Because of our own mental associations or our memories of similar objects, its presence may upset or repulse us. Even an object not perceived through ordinary sense channels may influence us by its radiant energy. The qualities of energy streaming from an object may influence both mind and body. Pollutants in the atmosphere, though unseen and unknown to the mind, can influence body chemistry and mental processes. Constructive emanational influences can also benefit us without our conscious awareness of their presence.

Memories and thoughts are objects in relationship to the mind and have power to influence. States of consciousness are objects in relationship to the mind and exercise influence. Whether these are known or unknown depends upon the soul's ability to perceive through the mind.

18. Due to the changeless nature of the soul, all mental modifications are always known to it.

The soul nature is never modified by what is presented to it. Apparent modifications of soul awareness are due to its identification with the mind which is subject to modification. The soul is referred to as the seer: the observer, the witness. It observes mental processes and always knows about them, just as God is always aware of phenomenal processes and knows about them.

When reminded of a circumstance or a fact we say, "Oh, I knew that," affirming prior knowledge, or, "I know that," affirming present knowledge. The soul undergoes no mutation, no transformations. If it did, it would not be changeless. It would instead be of material substance, subject to modification according to influences from external sources.

19. Since the mind is an object which is perceived by the soul, it cannot be self-luminous and self-conscious.

The soul is not mind. It observes and uses mind for its purposes. The mind is only given light and life because of the presence of soul consciousness. Unenlightened people err in assuming the mind to be their real nature and that the mind has power of its own. Thus, some metaphysicians assert, "God is Cosmic Mind and I am individualized God-mind." God is more than Cosmic Mind—God's Mind is a creative medium through which God expresses. In spite of lack of complete knowledge many people who believe themselves to be a mind in relationship to God as Mind, are able to function somewhat effectively because of using mental laws of causation. Their achievements, however, are not proof of their understanding of God; only evidence of their degree of understanding of mental creative processes. Devotees at this level often admit that they persist in their metaphysical practices because such practices are beneficial to them, enabling them to gratify their desires and somewhat control their lives.

20. Complete, simultaneous identification of the mind with God and external objects is impossible.

The qualifying words here are *complete* and *mind*. Only the soul can completely experience simultaneous perception of God and external objects. The mind is the transmitting medium through which information is processed. The mind, not being self-conscious, cannot know anything but can identify with things. When completely identified with the senses and their objects it cannot at the same time be completely identified with Higher Reality. When completely identified with Higher Reality it cannot be similarly identified with externals. There may be partial, simultaneous identification with Higher Reality and objective phenomena, but not complete identification.

Because the mind can only completely identify with its primary object of contemplation, during meditation we turn away from outer sources of attraction to provide an opportunity for the mind to be exposed to superconscious influences. Some people say they do not meditate by turning within because they can meditate while quietly involved in sensory relationships. They are not really meditating—as meditation is taught in this text— they are observing or being open to insight, and perhaps experiencing a degree of harmony or unity with life processes. This can be a beneficial practice when we are not engaged in internalized meditative contemplation. To offer the mind a useful environment in which to identify with divine qualities which are transcendent, meditation practice as described in this text should be regularly scheduled.

When the mind has been purified and the brain and nervous system refined, soul consciousness can express in relationship to externals while being fully aware of the reality of God.

21. If all minds could be aware of the contents of all other minds, confusion of memories would result.

I do not know your memories and you do not know mine. If individualized minds fully identified with all other minds, with their modifications and memories, all minds would be confused.

While we can have access to Cosmic Mind for creative purposes, for routine purposes we function through an individualized mind. A mind can be illumined but is not itself the source or cause of illumination. When a guru attunes his or her consciousness to the disciple's to share illumination, it is the guru's consciousness which imparts illumination, not the guru's mind.

22. The Supreme Soul (God) is omnipresent, omniscient, omnipotent, and eternal, but due to Its reflections becoming involved with the material organ of intelligence, It identifies with them.

Reflected light of God shining on the field of primordial nature becomes involved with nature. Individualization occurs when the reflected light identifies with the organ of determination (intelligence).

The meaning of this sutra should be contemplated because insight into it will result in Self-knowledge. We may, when meditating, succeed in calming mental waves and experience a degree of peace without understanding, or we may use our powers of discernment while still under the spell of being individualized. However, by correctly understanding and experiencing that we are a ray of conscious light and not the mind or its faculty of determination, we can experience release from the operations of the mind. Released from the mind's operations the soul can then explore higher superconscious states and experience true spiritual freedom.

23. The mind influenced by the seer (soul) and the seen (objective sense-perceived circumstances) is all-apprehending.

The mind is influenced by impressions conveyed by the senses and by soul awareness and its knowledge. It can thus apprehend or mentally grasp such impressions but does not comprehend or understand them. The mind processes information; the soul is alone capable of comprehending.

24. The mind, with its varied and innumerable forces, exists to serve the soul.

Every aspect of nature serves the needs of consciousness. For the mind to well serve the soul, its impulses have to be regulated and its processes ordered so that consciousness can express through it with minimum interference.

The mind has two main purposes: 1) it serves as the medium of communication through which the soul perceives and relates to the material realms; 2) it serves as a vehicle through which the aspiring soul can realize release from involvement with matter. In the latter instance, if the soul were identified with a material body but did not have a mind through which to express, it would tend to remain unconsciously identified with that body until the body died. It is with the mind's subtle organs of perception, including that of intelligence or determination, that the soul can analyze its relationship to matter and explore higher levels of consciousness. Thus, while embodied, the soul can pursue higher knowledge and relate to the world in useful ways. After leaving the physical body, while functioning in an astral sphere, the mind continues to serve the soul's aspirations.

25. When, by discrimination, the soul experiences complete separation from body, senses, and mind, it is free.

The *Mundaka Upanishad*:

For that one who has seen the Supreme Reality and the manifested aspects of this Reality and is engrossed in this knowledge, the heart-strings of attachment and bondage are severed, doubts are removed, and effects of prior actions are eliminated.

The matter of personal identity is very subtle. So long as we think of ourselves as independent entities, we search to satisfy our needs and wants. Thinking "I am somebody," we want what we want when we want it, and we usually want everything on our own terms. When trends go our way we are happy; when they do not, we are unhappy. We identify with our sense urges and our addictions and have one problem after another. Conditioned life is like this. The only end to it is Self-realization and surrender in God.

26. **Having overcome identification with the body, senses, and mind, consciousness becomes serene and calm and awareness flows in the direction of absolute freedom.**

Here is described the inner condition of one capable of consciously experiencing liberation of consciousness. The major obstacles to success on the spiritual path are attachments of various kinds which support addictive attitudes and behaviors, emotional upsets which disturb the mind, and the varied forces flowing through the mind causing transformations and fluctuations. It is difficult to regulate these processes and transformations through will power alone. The easier way is by behavior modification and training of the senses, reinforced by regular practice of superconscious meditation. When internal forces are directed away from the senses and to the higher brain centers, some relief is experienced and the devotee is provided freedom to acquire conscious control. By doing everything possible to contribute to wellness and internal balance, and by meditation and discernment, one's consciousness finally becomes serene and calm.

In the process of Godward-flowing one must be alert and use powers of discernment until transcendence is experienced. Along the way there may be a variety of phenomenal perceptions which are usually projections of one's own mental states. Therefore, the meditator must be willing to avoid fantasy and to confirm the validity of perceptions if any doubt about them remains. During final stages, when dormant mental impressions become activated, one may see beautiful visions of celestial spheres, or visions of threatening circumstances. Both are mental productions and can be renounced. One may also be tempted to settle into a comfortable mood instead of awakening to transcendence.

27. Even when inclined in the direction of absolute freedom, interruptions of contemplation may result during intervals when the mind experiences an invasion of thoughts because of old habits, tendencies, and impressions which retain some influential force.

When the devotee is completely surrendered in God, and is patient, persistent, and committed to final freedom, interruptions of divine contemplation will be few and those which do occur will not overly challenge the soul. All manifestations of disturbance are due to inability to keep attention focused and the occasional influences of habits, tendencies, and karmic impressions which retain some driving force.

These disturbances do not always manifest during meditation—they may manifest at other times when we are not centered and aware. We may enjoy profound meditation states during inward contemplation, and later discover when involved in routine matters of the day that habits still dictate behavior and unwanted thoughts surface in the mind. We may notice that restlessness and inertia cause conflict, or desires which have nothing to do with our intended lifestyle make themselves known. We may confront circumstances which require discernment to understand, or avoid. We may be unclear about our understanding of who we are, what our relationship to God is, or about our present status of spiritual growth. Memories of past mistakes, past hurts, or past occasions of grief may surface along with the full force of emotion which first caused us sorrow, guilt, or a sense of unworthiness. We may doubt the validity of our spiritual path. We may experience fear of the unknown. We may become aware of the necessity of letting go of restrictive attitudes and behaviors and may not want—or know how—to do so.

These symptoms are evidence that transformation is occurring; that the last remaining restricting influences are being brought to light, to be recognized and released. It is not always easy to release them because they have been with us for so long. They are almost like friends—not always welcome friends, but companions to the mind just the same.

In the first chapter of the *Bhagavad Gita*, Arjuna is portrayed as having to confront conditions like these. He was advised by his guru, Krishna, to arm himself with fortitude, wisdom, devotion, and righteous action, and to slay his enemies—the destructive inner drives and habits. He wanted to, because he knew he must, yet at the same time he did not want to vanquish those parts of his personality which had become like members of his family. Indeed, early on, when confronting the task before him, he became despondent and put aside his bow as a gesture of defeat. The symbolism of that gesture is that, when confronted with the sometimes awesome challenge of overcoming the very things which stand in the way of success, the meditator will put away spiritual routines and avoid meditation practice.

It is conditioned human nature to sometimes make excuses. We may say, "I'm not yet ready for enlightenment. There are many things in life I want to experience before continuing my spiritual practices. Spiritual practices interfere with my personal life; my social life; my plans for myself."

What can we do to remain steady on the path? We can resolve to remain clear-minded, purposeful, and consistently attentive to procedures and practices we know to be helpful. Habits and tendencies are regulated by intentional behavior and will not overly influence us if we are true to our high calling. We should live a balanced life to regulate mental, emotional, and physical processes. It is in the arena of daily living that we are able to actualize our knowledge and our soul abilities.

Avoid behavior which is not compatible with aspiration for God-realization. Maintain a regular program of exercise and rest. Avoid prolonged fasts which may weaken the body and disturb prana flows and their influences. When pranas are imbalanced we may become unwell, and mental and emotional states may become erratic. We may behave in strange, inappropriate ways, and more easily be subject to confusion and fantasy.

Be willing to renounce attitudes and beliefs which interfere with spiritually appropriate behavior. Paramahansaji privately told me how he helped an advanced disciple clear his mind of a final restricting attitude. The disciple had been experiencing higher superconscious states with regularity for many years and was very near to being liberated. His personal challenge was his relationship to money. He had been born in poor circumstances and in later years had become wealthy, the head of several large business enterprises. He was attached to his personal accomplishments and to his possessions. Although a generous giver, he did not always give freely and selflessly. Paramahansaji talked with him and made him confront his attitude and behavior. My guru said to me, "That was the last little thing he had to overcome. He will be liberated now."

When sattva guna prevails in the mind, challenges and delusions will be of a more subtle nature, requiring keen discernment and surrender to overcome them. When rajas guna prevails, challenges and delusions tend to be obviously dramatized. There is usually more emotion involved because of restlessness and abundant energy driving the forces in the mind. When tamas guna prevails, there may be a tendency to become lethargic, dull, unconscious, and undiscerning.

Strong desires may manifest when meditating. We may yearn for experiences to satisfy desires or whims. Sexual desire may become pronounced, causing fantasies during meditation or frequent urges for gratification at other times. Interestingly enough, when desires of any kind are present, circumstances often unfold in our environment which provide an opportunity for their satisfaction. These temptations should be recognized for what they are: the orderly working out of causes, and their influential forces used for constructive purposes.

If we are to remain steady on the enlightenment path it is essential that we cultivate purity, morality, regularity in study and meditation practice, and spiritually appropriate living.

28. One must renounce these beliefs, fantasies, and untruths, as they are obstacles to final enlightenment.

The removal of all mental fluctuations is accomplished in the same way that any other restricting influence is removed.

Renounce them by removing attention from them.

Some harmless desires can be fulfilled and their force thereby spent. Harmless desires are those which cause no injury to self or to another. Paramahansaji referred to them as "desireless desires": small whims which are not important and can be experienced for enjoyment or easily ignored.

When mental fluctuations cease, the remaining delusion can be the sense of I-ness. "Now I have attained," one's individuality asserts. This delusion must be renounced. When it is, soul awareness perceives no individual self and no independent universe. Souls are rays of God's light and the universe is God's manifesting energy. When the contents of the mind are renounced, their forces flow into the unmanifest field of primordial forces.

29. Having renounced even the craving for liberation, one experiences higher knowledge.

One who is subject to influential mental drives and karmic impressions cannot renounce liberation and experience freedom, for the giving up of the desire for liberation would result in individualized consciousness being overcome by mental influences. However, when the nearly enlightened soul surrenders the desire for liberation, it occurs by grace. By grace are we saved (liberated), not by works (personal endeavors) or by faith alone.

The result of this renunciation is apprehension of "the rain cloud of knowledge, the cloud that pours virtue." Divine forces flow into the mental field and cleanse it. As a cloud pours rain, so refined superconsciousness floods the mind with redeeming influence, eliminating root-causes of destructive drives and harmonizing the gunas, the cosmic forces in the mental field.

With final renunciation of self-consciousness, the devotee's attitude is that of surrender in God: "I want nothing for myself. I give my all to You. With ego-boundaries dissolved, I know and experience only wholeness."

30. With the dawning of true knowledge, all restrictions cease.

When restricting influences are neutralized and their causes removed, the devotee is free while embodied. If residual tendencies remain, their eventual removal is assured. Established in knowledge of absolute oneness the devotee lives in the world as a gift of God. Thoughts and actions are spontaneous and appropriate. If any sense of individuality remains, the inner awareness is, "I live in God; God lives and expresses through me." Paramahansaji told a few disciples, "I banished the Yogananda personality long ago. Only God dwells in this body temple now."

31. With the dissolution of mental restrictions, individual mind is transformed into Cosmic Mind.

Rajas and tamas veil sattvic characteristics. When restlessness and inertia come under the influence of sattva, individual mind is transformed into Cosmic Mind, becoming all-pervasive and the repository of knowledge.

A liberated soul is not compelled to incarnate again, for there are no corresponding characteristics in the mind to bind it to gross matter. A liberated soul may incarnate for special purposes due to God's inclination. Now liberated, it does not matter to the soul whether or not it expresses through a mind and body. Without karmic compulsion, only the gunas prevail in the mind, contributing to the soul's involvement with matter.

32. With the dawning of knowledge, the cosmic forces, having served their purposes, cease to be influential.

With soul liberation, the purposes of the gunas have been served and they cease to be influential. This represents the final stage of soul unfoldment. Beyond this there is nothing more to be realized, for beyond the cosmic forces is pure consciousness.

The cosmic forces active in the mind serve useful purposes. They enable the devotee to have experiences and to unfold consciousness. When absolute knowledge is experienced the gunas are no longer necessary. Soul awareness fluctuates when identified with the mind comprised of cosmic forces. These forces can influence the mind but not the soul. The soul is more subtle than cosmic forces and, when no longer identified with mind, cannot be influenced by cosmic forces. Cosmic forces are not needed for the soul's perception of Higher Reality and cease to be influential to the soul established in absolute knowledge.

33. No longer perceiving changes from moment to moment, soul awareness is restored to absolute knowledge beyond time and change.

Supreme Consciousness is called "eternally immutable" and the field of nature is called "eternally mutable." Transcendental Consciousness, being devoid of characteristics which allow transformative change, is eternally immutable. Because cosmic forces persist and are involved in transformation, or have that potential, they are eternally mutable.

Eternal existence for the liberated soul is not forever-awareness of time. Perception of successions of moments which give rise to time-sense are not experienced by the liberated soul removed from identification with nature. This is why soul liberation is incomprehensible to the mind involved with concepts of time and influenced by the gunas.

34. When cosmic forces, having no further purpose to serve, return to the field of cosmic forces, the soul experiences absolute freedom.

Soul freedom is the removal of identification of soul awareness from matter. Two descriptions of the liberation process are: 1) when cosmic forces no longer influence soul awareness; 2) when soul awareness is established in realization of the Supreme Self.

35. This is absolute liberation of consciousness.

This is the final conclusion of spiritual practice; the end of all sorrows due to former delusion. As we have learned, life without understanding is painful. We feel discomfort when we are unwell. We may be physically and mentally functional while spiritually unaware, and testify to feeling a divine discontent—a kind of subtle pain. And what is the solution to the problem of pain? It is to restore awareness to wholeness. The final freedom is liberation of consciousness.

36. Liberation of consciousness is that state in which only pure consciousness remains.

The soul's innate state is pure consciousness. A meditative theme for contemplation is, "How was it with me before I became involved with mind and matter?" By such contemplation, the devotee flows attention beyond thoughts and mental fluctuations, to the field of pure consciousness. Memories of initial involvement with matter may surface, and discernment may allow insight.

37. When liberated while embodied, one perceives the universe as existing in God and God in and as the universe.

Before liberation, we may intellectually know the universe to be a manifestation of God's creative power and may somewhat understand that the regulating influences of God govern universal processes. With liberation, everything is truly known and comprehended. We no longer have to "practice" the presence of God or endeavor to remain centered and perceptive. Knowledge is complete and permanent.

38. Eternal existence, consciousness, and pure bliss of being are the attributes of God; the field of Absolute, Pure Consciousness is beyond attributes. Here ends this exposition of yoga.

The Oversoul, has attributes because of the actions of cosmic forces within its field of being. The Absolute, because removed from cosmic forces, is devoid of attributes. Knowledge of God and realization of Absolute Reality is the final consummation of dedicated, proficient Kriya Yoga practice surrendered in God.

PART THREE

PRACTICE

Routines, Meditation Techniques and Lifestyle Guidelines

CHAPTER ONE

Guidelines to
Enlightened Living

If you would be surrendered in God, let your life reflect your complete dedication on the enlightenment path. Behavior which reveals your understanding is the most reliable indicator of your degree of spiritual awareness. You can easily know your level of soul awareness by how you choose to live. You can determine your emotional maturity by how you relate to others and to your environment and circumstances.

Let your lifestyle be pure, natural, and in harmony with your chosen and destined purposes. Let most of your choices be determined by your awareness of soul destiny. The practical way to experience desired unfoldments and the fulfillment of soul destiny is to live in harmony with the rhythms of nature and with the causative laws of mind and consciousness which determine effects and results.

Four complimentary applications of our understanding can assist us to total wellness and creative, functional living:

1. *Cultivation of Spiritual Awareness* – This is basic to everything else we do. Without spiritual growth and expanded awareness, life in this or any world is superficial and wasted. Live righteously, attend to spiritual practices and be aware of the reality of God at all times.

2. *Reduction of Stress* – Stress due to inner conflicts can be reduced by meditation and natural living. Stress from reactions to environmental circumstances can be reduced by coming to terms with our relationships and improving personal, environ-

mental, and social conditions. We may attend to personal routines chosen for their life-enhancing influences but if family, social and work-related circumstances are not harmonious these may contribute to emotional conflicts and disturb our peace of mind.

3. *Behavior Modification* – Because our behavior reflects our psychological condition and states of consciousness, intentional modification of behavior can contribute to adjustments in psychological states and states of consciousness. Many devotees remain small-minded and frustrated in spite of their good intentions and their devotion to God because they choose to remain emotionally immature or they lack the will and the courage to modify their behavior. They hope for spiritual growth without having to change attitudes and behavior. They are either unwilling to adhere to recommended and proven guidelines or they are unable to do so because of self-defeating attitudes. The most useful approach to behavior modification is to do what should be done as a matter of duty, as evidence of surrender in God.

4. *Specific Routines* – If we are not already spontaneously living in harmony with the rhythms of nature, we will have to learn and adopt routines which, while perhaps novel or different at first, will prove helpful to the accomplishment of our higher purposes. Several routines follow.

A Recommended Daily Routine to Stabilize Your Life and Support Spiritual Growth

If you will do these things you will live as enlightened people live. You will remain anchored in spiritual awareness and be in harmony with the rhythms of nature. Sattvic qualities will become influential, physical and psychological health will be nurtured, and your worthy purposes will be more easily fulfilled. You will be happy in this world and your presence in it will be a blessing to others.

1. *Awaken Early in the Morning* – After restful sleep, awaken just before dawn. Attend to bathroom routines, rinse your mouth and drink a glass of warm water to encourage stimulation of the intestinal tract to regulate bowel movements. Subtle cosmic forces

are active in nature before 6 a.m. which contribute to processes of elimination and the movements of prana in the body.

2. *Meditate* – The duration of your meditation practice will determine how early you begin your day. Allow sufficient time to practice deeply and to enjoy the tranquil aftereffects of Kriya Yoga meditation practice.

3. *Begin the Day's Activities* – Have a light breakfast and proceed to your duties or work. Plan the day before what you will do, so that you can begin with clear intention and be productive.

4. *Live Constructively* – The work you do should be constructive, meaningful, and done in the spirit of service. Your social relationships should be wholesome and worthwhile, with no destructive emotional dependency so that you and everyone with whom you relate benefit from the relationships.

5. *Meditate in the Evening* – This is optional. Early in the evening or before bedtime, meditate. Before sleeping, turn your thoughts to God and relax into the Infinite. Retire early enough to obtain adequate sleep so you can awaken early the next day to begin your routine.

Family life and social interactions should be enjoyable and mutually supportive. On weekends, and during occasional or annual vacations, maintain your personal schedule of study and meditation while relaxing and being mentally and physically renewed. Now and then, when possible, spend time at a spiritual retreat center to further your spiritual education and experience more intensive meditation.

Select wholesome, natural foods in accord with your needs and basic constitutional nature. Avoid alcohol and other substances which poison the body or interfere with its functions. Enjoy moderately vigorous exercise several times a week. Sexual activity should be moderate, spontaneous, and natural. Celibacy, if desired or required because of lifestyle, is all right but is not necessary for success on the spiritual path. What is important are respectful, supportive relationships.

Millions of people live without plan or purpose. Caught up in a multitude of details and overly involved in outer circumstances, their accomplishments are few. If you are committed to discipleship, plan your life and live it with intentional purpose. While enjoying life and relationships, eliminate all nonessentials and focus on important matters. By doing this you will experience the equivalent of several lifetimes in the present incarnation, accelerate spiritual growth, and fulfill your destined purposes.

In a personal notebook write a list of your hopes and dreams for this incarnation and beyond. Cross out the ones which are not relevant to higher purposes, focusing on the ones which are meaningful. Write what you need to do to accomplish your purposes, plan a program which will enable you to fulfill your dreams, and involve yourself with the process. To clearly write a list of hopes and dreams can be useful. As you do this, your mental concepts and intentions are impressed in the field of Cosmic Mind and can then be actualized because of the relationship you have through your mind with Cosmic Mind. Anything you can envision and believe—if it is in accord with the laws of nature and with metaphysical laws—can be experienced. If you need a miracle, don't just hope for one—expect it!

Use your God-endowed ability to exercise creative imagination to help you experience the fulfillment of worthwhile hopes and dreams.

1. *Meditate* – After a brief centering meditation or after your regular session, remain in the tranquil silence. Feel yourself to be surrendered in God and one with Cosmic Mind. You are now consciously resting at the seat of power and creativity which enlivens the universe.

2. *Vividly Imagine Desired Ends* – This is not the time to think about how to fulfill your goals. Mentally picture results. If you cannot imagine specific end results, or do not care to, imagine and *feel* as you would feel were your dream already totally fulfilled.

3. *Rest in this Experience* – Rest in this imaginal state for as long as comfortable, or until you are firmly satisfied that in your consciousness the end results are already established.

4. *Conclude the Practice Session* – *Feel* and *know* the project to be complete. Do not overly analyze the process, worry about it, or talk about it with anyone else. Your inner work is first in consciousness, in cooperation with Cosmic Mind from which all objective manifestations emerge into physical expression.

After the practice session, if you are inspired to engage in constructive actions to assist the outcome, follow through. If you do not know what to do, hold firm to your realization and let the universe perform the necessary actions.

The key to the process is to work from the level as near to the field of pure consciousness as possible. Superficial use of the technique may enable you to accomplish some results. Willful use of the procedure will only enable you to be a fairly competent sorcerer, not a surrendered devotee of God. By opening your mind, expanding your consciousness, and learning to accept life's blessings, you help yourself to the fulfillment of desired ends and worthwhile purposes. Do not be afraid to take responsibility for your life. If you are God-surrendered you will not be ego-driven nor will you have to be concerned about making mistakes. If your mind is closed to the possibility of good fortune, if you expect God to do the work you should do for yourself, you will have to live with your illusions.

When you are surrendered in God your every need will be provided to the extent that you are able to accept your blessings. *Anchored in God, if your inner peace is disturbed because of a need of any kind, the universe will respond to provide that need to restore you to harmony.*

What your states of conscious awareness are, determines what will be reflected as your experiences. If you are subject to moods, inclined to physical illness, accident-prone, or feel unloved, insecure, and unworthy of fulfillment, these are the experiences you will tend to create or attract to yourself. If you feel prosperous, emotionally stable, healthy, in harmony with the rhythms of nature, and worthy of enlightenment and happiness, these are the experiences you will have.

Accept your available good so that you can be free from limitations and accomplish every worthy purpose you are inspired to accomplish. Be bold and confident. Live as the divine being you are. Share your consciousness of wholeness with planetary consciousness and serve the cause of evolution by dedicating yourself to serving others and the processes of life. Without emotional compulsion, help others fulfill their purposes. Be willing to see needs and fill them, to see hurts and heal them. Be involved in practical ways without impoverishing yourself or depleting your spiritual forces. Bless others by seeing the good and the possible for them, and acknowledge their innate divinity. You cannot force others to change but you can bless them with your compassion. On their behalf, see their potential and their possibilities. Help people at their level of need, while doing what you can to encourage their spiritual growth.

Whatever your present degree of prosperity, share a portion of it with others. If you have an abundance of resources, fund worthwhile projects. Support enlightenment movements which are contributing to the spiritual education of truth seeking souls. As you have been blessed, be an agent through which others can be blessed. Be God-surrendered. A self-centered person can never know personal fulfillment or experience satisfying progress on the spiritual path until egoism is renounced in favor of expanded awareness.

While attending to basic routines and daily duties, be ever aware of the redeeming influence of grace in your life. Doing your part to help yourself and others is your duty; the activity of grace in your life is a gift. It cannot be earned, it can only be accepted.

Life-Enhancing Routines to Support Spiritual Unfoldment

The following routines can be included in your daily schedule according to your inclination or need. After learning these procedures you will be the best judge of what is of value to you. These basic procedures will remove restrictions to free flows of awareness, contribute to wellness, and enliven body and mind.

When all conditions are ideal, the body's systems will be balanced and a natural, spontaneous flow of thoughts, feelings, and life forces will occur. Imbalance or restrictions at any level can interfere with these flows.

In the traditional yogic approach, while emphasis is upon spiritual awakening and growth, the foundation practice is at the physical level, to encourage wellness and vital function so that possibilities of physical problems are reduced or eliminated in order to allow the soul qualities of expression. By using these basic procedures we afford ourselves the opportunity to learn about spirit-mind-body interrelationships and to release awareness for contemplation of higher Realities. They are not ends in themselves and adherence to them will not alone guarantee spiritual unfoldment. Understand them for what they are: processes which can assist you in moving on to more advanced practices and insightful realizations.

Yoga practices include routines to ensure physical health and vitality. Their purpose is to enable the devotee to progress to mastery of mental states and contemplative meditation. In Hatha Yoga texts it is clearly stated that preliminary practices are for the purpose of preparing body, mind, and awareness for the unfoldment and experience of superconscious states.

Body Cleansing Procedures:
Regular and Occasional

Consider your body to be a temple of the Holy Spirit. Keep it clean and always be fresh and well-groomed. A useful procedure, daily or a few times a week, is to brush the skin of the entire body just before bathing, using a natural bristle brush for this purpose, or a dry towel. This will remove dead skin cells, improve blood circulation, and stimulate the circulation of lymphatic fluids. Massage the scalp, head and face, neck and shoulders, upper back, chest and abdominal regions, legs and feet, with sesame seed (or some other) oil. Massage the feet last, probing firmly but gently with your fingers and thumbs into tender areas. Stimulation of the reflex points of the feet, including heels, toes, and bottoms of the feet, can trigger a release of life forces throughout the body, contributing to normalizing their flows. Do this in the morning as part of your regular routine, or in the evening before bedtime.

As part of your cleansing routine, now and then wash the nasal passages with body temperature water in which a pinch of salt or sea salt has been stirred. Use a small tea pot or other suitable water receptacle. Lean over the sink, insert the spout into one nostril, bending the head slightly in the opposite direction to allow the water to flow out through the opposite nostril. Then reverse the procedure. Gently blow out the remaining water through both nostrils, bending forward to allow drainage. Avoid blowing the remaining water out through one nostril while holding the other one closed, as this could force water into the inner ear.

The mucous lining of the sinuses and nasal passageways performs the functions of keeping membranes moist, thus protecting the body against bacteria, viruses, and pollutants in the atmosphere. Mucous secretions are ordinarily rather thick, sufficient to coat the linings and trap invading substances which are then drained into the throat and stomach. Eye secretions from the tear ducts which keep the eyes moist are also drained into the nasal passages. When mucous secretions are insufficient, resulting in dryness, the body becomes more easily prone to colds and various respiratory problems.

Basic Pranayama Routines

Pranayama cleanses the channels (nadis) through which prana is distributed, balances prana flows, and can contribute to the awakening of dormant soul forces. When prana flows are strong and balanced one is said to "shine like a god."

For pranayama practice, assume a comfortable, seated posture. Be relaxed, in a meditative state.

Whenever the fire influence in your body needs to be stimulated (after meals to encourage digestion, or when you want to be more left-brain influenced) close the left nostril and breathe through the right nostril three to five minutes. To stimulate the lunar influence (when preparing to sleep, or whenever you want to be more right-brain influenced) close the right nostril and breathe through the left nostril three to five minutes.

DIAPHRAGMATIC BREATHING

If you have the habit of breathing in a shallow, rapid, and irregular manner, restore your system to balance by learning to breathe naturally from the diaphragm. This will ensure an abundant supply of air in the lungs, allowing for adequate exchange of gaseous elements and improving blood circulation. Place your hand on your upper abdomen just below the rib cage. As you breathe you should feel the diaphragm expand and push outward with inhalation and contract and recede with exhalation. There should be no forced upward movement of the shoulders or any special effort involved. Breathing in this way will, in itself, contribute to deep relaxation. Doing this for a few minutes during the day or just before going to sleep will prove beneficial.

ALTERNATE NOSTRIL BREATHING

This is said to cleanse the nadis or channels through which prana circulates. Because the force of prana flows more strongly through the right side of the body for relatively short durations each day, then changes over to flow more strongly through the left side, somewhat contributing to mood fluctuations and attitude changes, we can somewhat master these flows by practicing alternate nostril breathing.

Hold your right hand near the nose. Breathe in deeply and exhale. Relax. When inclined to breathe, close the right nostril, inhale through the left nostril. Experience a natural pause without intentionally holding the breath, close the left nostril and exhale fully through the right nostril. Experience a natural pause. Inhale through the right nostril. Pause. Exhale through the left nostril. This is one complete round of practice. Continue five to ten times. Inhale through both nostrils and exhale. Relax. When doing this pranayama you will inhale and exhale a little more deeply than usual. Stay within your comfort range, without forcibly holding the breath after inhalation and exhalation.

This practice neutralizes the force of prana flows along the left and right channels in the spinal pathway, encouraging prana to flow in the sushumna, contributing to physical relaxation and mental calm. When practiced at the beginning of a meditation session, concentration will flow more easily.

SUSHUMNA BREATHING

This is useful to do at the beginning of meditation or at interludes during longer meditation sessions when you want to deepen your practice and further internalize attention. It is helpful preparation for learning and practicing the more advanced Kriya Yoga pranayama technique.

Sit upright with closed eyes and attention focused at the spiritual eye and crown chakra. Be aware of the spinal pathway and chakras. Inhale and exhale a few times to cleanse the lungs and elicit relaxation.

Let your normal breathing rhythm be established. After a complete exhalation, breathe in through slightly parted lips, letting the air flow against the throat behind your tongue. Feel that you are gently "sucking" life force upward through the sushumna, from the bottom chakra to the crown chakra, in a steady flow synchronized with natural inhalation. Breathe a little more deeply than usual. You will find that a natural rhythm occurs as you settle into the process. Draw the current up with inhalation and let it descend when you gently and naturally exhale. Experience a natural pause, if one occurs, after inhalation and exhalation. Continue for several minutes or for as often as practice is comfortable. To conclude, draw the current into the spiritual eye and crown chakra, and meditate.

As your practice progresses, you will experience a soothing flow of current ascending and descending the spinal pathway. It will be extremely pleasant, even blissful.

**Basic Procedures for Enlivening
and Directing Vital Forces**

These should not be practiced if there is any problem with high blood pressure, ulcers, hiatal hernia, or heart disorders. Women should not practice during menstruation or during pregnancy. (The reason for this is that techniques used to encourage prana to flow upward may interfere with normal actions of downward flowing prana which regulates processes of elimination.)

These techniques are known as mudras (*mudra*, seal, sign, or gesture). Ritual hand gestures are also referred to as mudras. A familiar mudra is the one in which the hand is held upward, palm facing out, to communicate the message "fear not." For yoga practice, the word refers to techniques used to acquire voluntary control over vital forces. They usually require the use of a *banda* (lock) to restrain inner forces.

The "chin lock," for instance, may be done during the practice of pranayama to retain air and stabilize prana during a pause in practice after inhalations. For this, one breathes in, closes off the glottis and drops the head into the notch in the neck. This prevents air from flowing out and is more effective than merely holding the breath. These techniques are to be practiced with firm control but without any evidence of strain.

UDDIYANA BANDHA (*Abdominal Lift*)

For this procedure the abdominal cavity is lifted up and a chin lock is utilized to close the throat. To the beginning student it may appear quite impressive but is really moderately easy to accomplish. Its practice increases powers of digestion by stimulating the "gastric fire" and lumbar chakra, massages internal organs, tones abdominal muscles, and awakens and draws vital forces in the lower chakras upward. It is useful for awakening awareness in the spine and enlivening the body.

Standing, bend over, placing your hands on your thighs without pushing against them. Inhale rather deeply. Exhale completely. Hold the breath, make the chin lock and press your chin into the notch at the throat. Lift the rib cage and elevate your shoulders. Your diaphragm will be pulled inward and upward, resulting in a "sucking in and up" effect. Hold for a moment and relax. Resume normal breathing. Repeat.

With practice you will be able to do five, ten, or more, complete movements (that is, drawing in and up and relaxing, then repeating) on one breath. Do not strain to hold the breath.

MAHA MUDRA

Maha means "great" and this technique is highly extolled in basic yogic literature. It is also recommended as a preliminary practice to Kriya Pranayama. It enlivens the entire system, imparts flexibility to the spine and legs, and directs prana into sushumna.

Sit on the floor with your legs extended. Tuck the left heel under the body at the juncture between the genitals and anus. Inhale, exhale. Hold the breath out. Perform the anal sphincter lock by drawing the sphincters up and retaining the contraction. Inhale, perform the chin lock, bend forward and grasp your ankles (or your feet if you can), stretching the spine. Sit upright, relax completely, releasing the chin and sphincter locks as you exhale. Change leg positions and repeat. Repeat the process with both legs extended.

If you are a Kriya initiate, when doing this procedure, after performing the anal sphincter lock, draw the current upward with inhalation and proceed as described. Relax into the process, avoiding any tendency to exert yourself.

If any physical reason exists which prevents the performance of this technique (obesity, stiffness, weakness, or any other reason), use this alternative procedure. Sit upright with awareness in the sushumna and attention directed to the spiritual eye and crown chakra. Inhale. Exhale. Perform the anal sphincter lock and draw the current upward at least to the navel chakra. Let the current descend with exhalation and relax the sphincter lock. Pause. Repeat three or four times. This will somewhat awaken forces in the lower chakras and send them upward through sushumna. When practicing this (and later, Kriya Pranayama) you may feel an "electric" surge in the spinal pathway.

Recommended scheduling of Alternate Nostril Breathing, Sushumna Breathing, and Maha Mudra is explained in the following chapter to enable you to use these procedures along with your meditation practice.

CHAPTER THREE

Kriya Yoga Meditation
Techniques and Routines

These meditation routines are taught by the masters of Kriya Yoga in the guru line of Mahavatar Babaji, Lahiri Mahasaya, Sri Yukteswar, Paramahansa Yogananda, and their spiritual successors. Practice should be according to your needs and ability, allowing progressive spiritual growth, experience, and God's grace to determine progress. After practicing as instructed for a number of years, your own inner guidance will enable you to discover subtle procedures which will be helpful in attaining more refined states of superconsciousness.

Success in meditation can unfold by: 1) giving attention to procedures and techniques for the purpose of adjusting the body's physiology and regulating mental states and states of consciousness; 2) spontaneous awakening and unfoldment. Both are included in the Kriya Yoga system. Until inner surrender and kundalini activity produce spontaneous meditation, use the procedures so that adjustments in mental states and states of consciousness can occur.

As a disciple on the enlightenment path, you should be totally committed to living a righteous life and to daily spiritual practices and meditation. Even the masters who have transcended karmic influences, regularly withdraw from outer involvements to rest in pure consciousness. Paramahansaji, for instance, maintained a balanced schedule of activity and meditation. He slept but three or four hours a night—not ordinary sleep but superconscious sleep—then meditated to experience samadhi states for at least four hours. Occasionally, he would withdraw into total seclusion for several days, or a few weeks, to do inner work during extended periods of meditation.

Beginning meditators are advised to meditate for twenty to thirty minutes twice a day. Useful times to do this are the morning and evening hours. In the morning, after awakening, thoughts and feelings are still somewhat dormant and it is then easier to meditate. In the evening, when the day's work is done, meditation helps to reduce stress and clears the mind and consciousness for restful sleep. Regular meditation maintains a flow of superconscious influence to the nervous system and body.

A daily meditation schedule will anchor your life and keep you on course. It will provide a quiet time during which you are in control of your life, no longer at the mercy of external influences. You will be better able to live as a God-centered, Self-reliant person. Your daily meditation schedule will protect you from diversions and temptations. You will not as easily be attracted to useless, time-wasting, and potentially destructive involvements and behaviors when you are centered as a result of daily devotions and meditation practice. In almost every instance of confusion and personal challenge reported by a devotee on the path, it is noted that the individual usually has not been attentive to regular meditation practice.

Any quiet place where you can be alone and comfortable is suitable for meditation practice. When meditating, be intentional, alert, and focused. Only "gentle endeavor" is required. Avoid any tendency to be self-centered or motivated by petty thoughts or feelings. You are a divine being, meditating to open yourself to the Infinite. Do not overly analyze the techniques or your perceptions. Enter into the process, experience it, conclude the session, and attend to your daily routine with thoughts of God in the background of your mind. Let the calm of meditation remain with you as you perform duties and experience relationships.

Shorter meditation sessions for centering and attunement can be experienced at any time. When you meditate during your regularly scheduled times, allow a few minutes for relaxation before meditation. It is best to meditate when you are rested, relaxed, alert, and inspired. Anticipate the meditation experience, without being overly anxious about results. Do your part, surrender in God, and leave the results to grace.

Kriya Meditation Techniques
and How to Practice Them

While basic meditation procedures can be learned and practiced with a degree of benefit by reading about them, advanced practices should be learned from a qualified teacher who is proficient in practice and who lives the teaching. Accurate information is then more likely to be acquired and some of the teacher's realization can be transmitted to the student.

During Kriya Yoga initiation the disciple is taught basic philosophical principles, lifestyle guidelines, appropriate meditation methods and techniques, and is infused with spiritual force which pervades the environment in which initiation occurs. The initiator invokes the presence of God and the line of gurus while conscious of the fact that he or she is but the vehicle through which the teaching is transmitted and God's grace shared. The disciple, in turn, absorbs the instruction and commits to being surrendered in God and steadfast on the path.

Initiation is not to be taken lightly. It is not a merely a matter of going to an available teacher who claims knowledge of God. It is not something to do to see if it might prove helpful. The disciple is to seal the initiation instruction and experience in mind and consciousness, and practice with diligence to allow spiritual growth to occur.

In this tradition a disciple becomes qualified to initiate others as a result of inner realization. The guru will acknowledge the disciple's qualifications and give permission to initiate. One who has departed from the guru line because of inability to adhere to the teaching tradition cannot successfully transmit the teaching. If you are invited to be initiated by a person who does not honor the guru line, or who is being promoted as a special teacher without legitimacy, avoid that relationship. You will only waste your time and results will be unsatisfactory.

Personal instruction varies according to the experience and insight of the guru and the needs of the disciple. Among Kriya gurus, minor differences in teaching emphasis may be noted. At the core, the essential teaching and fundamental practices are the same.

To new Kriya students, mantra is invariably taught as the

first meditation technique to use. There are many mantras and the one given by the guru should be considered sacred. All mantras derive their potency from Om.

Mantra meditation provides an attractive inner sound which fascinates the meditator's attention and disengages it from random thought processes, enabling transcendence of mental processes. The sound frequency of the mantra pervades the mental field and nervous system with beneficial influences which order thought processes and refine the brain and nervous system. The meditation mantra is a pure sound which originates in subtle spheres and brings their influences into the physical realm. It has transforming effects and leads the meditator's attention from gross to subtle levels of perception, then to refined levels and to transcendental realizations.

The recommended mantra given through my guru line is *Hong Sau* (hong-saw). It is the natural sound of the inflowing and outflowing breath. Paramahansaji said that mantra meditation alone could result in samadhi states. Indeed, in some teaching traditions, mantra meditation is the only technique taught to devotees. It is easily learned and practiced and is suitable for almost everyone.

After the mantra has been taught and one knows what it sounds like when verbalized, it is listened to mentally; it is not audibly or mentally chanted during internalized meditation practice. The devotee listens to the sound of *hong* during natural inhalation and to the sound of *sau* during natural exhalation. After extended practice, when one is relaxed and internalized, listening to the mantra is replaced by contemplation of the sound current (Om) and expansion of awareness which allows unfoldment of superconscious states.

For devotees who prepare themselves to learn and practice advanced meditation procedures, several are given according to the qualifications of the devotee. One is advised to acquire proficiency in the practice of preliminary procedures before proceeding to practice of higher Kriya techniques. Progress should always be monitored by the guru. If the guru is not available, because of having withdrawn from the world scene or for some other reason, the devotee may request instruction from a qualified representative of the guru's lineage.

1. *Inner Sound and Light Technique* – Paramahansaji referred to this as the "Om Technique." It is usually spontaneously practiced after mantra meditation leads the devotee's attention to subtle levels of awareness, or it can be taught by the teacher. When prana flows upward through the sushumna, the inner sound naturally arises in the meditator's awareness. This is to be listened to as the "manifesting indicator" (sound) of God's creative force. Awareness of light at the spiritual eye often accompanies awareness of sound.

2. *Kriya Pranayama* – This is the procedure generally referred to by gurus of this tradition as "kriya." It is an advanced process of sushumna breathing, during which one directs ascending life force through the chakras with inhalation and allows the force to descend during exhalation. This procedure clears the mental field and purifies the channels (*nadis*) through which prana circulates in the subtle body. Paramahansaji taught that one circulation of current is considered to be the equivalent of the beneficial influences of nature acting upon the body and subtle sheaths during the course of a solar year. (It is sometimes taught that one circulation of current is equivalent to the mind-renewing effects of one lunar month.) It is recommended that new initiates practice Kriya pranayama fourteen times twice a day for the first year, then increase to twenty-eight times twice a day, then increase the number according to the guru's instructions until perhaps hundreds of "kriyas" are routinely practiced. This technique, as with the following ones, is to be learned from the guru, to ensure precise instruction and the transmission of grace flowing through the guru line. Its practice may be preceded by Maha Mudra and mantra meditation.

3. *Yoni Mudra* – Paramahansaji referred to this technique as *Jyoti* (light) *Mudra* because it enables the devotee to more clearly perceive the reflected lights of the chakras and the brilliance of the spiritual eye. *Yoni* means "the path through which one is born." In general usage the word is used to refer to the vaginal canal through which one is physically born. As an esoteric keyword, it is used to refer to the spiritual eye center through which the meditator's consciousness flows into subjective levels of consciousness. This technique is practiced after Kriya Pranayama and after resting in the tranquil silence. Closing the ears, while

focusing attention at the spiritual eye, the current is drawn upward with the Kriya breath and held at the spiritual eye while the breath is suspended for a comfortable duration. The devotee then flows attention into the spiritual eye while chanting Om several times, each time probing into the spiritual eye with gentle mental thrusts. The current is then allowed to descend, breathing rhythm is restored, and the process is repeated a few more times. The meditator then remains poised at the spiritual eye and crown chakra while meditation deepens.

4. *Ascending the Chakras* – Sometimes referred to as the second Kriya meditation technique, this process enables the devotee to consciously ascend awareness through the chakras and clear the field of awareness to experience superconscious states. It is also used to consciously withdraw from the body at the time of transition. During the practice of this technique, appropriate mantras may be mentally chanted at each chakra and inner lights and sounds emanating from the chakras are observed. Awareness is progressively removed from lower chakras to higher ones as successive levels of soul awareness are experienced and transcended, until cosmic consciousness and pure consciousness are experienced.

5. *Higher Kriya Techniques* – These involve subtle variations of the procedures already explained and are either taught after the disciple has become proficient in the practice of preliminary Kriya routines or learned spontaneously by inner revelation. Some of these include the basic Kriya Pranayama with attention given to the higher chakras, along with mental chanting of prescribed mantras.

For the devotee who is initiated and who attends to regular and attentive practice, progress is rapid. Without initiation—or with initiation but without diligent practice—progress is seldom satisfactory.

The Kriya techniques are graded according to the capacity of the meditator and used according to need and inclination. Advanced meditators may meditate three or four times a day. The recommended times for meditation are dawn, noon, dusk, and midnight.

Because it is not always convenient for one to schedule meditation practice at the recommended times, any other suitable time will suffice. Many devotees are able to utilize the hours of night for deep meditation. They retire early, to rest, then later awaken to meditate for one or more hours, followed by a period of restful sleep until the usual waking time. One should not carry this practice to extremes, to the point of denying the mind and body needed sleep and refreshment. Sleep, also, can be an occasion of wakefulness when one learns to sleep superconsciously.

CENTERING AND ATTUNEMENT MEDITATION

A basic procedure for anyone, at any time. If you are a new meditator, meditate like this for several weeks until you acquire proficiency and are able to accurately discern the physiological and psychological changes which occur during meditation. If you have been meditating for an extended period of time but have been neglecting the basics, use the following routine for a few days, or weeks, until you are restored to balance, then proceed with a more advanced routine.

1. *Sit upright* in a comfortable posture, with your spine straight and head erect. Awareness should be in the spinal pathway, spiritual eye, and higher brain centers. Feel that you are immersed in the ocean of God's life and presence.

2. *Pray,* according to your inner guidance, invoking awareness of the reality of God. If you are an initiate disciple, also invoke the presence of your guru line.

3. *Use the meditation technique or procedure of choice,* the one which is the most result-producing for you, or given by your guru—mantra or contemplation of God in whatever form that satisfies your heart. Thoughts will usually persist during early stages of meditation even when your attention is involved with mantra or other forms of contemplation. Let them be thoughts of God. If using *Hong Sau* mantra, let the mantra flow in harmony with the body's natural breathing rhythm. Exhale, then listen to *Hong* with inbreathing and *Sau* as the breath flows out. The body will establish its own breathing rhythm—just flow with it. As breathing becomes slower and refined, thought processes will become more subtle and concentration will be more easily

focused at the spiritual eye. There may be interludes of suspended breathing, when you are motionless and pranas are balanced. During these intervals, thoughts will be minimal or nonexistent. At such times, surrender completely in God and experience tranquil pure consciousness. Lahiri Mahasaya taught these intervals of spontaneous breathlessness to be ideal occasions for "slipping through" thought-streams which are temporarily stopped during the breathless state. Let the body's innate intelligence regulate the breathing rhythm as you give your attention to meditation practice and superconscious experience.

4. *When the mantra* is transcended and you experience a degree of pure awareness, or inner sound, merge in pure awareness and/or inner sound. The purpose of mantra is to lead your attention to refined levels of consciousness. Rest in the "peak experience" as desired, or for as long as it persists.

5. *Conclude your practice* by sitting for a few minutes after meditation to allow the experience to be integrated with your thoughts, feelings, and body awareness.

This easy procedure can be used for relaxation, centering, and attunement. It will contribute to reduction of stress, clear the mental field, order mental processes, balance emotions, strengthen the body's immune system, awaken vital forces, and help you to be more discerning, intuitive, and purposeful. Allow twenty to thirty minutes for practice to elicit the relaxation response and meditative calm. If you want to pray for others, examine your goals and purposes, do possibility-thinking and use creative imagination, or engage in philosophical reflection, the interlude after meditation is ideal for these purposes.

If adhered to with diligence, meditation practice can contribute to spontaneous and progressive spiritual growth. It can, if meditation sessions are extended, enable you to experience higher states of superconsciousness because awareness will literally transcend identification with mental operations.

ROUTINE FOR ADVANCED MEDITATION #1

Meditate longer, at least for one hour. Assume your meditation posture and practice alternate nostril breathing a few times.

Meditate to the point of deep relaxation. Listen to Om, contemplating at the spiritual eye. Explore inner states of consciousness and contemplate your relationship with God, the field of God, and the unmanifest field of consciousness.

ROUTINE FOR ADVANCED MEDITATION #2

Proceed as recommended above. After alternate nostril breathing, do twenty or more cycles of Sushumna Breathing. Relax into the process and in this way enliven the chakras and encourage life force to ascend to the higher brain centers. Then proceed with mantra and sound and light contemplation.

KRIYA YOGA PRANAYAMA ROUTINE FOR INITIATES #1

Proceed as recommended with preliminary routines. After alternate nostril breathing, practice Kriya Pranayama for the prescribed number of times. Avoid strain while practicing. Let the flows be smooth, yet dynamic. After Kriya Pranayama sit for a long time, absorbed in tranquil silence and surrendered in God. After a while, practice Yoni Mudra, giving more attention to the spiritual eye and inner sound. Meditate deeply.

KRIYA YOGA PRANAYAMA ROUTINE FOR INITIATES #2

Proceed as recommended above, but sit longer. After Yoni Mudra practice, when you begin to come out of meditation listen to your mantra or practice Sushumna Breathing. Cease Sushumna Breathing when effort in practice becomes obvious. For extended meditation sessions, use all of the techniques except the Kriya Pranayama routine (which is only practiced once during each meditation sitting for the prescribed or chosen number of times) as often as you like and in whatever sequence feels best, to deepen your concentration and afford intentional and conscious involvement in meditation. You may even want to engage in devotional chanting before you meditate or between interludes of deep meditation when sitting longer. Or you can pray to cultivate devotion and deepen concentration. This routine can continue for one or two hours, or longer.

ROUTINES FOR SPECIAL PURPOSES AND OCCASIONS

Regardless of your present meditation routine, now and then meditate longer than usual. Once a week, every two weeks, or once a month, meditate longer and deeper. If you are a new meditator and your daily sessions are approximately thirty minutes each, meditate for at least an hour during longer sessions. If you already meditate for an hour at a sitting, occasionally meditate for two hours. Advanced meditators may want to meditate occasionally for three or more hours at a sitting.

Other suitable days for special meditation practice are the regular religious holy days, the eve or the day of a new year, the birthdays of the gurus in your lineage, and the anniversaries of their transition from the body.

Supportive Practices on the Awakening Path

Natural living routines and cleansing procedures vitalize the body and help to maintain biochemical balance. Pranayama stimulates the brain stem and regulates pranas in the body and subtle sheaths. Meditation techniques and contemplation contribute to abstract thinking, inspiration, and superconsciousness. Pranayama actively brings the five lower chakras into harmony; ritual regulates emotions and finer sentiments associated with the fourth, fifth, and sixth chakras.

Actions without conscious intent are often impotent, so be sure you know why you are performing a chosen ritual. The inner "fire rite" which facilitates psychological transformation and dissolves karma, purifies the mind, and restores consciousness to awareness of wholeness, is performed by the practice of Kriya Pranayama and the resulting samadhi states.

How you pray is a matter of the heart. If your outlook is transcendental, you may pray to invoke awareness of the presence of God into your mind and consciousness, or pray to withdraw awareness from mental processes, then contemplate the unmanifest field of pure consciousness. If you are devotional, you may pray to a preferred form or aspect of God—as Heavenly Father, Divine Friend, Beloved Presence, or Divine Mother.

Prayer is entirely a matter of personal inclination. A prayer used by some Kriya Yoga devotees, prior to meditation, is:

Infinite God, Divine Mother, all saints, Mahavatar Babaji, Lahiri Mahasaya, Sri Yukteswar, Paramahansa Yogananda, (and your own guru if you have one), I reverently acknowledge you. May your love shine within me, and may I behold its radiance shining in all hearts. Quicken my heart, awaken my devotion, elevate my consciousness to the reality of the Divine Presence.

As you progress in prayer practice use words which are meaningful to you, or flow spontaneously as impelled by your devotional ardor. After meditation you may want to pray like this (or using words of your choice, if you prefer, in a similar spirit):

Infinite God, Divine Mother, all saints, Mahavatar Babaji, Lahiri Mahasaya, Sri Yukteswar, Paramahansa Yogananda, (and your own guru if you have one), I reverently acknowledge you. Thank you for this quiet interlude of communion and realization. I will carry you in my heart (my innermost being) and mind as I attend to my duties surrendered in the Infinite.

You may want to conclude your meditation practice with an affirmation, using words suitable for the moment, such as:

I am surrendered in God and open to the nurturing and enlivening flows of grace. I am spiritually awake, mentally clear, emotionally calm, physically healthy and vital, on friendly terms with a friendly world, and prosperous and successful in all ways. I am peaceful, happy, and thankful.

Guidelines for Kriya Students and Disciples

The Kriya path is the direct route to God-realization. It includes the core guidelines and procedures taught by every enlightenment tradition, with emphasis on meditation and superconscious experience. The recommended guidelines are for the purpose of assisting Kriya students and initiated disciples to be regular in practice and unfold steadily and quickly to higher levels of understanding and awareness.

1. *Be Surrendered in God* – Surrender nurtures humility. Clear understanding allows a supportive relationship with nature.

2. *Respect Your Guru and the Guru Line* – Honor those through whom knowledge and encouragement flows to bless your life while knowing God to be the source of all good.

3. *Live a Righteous Life* – A simple, natural, lifestyle is most suitable. Let purity of motive and clear knowledge of meaningful purposes determine your behavior.

4. *Attend to Daily Spiritual Practices* – Anchor your life in God by regularly and correctly participating in your spiritual practices. Overcome resistance to practice by cultivating devotion to God, being courageous, and doing things which contribute to inspiration-to-right-action. Review the techniques and procedures to be sure you are practicing correctly. Ask your teacher or guru to check your practice.

5. *Maintain Your Privacy* – Share helpful how-to-live principles with your friends and associates, when asked, but maintain personal privacy in relationship to your spiritual practices. Do not share advanced Kriya meditation techniques with persons who are unprepared to practice them. Until you are given permission to teach by your guru, refer interested persons to a qualified teacher or guru.

6. *Practice Kriya Pranayama Only as Advised* – Do not mix Kriya techniques with meditation procedures which are not included in the Kriya system. Avoid practicing Kriya Pranayama when overly tired, physically ill, or psychologically disturbed. If you are unable to practice Kriya Pranayama, use alternative meditation techniques. Centering and attunement meditation can be practiced anytime. Awareness of the Presence of God should be cultivated always.

7. *Be Patient with Yourself* – Yearn for God-realization and attend to your spiritual practices until realization is experienced.

Cultivate soul contentment as you persist on your path. When challenged, confused, or despondent, go deeper into God.

YOUR PERSONAL MEDITATION SHRINE

This is optional: a matter of personal choice. It can be helpful to set aside an area in your home or apartment, or any other convenient place, as a personal meditation sanctuary. This can be arranged to suit your purposes. As a central focus a small altar can be placed, with photographs or pictures of the gurus or saints who are an inspiration to you. Perhaps a single candle and an incense holder could be placed on the altar. An altar is traditionally "the place where man meets God." We commune with God in the sanctuary of the soul. An altar as an outer symbol of God communion can be helpful. Let your shrine room be simple and clean. Have a comfortable chair or meditation seat placed before the altar. Reverently clean your shrine at least once a week. Allow only devotional practices and meditation there. If others meditate with you from time to time, have extra chairs for this purpose.

Consecrate your sanctuary after you have prepared it. As a prelude to your first meditation there, light the candle, bow to the altar and pray that this may be a divine place where you will daily experience God's presence and awaken steadily in the direction of final soul realization. As you progress in your devotional practices and meditations, your sanctuary will become a sacred place for you. When you go there your thoughts will easily turn Godward. It will become charged with spiritual energy which will beneficially influence you, others who may meditate there, and the immediate environment.

You now know what the enlightened masters of yoga know. You have the information you need to proceed on the awakening path and the procedures to use to contribute to your total wellness and spiritual growth. As you remain steadfast, anything else you need to know will be revealed to you. God's grace will abound. The waves of blessings flowing from enlightened souls will nourish you. You will experience the fulfillment of soul destiny without fail.

APPENDIX

Mahavatar Babaji

The Transmission of the Kriya Yoga Tradition in the Current Era

The impulse for the transmission of the Kriya Yoga tradition to an increasing number of devotees in the current era can be traced to an illumined master known as Babaji. The name is a common one, and means "revered" or "holy" father. Little is known about this legendary personage because he prefers to work behind the scenes, communicating directly with advanced disciples and sharing his spiritual radiance with planetary consciousness. Many saints consider Babaji to be a *mahavatar* (a "great" incarnation).

There are several illumined masters on earth through whom planetary consciousness is infused with divine light. Many of them are assisted by Babaji, for it is his role to inspire people who are actively nurturing planetary consciousness, uplifting humanity, and ministering directly to seekers on the spiritual path. While acknowledged as the spiritual head of the current era Kriya Yoga tradition, Babaji is not limited to this enlightenment movement. His influence flows to any agency through which God's will can be done. He is fully illumined, with no karmic ties to the world, and embodied only to be a conduit through which enlivening forces can express to cleanse planetary consciousness.

Babaji has been in his present body for several centuries and has been known by various names at different times and places. Lahiri Mahasaya confided to a few disciples that Babaji played the role of Krishna, writing in his diary, "The old baba (father) is Krishna." When leading devotees in responsive prayer, Paramahansa Yogananda referred to Babaji as "Babaji-Krishna," in affirmation of his understanding.

Babaji told Swami Kebalananda, a disciple of Lahiri Ma-

Reputed photograph of Mahavatar Babaji

hasaya, that he had initiated Shankara, who lived over a thousand years earlier. Other masters initiated by Babaji in times past are Kabir and some of the masters who wrote basic texts on the various yoga systems. Lahiri told a few of his disciples that he remembered a previous incarnation when he was known as Kabir, the poet-saint (1440–1518 A.D.) who extolled surrender to the guru and meditation on inner sound and light.

Avatars play their roles according to planetary and human needs. Babaji's role is that of an avatar of Shiva. His mission is to enliven planetary consciousness during the present transition from the Dark Age to the Age of Enlightenment thousands of years hence. He is influential in accelerating the awakening of the multitudes to spiritual values, and works to somewhat neutralize the stress caused by the actions of misguided individuals and materialistic societies. The presence of selfless spiritual masters on earth is our assurance that evolutionary trends will continue on a steady course.

Until well into the present century Babaji has resided in northern India, in the Himalayan Mountain area near Badrinarayan, not far from the border of Nepal. It was in this region, on Drongiri Mountain, during the autumn of 1861, that Babaji initiated Lahiri Mahasaya into Kriya Yoga practices and counseled him to return to society and teach others the sacred science. During a two week stay with Babaji, Lahiri witnessed many miracles and met several advanced disciples.

In 1893, at a Kumbha Mela (a periodic, major religious gathering convened for the purpose of bringing together saints and truth seekers) at Allahabad, where the Ganges, Jumna, and now extinct Saraswati rivers come together, Babaji met with Sri Yukteswar and asked him to write a book revealing the underlying unity of religions. The book was soon published as *The Holy Science*. Babaji also told Sri Yukteswar that, a few years later, he would send him a disciple who was to be trained to take the message of yoga to the West. That disciple was Paramahansa Yogananda.

Several close disciples of Lahiri Mahasaya also had personal contact with Babaji over the years, in the Himalayas or when the master would visit them in subtle form. Babaji can appear to persons in his light body and he can dematerialize and materialize his physical body at will. Some titles of respect given Babaji by disciples of Lahiri and others, are Mahamuni Baba ("Supreme Ecstatic Master"), Mahayogi ("The Great Yogi"), and Trambak Baba or Shiva Baba (titles denoting avatars of Shiva). There is substantial evidence to connect him with a more recent appearance (until the second decade of the 21st century) with a saint known as Hariakhan Baba; so named by people because of the abundance of myrobalan (harra) which grew in the vicinity he had chosen for his temporary abode.

The master arrived in the small village of Hariakhan, in the Nainital district, and settled there around 1894. No one knew who he was or from where he had journeyed. Because of his style of dress, and the fact that he spoke a dialect which was a mixture of Kamaonee Pahari and Nepali Doti, he was considered to have come from Nepal. A specimen of his handwriting reveals what appears to be a mixture of Pali and Tibetan characters. His age was unknown.

An accomplished master of yoga, he was often observed "rapt in immense peace and calm" during extended occasions of meditative samadhi. Wherever he went, people flocked for his blessing. He was a strict disciplinarian and possessed yogic powers which he used to bring good fortune to people and to heal many of their ailments. He restored sight to the blind, revived persons who were near death, and could control the elements. It was said that he could "ride the air" as he would sometimes quickly traverse great distances. He was known to appear at two or more places at the same time. When Lahiri was with Babaji, decades before, he reported that those close to the Master often did not have to prepare meals; Babaji would point to a container and whatever food the disciple desired would be materialized therein.

Public ceremonies were encouraged for the welfare of the people and to encourage a harmonious relationship with the forces of nature. When asked by a devotee if a personal problem would be solved, the saint would say, "Your wish will be fulfilled if you sincerely rely upon God."

Before leaving the area, during the early years of the second decade of the twentieth century, Sri Hariakhan Baba toured several Himalayan areas, concluding his travels at the border town of Askote. Bidding farewell to those who had accompanied him, he crossed over the river to Nepal. While in the Himalayas he established several ashrams which are used to this day. Some of them are located at Katgharia, Shitlakhet, and Nainital.

After his physical departure, he was occasionally seen in his subtle form and as a mass of moving light during special public holy day occasions. Until the middle of the twentieth century, reports by disciples of Lahiri Mahasaya placed Babaji at several Himalayan locations, as well as in remote Siberia. Lahiri Mahasaya, Sri Yukteswar, and Paramahansaji often counseled disciples not to travel to the Himalayas to attempt to meet Babaji, but to deepen their meditation and learn to commune with him on inner levels of awareness.

Of Babaji's protective influence, Paramahansaji told disciples that, if they were faithful to their spiritual practices, when they made their transition, Babaji, or at least one of the gurus in this lineage, would be present to "usher them into the Infinite."

Sri Shyamacharan Lahiri (Mahasaya)

In the village of Ghurni of the Nadia district in Bengal, India, Shyamacharan Lahiri was born on September 30, 1828. As a young boy he would often seek out quiet places for meditation and contemplation. His family was devoted to God in the aspect of Shiva, and had several temples constructed for private and public worship.

At school in Varanasi (Banaras), Lahiri was exposed to the English, Sanskrit, Urdu, Hindi, Bengali, and Persian languages. Possessed of abundant vitality, he was active in sports and would often swim in the Ganges River. At eighteen years of age he was married to Kashimoni Devi. Although they did not begin their family until after he had been initiated by Babaji several years later, they became parents of two sons and three daughters.

Lahiri Mahasaya, as he became known to devotees (*Mahasaya* is a title bestowed by disciples and means one who is large-minded or cosmic conscious), was employed as a clerk of the Military Engineering Department of the Government, which supplied materials for the Army's road building projects. Lahiri also taught Hindi, Urdu, and Bengali to several engineers and officers of the department. Responsible in family and social matters by day, at

Lahiri Mahasaya

night Lahiri met with truth seekers and Kriya Yoga disciples. By so doing, he demonstrated that it is possible to live a natural life and still attain the highest goal of Self-realization.

In 1861 Lahiri was transferred to Ranikhet, a forest region near Nainital in the foothills of the Himalayas. One afternoon, while wandering in the Drongiri Mountain area, he was hailed by a man who announced, "A saint wants to see you." Following his new guide he was led to a cave from which a youthful appearing saint emerged and greeted him with the words, "Shyamacharan, you have come!" The saint was Mahavatar Babaji, who had chosen the occasion to renew the guru-disciple relationship which had been established centuries earlier.

Lahiri was taken into a cave and shown the simple belongings of a renunciate yogi: a water pot, meditation staff, and other items. At Babaji's touch, Lahiri's memories of a previous incarnation flooded his mind and he remembered the various items as his, and the cave as the place where he had engaged in meditation practice. Babaji informed his disciple that the Kriya path was really his own (Lahiri's) because one of Lahiri's ancestors was the sage Shandilya. The *Shandilya Upanishad* is a short treatise on advanced yogic practices. Soon after their initial meeting, Babaji gave Lahiri some oil to drink and told him to go to the nearby river and rest until it cleansed his body. When prepared, Lahiri was initiated into Kriya Yoga teachings and practices. During the next two weeks he acquired proficiency in meditation procedures and experienced several episodes of transcendent samadhi states.

While with Babaji and his small group of disciples in the Himalayas, Lahiri observed many interesting incidents. On one occasion, he visited a nearby temple, at night, and observed a holy man coming to worship. A bright halo of light surrounded the holy man. Babaji later told Lahiri that the saint was the son of Dronacharya. The preceptor Dronacharya, of the Mahabharata era, once lived at this place with the Pandavas, the virtuous faction of a family dynasty which engaged in a epic struggle later popularized in poems and stories. The *Bhagavad Gita* is but a small part of the lengthy Mahabharata story. The holy man seen by Lahiri was, like Babaji, considered to be a mortal-immortal: one who remains on earth to fulfill certain spiritual obligations.

Before leaving Ranikhet, Lahiri initiated a few disciples into Kriya practices. It was characteristic of him to share the process with devotees who came to him with a sincere desire for spiritual growth. Men and women of many religious traditions were initiated by him in the years which followed. He said that Hindus could observe traditional rites, Christians could pray in accord with their understanding and aspiration, and Moslems could observe their religious regimens—all being true to their chosen path while living an exemplary life and practicing Kriya Yoga meditation. With Lahiri, the former age-old restrictions concerning yogic initiation were somewhat relaxed, as Babaji agreed that the current era was now more suitable for a wider dissemination of these teachings.

Lahiri taught his disciples to live responsibly in the world and to privately attend to their spiritual practices. Some learned swamis and spiritually advanced yogis were also initiated by the master, including Swami Sri Yukteswar, Swami Pranabananda, Keshabananda Avadhut, Sri Shastri Mahasaya, Srimat Bhupendranath, Dayal Maharaj, and Ram Gopal. So highly regarded was he, that Lahiri was once praised by a then famous saint, Swami Trailanga, who said of him, "I have renounced everything for that which Lahiri Mahasaya has been given by God."

Twenty-two books and commentaries on various scriptures were prepared by Lahiri and published by disciples for distribution to Kriya devotees. Although Lahiri did not write the books, he advised some disciples to record his comments and approved the finished manuscripts before publication. He would not allow any formal organizational efforts to be made for the spread of the Kriya message, recommending instead that the teachings be transmitted by qualified disciples to individuals who were sincere on the spiritual path. Lahiri streamlined and simplified Kriya Yoga methods for ordinary seekers. The fundamental techniques he taught are the basis for regular practice which can awaken latent forces in the devotee and be the means of liberation of consciousness. Several modest ashrams were founded by some of his disciples. The major emphasis, however, was upon encouraging devotees in society to fulfill their family and social obligations while living a God-centered life.

When Paramahansa Yogananda was one year old his parents, both disciples of Lahiri Mahasaya, took him to their guru's home to be blessed by the master. Holding the infant on his lap he said, "Your son will be a great spiritual engine and carry many souls to God."

Some unique incarnations of yoga come onto the world scene for a special purpose and leave when their mission is fulfilled. Thus it was that, at their 1893 meeting at a Kumbha Mela, Babaji told Sri Yukteswar to take a message to Lahiri—that the latter's earth sojourn was soon to be concluded. Six months before his transition, Lahiri told his wife about his plans to depart during the month of September, 1895. On the 26th day of that month, which was Mahastami, the second day of worship of the Divine Mother as Durga (one of the many aspects of God's creative energy), a ritual ceremony was being performed at the home of a neighbor. In this ritual, the most significant moment is at the transition of the phase of the moon as it becomes brighter from the eighth to the ninth day. At that moment, Lahiri opened his eyes, then closed them and retired into meditation to make his transition from the body.

The following day, after his body had been cremated at the Manikarnika Ghat by the Ganges River, a disciple, Swami Keshabananda, was in his room when a great light filled the space around him. Lahiri Mahasaya appeared in a material form, younger and more radiant in appearance. He said to his disciple, "My householder work in the world is done. I do not leave the Earth entirely. I shall now spend some time with Babaji in the Himalayas, and with Babaji in the cosmos."

Swami Sri Yukteswar

Because of his clear understanding, Swami Sri Yukteswar was often referred to by Paramahansaji as a Jnanavatar (incarnation of wisdom). His monastic name, Yukteswar, means union with Ishwara, the ruling aspect of God in relationship to nature. Born in 1855, his given name was Priya Nath Karar. As an adult, Sri Yukteswar married, and managed properties inherited from his father. He and his wife had one daughter. His two main ashrams were at Puri, near the Bay of Bengal, and Serampore, near Calcutta. He was initiated into the swami order after the

Sri Yukteswar

death of his wife.

This master of yoga was an accomplished vedic astrologer, studied Ayurveda and, while a young adult, attended classes at a medical college. He was versed in the art of prescribing gemstones and metals to be worn for therapeutic purposes and often advised disciples to do this when he discerned that it would be helpful to them. Sri Yukteswar carefully researched the theory of cycles (yugas) and published his findings in several journals. He also wrote a commentary on the first six chapters of the *Bhagavad Gita*, after conducting discussions with disciples on this scripture and asking Lahiri Mahasaya for his insights and comments.

An adept spiritual healer, Sri Yukteswar seldom openly displayed his yogic powers. Gentle, and of quiet demeanor, his devotional nature was usually overshadowed by his practical observations and emphasis on the usefulness of intellectual development. When Paramahansaji, as a teenage disciple, thought of forsaking his family relationships, Sri Yukteswarji counseled, "Why exclude family from your love of God?" He was known to sometimes visit disciples in his subtle form, appearing to them in dreams and visions in their time of need. Paramahansaji said of him: "He could have been the most sought-after guru in India if it were not for his strict training of disciples." Once, when a visitor looked at a portrait of Sri Yukteswar and remarked that he appeared to be a fine man, Paramahansaji exclaimed, "He was no man, he was a god!"

When Paramahansaji was preparing to come to America, Sri Yukteswar said to him, "If you go now, all doors will open to you." He expressed keen interest in the unfoldment of the work in America and, in 1935, asked Paramahansaji to return to India for a visit.

Sri Yukteswar left his body on March 9, 1935. In keeping with yogic tradition his body was buried in the garden of his Puri ashram. Instead of cremation, the general practice in India for the disposition of physical remains, the bodies of saints are usually buried because they are considered to have already burnt the body when they renounced their worldly attachments. Their burial sites are considered, by devotees, to be significant places of pilgrimage.

Three months after his transition, in a hotel room in Bombay,

Paramahansaji saw and conversed with Sri Yukteswar in his resurrected form. His guru gave him personal information about world trends, explained details about life in subtle realms, and said that he was presently active as a guru to advanced souls on Hiranyaloka, a highly evolved astral planet. There, most inhabitants are withdrawing from astral attachments as preparation for experience in even more subtle causal realms.

The *Amrita Bazar Patrika*, a Calcutta newspaper, carried the following story after Sri Yukteswar's passing:

> One of the great expounders of the *Bhagavad Gita*, Swami Maharaj was a great disciple of Yogiraj Sri Shyama Charan Lahiri Mahasaya of Banaras. Swami Maharaj was the founder of several Yogoda Satsanga centers in India, and was the great inspiration behind the Yoga movement which was carried to the West by Swami Yogananda, his principle disciple. It was Sri Yukteswar's prophetic powers and deep realization that inspired Swami Yogananda to cross the oceans and spread in America the message of the masters of India. His interpretation of the *Bhagavad Gita* and other scriptures testify to the depth of Sri Yukteswarji's command of philosophy, both Eastern and Western, and remain as an eye-opener for the unity between Orient and Occident. As he believed in the unity of all religious faiths, Sri Yukteswar Maharaj established the Sadhu Sabha (Society of Saints), for the inculcation of a scientific spirit of religion. At the time of his demise he nominated Swami Yogananda as his successor as the president of Sadhu Sabha. India is really poorer today by the passing of such a great man. May all fortunate enough to have come near him inculcate in themselves the true spirit of India's culture and sadhana which was personified in him.

A few months before Sri Yukteswar's mahasamadhi, Paramahansaji noticed a loose tile on the roof of his guru's ashram and asked permission to have it repaired. Sri Yukteswar replied, "As long as I am here, it will not fall." The day he passed, it fell to the ground.

Many of the centers established by Sri Yukteswar were merged into Yogoda Satsanga, the Self-Realization Fellowship organization in India, and continue to serve as vehicles through which his work prevails. Some of his disciples also continued as Kriya gurus without organizational affiliation.

Paramahansa Yogananda

My guru was born on January 5, 1893, at Gorakhpur, northeastern India; the second son and the fourth child of Bhagabati Charan and Gurru Ghosh, devoted disciples of Lahiri Mahasaya. His parents named him Mukunda Lal.

Baptized by Lahiri Mahasaya at the age of one, as he grew older the young Mukunda often visited saints and yoga masters, learning from them of God and being further motivated on the spiritual path. He once mentioned that he had been conscious in his mother's womb, and, later, recalled several previous incarnations as a yogi.

On one occasion during his twelfth year, in his attic meditation room of the family home in Calcutta, he was absorbed in samadhi for forty-eight hours. During that interlude he inwardly saw the manifestation and dissolution of the universe and experienced a variety of superconscious states. In his later years he lectured about the experience, referring to it as "My forty-eight hours in eternity."

Paramahansaji informed disciples that his mission was to make known the philosophy and practices of Kriya Yoga in the West, and that it was Babaji's intention that he do so. Even as Babaji had encouraged Lahiri Mahasaya to live an outwardly normal life while fulfilling his spiritual destiny, he prepared Paramahansa Yogananda for a more public work.

Few could have borne the strict discipline Paramahansaji endured under the watchful eye of Sri Yukteswar. No ordinary seeker on the path, my guru was in the world with enlightened purpose. His training by Sri Yukteswar, who had a keen interest in world enlightenment, provided the needed emphasis and direction for the ministry that was to later unfold. After receiving his college degree, Mukunda Lal Ghosh was initiated into the swami order by Sri Yukteswar, and chose Yogananda as his monastic name.

Paramahansaji assisted with his guru's organizational work and founded a residential boy's school for the purpose of provid-

Paramahansa Yogananda

ing a balanced approach to education, with emphasis on vedic philosophy and yoga practice. While meditating at the school at Ranchi, Paramahansaji had a vision in which he saw a vast number of people. He intuitively knew them to be disciples he would meet in America. A few days later, he received an invitation to be a speaker at a Congress of Religious Liberals to convene in Boston. Because of the generous financial assistance of his father, he was able to travel to America, by boat, and to remain after the conference was concluded.

Before leaving India to come to America, Paramahansaji prayed for Babaji's blessings. Babaji came to his house to assure him that his mission was divinely ordained and would be successful, saying, "Kriya Yoga, the natural way of God-realization, will ultimately spread in all lands, and aid in the harmonizing of the nations through humanity's personal, transcendental perception of the Infinite."

In Boston he taught classes and accepted his first American disciples. Before long, he was to tour the major cities, speaking to large audiences and initiating thousands of truth seekers into Kriya Yoga practices. Wherever he went he was hosted by civic and business leaders. During a Washington, D.C. lecture series President Calvin Coolidge welcomed him to the White House. Adapting himself to modern methods of communication Paramahansaji was extremely effective in introducing his teachings to large audiences. He always said that he taught both a quantity and a quality message. He was interested in educating new seekers and was ever attentive to recognizing sincere devotees of God to whom he could impart the quality work.

During an extremely successful Los Angeles lecture series, he looked for suitable property for the establishment of a permanent headquarters facility. While visiting the Highland Park district, he saw a hilltop estate, which included a sixty-room hotel building with a panoramic view of the city of Los Angeles eight miles distant. Leading those who were with him onto the property he said, "This place feels like ours!" A few of his companions tried to dissuade him, pointing out that there were no signs indicating that the property was for sale. Upon inquiry, however, they were informed that the property could be purchased. With the help of generous friends and students, negotiations went forward. The site remains as the international headquarters of the Self-Realization Fellowship.

While in India, during a visit of several months in 1935-36, Sri Yukteswar bestowed upon my guru the further monastic title of Paramahansa. While in India he spoke at several public meetings, visited ashrams, consolidated organizational activities, and gathered information to later include in is writings. Upon his return to America, he was presented with a hermitage retreat at Encinitas, California, a gift of one of his disciples, Mr. James J. Lynn (Rajasi Janakananda). Overlooking the Pacific Ocean, with lush flower gardens and lawns, it became a favorite place for Paramahansaji and many of his close disciples. In the early 1940's two churches were founded, in Hollywood and in San Diego. Paramahansaji designated each facility as a Church of all Religions and alternated Sunday lecture services between them for several years. Ten years later an addition was added to the Hollywood church, and a new Self-Realization Fellowship Lake Shrine was dedicated at Pacific Palisades just a few hundred yards from the ocean.

As his California work progressed, printed lessons were published and sent to thousands of students in America and other countries. His major literary work, *Autobiography of a Yogi,* first published in 1946, is currently available in more than seventeen major world languages. It is estimated that well over one hundred thousand people were personally initiated into Kriya Yoga by Paramahansaji during his thirty-two year ministry. Additional millions have since been blessed by reading his books and by learning Kriya Yoga practices from disciples ordained by him.

In early 1950, Paramahansaji retired from public activities and secluded himself at his desert retreat near Twentynine Palms, California, about one hundred miles east of Los Angeles. There he met with disciples and wrote an extensive commentary on the *Bhagavad Gita.* I used to visit him there, usually talking with him during the early evening hours in his living room or while walking on the property. One evening, as he sat in a large reclining chair, he said, "I finished the *Gita* today!" Then, after a pause, "Just a little while ago, as I sat here meditating, I saw a gold circle of light in the spiritual eye. Opening my eyes I saw the light up there." As he said this he pointed to a place high on the wall in front of him. "Babaji, Lahiri, and Sri Yukteswar appeared in that light, smiling their blessings. They are pleased."

During my last visit, a few weeks before his mahasamadhi, he counseled, "Don't allow your mind to be influenced by anything anyone says. Don't look back, or to the left or right, but [look] straight ahead. You must go all the way [on the spiritual path] in this incarnation—and you can!" He also told me of his feelings about Sri Yukteswar's mahasamadhi in 1936 and hinted of his own soon passing.

In the late evening of March 7, 1952, I was at the Self-Realization Fellowship Center in Phoenix, Arizona. Herbert Freed, a brother disciple, telephoned me from Los Angeles. "Master left his body tonight," he said. Herbert then instructed me to conduct a memorial service for devotees in Phoenix, where I then served as the assistant minister, and to attend Paramahansaji's memorial service in Los Angeles a few days later.

During the months preceding his mahasamadhi, Paramahansaji confided to several disciples that his mission had been successfully accomplished. His organization was established on a firm basis and he had prepared his successors to represent the Kriya Yoga tradition. On March 7, he attended a dinner, arranged in honor of India's Ambassador to the United States, Binay Ranjan Sen. After a short talk, Paramahansaji quoted one of his poems, lifted his eyes, and left his body. Years before, he had said to some disciples [using an American expression], "When I go, I want to go with my boots on, speaking of God and the masters."

After the funeral service at the Self-Realization Fellowship headquarters, his body was taken to Forest Lawn Memorial-Park, to await placement in a crypt. Some representatives of the India branch of his organization had communicated their intention to travel to Los Angeles to view it a final time. Approximately three weeks later, an official of the mortuary sent a notarized letter to Self-Realization Fellowship stating: "The absence of any visual signs of decay [of Paramahansaji's body] offers the most extraordinary case in our experience." Years before, when a few disciples had witnessed one of his ecstatic states, Paramahansaji told them, "The same energy [shakti] you saw manifesting today, will keep my body intact after I am gone."

He assured disciples that his teachings and spiritual influ-

Paramahansa Yogananda and
James J. Lynn (Rajasi Janakananda)

ence would continue to benefit seekers of truth for centuries. To those who asked about their future relationship with him, he said, "If you think me near, I will be near."

A Path of Light for All People in Our Awakening World

Kriya Yoga is for anyone who is able to understand the philosophical principles upon which its practices are based and who will dedicate themselves to practicing its precepts. There are committed disciples of this path of light in all walks of life who attend to their secular duties while improving their relationship with God. The gurus of this tradition radiate blessings to the world, their representatives continue to instruct and initiate responsive disciples, and the enlivening, redemptive actions of God's grace are increasingly expressive in the lives of devotees who are ever receptive to them.

To inform interested people about spiritual growth opportunities and to support their practices, some organized endeavors are necessary: public information programs, printed materials and other communications media, classes and retreats, occasional gatherings of devotees who meet for the purpose of meditation and supportive fellowship if desired, and personal instruction and initiation. An organized body of servers and devotees, however, is only the vehicle for the transmission of information and has little value if devoid of spiritual vitality. My guru often said, "God is the honey; a formal, organized activity is the hive. If the organization is devoid of the honey of God, it has no spiritual value."

A world enlightenment tradition will never be a massive, structured movement because its emphasis is upon the inner way of soul remembrance, God-relationship, and dedicated living. To promote the ideal of large numbers of adherents for the purpose of socializing the teachings would be a mistake, regardless of the good intentions of participants. What this approach calls for is honest, responsible inquiry into the questions of why we are in this world and how to fulfill our purposes while here. One who is intent upon discovery should not desire to be pacified or catered to; the focus should be upon learning how to remove (or be removed from) physical, mental, and circumstantial obstacles to being knowledgeable and functional, in order to live effectively and experience rapid spiritual growth. What is necessary, then, if we are to be truly fulfilled, is discipleship: commitment to learning and to the application of what is learned.

The requirements of discipleship eliminate the possibility of mass, socialized movements because sincere truth seekers, intent upon exploring possibilities of awakening to transcendent realities, are not in need of perpetual emotional support, personality reinforcement, or diversions. General information can and should be provided to anyone who wants to know how to live a wholesome, honest, successful, self-conscious life; the kind of life which is considered to be normal by most people.

Discipleship commitment may be mild, more focused, or intensive, and progress will be in accord with one's involvement. It is not usually possible for the truth student or disciple to constantly live near the teacher or guru, nor is it necessary. What is essential is that one live the teaching. Although the requisites needed for success on the discipleship path are few, they cut to the very core of the cause of why it is that, of the many seekers who may be interested in discipleship, few actually enter into the learning and growing process, and few among them persist to its conclusion. Some requirements for discipleship are:

1. *A Sincere Desire to Learn* – It is easy to commit to the learning process when one is sincerely motivated. Curiosity, open-mindedness, and adaptability are qualities usually apparent when a sincere desire to learn is impelling.

2. *Ability to Learn* – Along with willingness to learn, one must be capable of learning. Progress can then be in accord with the disciple's capacity to acquire knowledge and successfully apply it. It is not necessary for one new on the path to immediately, intellectually comprehend the entire range of the categories of cosmic manifestation. A little understanding will be helpful in the beginning; more knowledge will unfold with the passage of time. The important matter is to use what is learned and to be steadfastly committed on the discipleship path. Rational thinking should be cultivated, as well as intellectual and intuitive skills. Mental perversity—a tendency to distort what is learned

for self-serving purposes—is an obstacle to learning. Other obstacles are inattention to details, mental laziness, emotionalism and moodiness, addictive attitudes and behaviors, delusions, and illusions. All physical, mental, and circumstantial obstacles are definitely eliminated or transcended by dedicated practice.

3. *Respect for the Teaching and the Teacher* – One who approaches the learning process without respect for the teacher or the teaching, has little or no self-respect. Therefore, little or nothing of real value can result from such an unfortunate endeavor. What is most helpful is a healthy-minded, respectful attitude, devoid of any emotional need to worship either the teacher or the teaching. The outcome of the ideal learning relationship is that the seeker of truth becomes a knower, established in Self-knowledge.

4. *Persistence* – Having chosen to be a disciple, aspiration to enlightenment should be nurtured and commitment should be unwavering. If we are not well, we need to be healed. If we are not successful, we need to learn how to be successful. If we are dysfunctional, we need to learn how to be healthy-minded, self-responsible, and effective. If we are not enlightened, we need to awaken to knowledge and realization of our innate condition and experience a relationship with God.

There are several hundred thousand Kriya Yoga meditators in the world today. In the centuries before us, there will be hundreds of millions. Because this tradition provides accurate information about matters essential to total well-being, and proven regimens to facilitate spiritual growth, it is the most result-producing way to personal fulfillment and illumination of consciousness. By the "way," I mean the process of awakening from self-consciousness soul awareness. Whether or not it is referred to as Kriya Yoga is of little consequence. What is important, is that dedicated spiritual aspirants have an opportunity to be informed of the facts of life so they can fulfill their life-enhancing purposes in this world and actualize their spiritual destiny as efficiently as possible.

Since being ordained by my guru, in 1951, I have written extensively, traveled the world to teach these processes, and initiated many devotees into Kriya Yoga meditation practices. I am fully aware that all personal endeavors are but preparatory to the influence of God's grace which alone is redemptive. No one can do for us what we must do, and no one can do for us what God's grace can do. Our role in the awakening process is to learn how to live effectively, while wholeheartedly aspiring to knowledge and experience of God which satisfies the heart.

It is a mistake to naively believe that mere adherence to regimens, practice of meditation techniques, or association with other devotees on the path, will guarantee psychological growth and illumination of consciousness. Living with conscious intention can be helpful, as can proficiency in meditation practice. What ultimately assures enlightened understanding and soul liberation is an adjustment of viewpoint that enables us to flawlessly perceive ourselves as spiritual beings in relationship to a Reality which is infinite because without boundaries.

The stages through which we awaken to Self-knowledge can be determined by observing states of consciousness, mental states, and preferred behaviors. Until established in pure consciousness, characteristics of various levels may be present. For rapid spiritual growth to be facilitated, it is recommended that restrictive psychological characteristics and personal behaviors be renounced in favor of those which allow spontaneous soul unfoldments. A review of the stages of soul unfoldment follows:

• *Unconscious Self-Consciousness* – Mental dullness, apathy, and boredom are common symptoms. The physical body is assumed to be the real being, birth and death are considered as beginnings and endings of existence. Awareness of spiritual matters is usually absent. If religious, prayer is usually directed to a concept of God and belief is more important than knowledge. Activities and relationships are usually determined by needs, desires, or whims. Intellectual powers are limited. Memories, mental conditionings (karma), habits, and learned or acquired behaviors strongly influence one's lifestyle. Small-mindedness and self-righteousness may be dramatized. Characteristics of first chakra awareness.

• *Dysfunctional Self-Consciousness* – Mental confusion and conflicted emotional states are normal conditions. Egocentricity prevails. Meditation may be practiced for the purpose of having phenomenal perceptions. Illusions and fantasy are common: also attachments, dependency, addictions, and self-defeating attitudes and behaviors. Actions are often irrational and behaviors unpredictable. Neurotic needs, complaints, blaming others or circumstances, and irresponsibility are common. Subconscious influences dominate mental and emotional states. Characteristics of second chakra awareness.

• *Functional Self-Consciousness* – Healthy-minded, superior self-conscious condition. When meditating, the major purpose may be to elicit a relaxation response and actualize psychological and physiological benefits only. Normal activities and relationships are rational, nurturing choices. Intellectual powers may be well-developed. Actions are performed skillfully. Unclear understanding of God and higher realities may be present. A pronounced sense of individuality may be present, supportive of self-responsible behaviors but may be difficult to renounce in favor of cultivating soul awareness. Characteristics of third chakra awareness.

• *Superconsciousness* – Partial or complete Self-realization. Knowledge and experience that one is a ray of God's consciousness. When meditating, refined superconscious states unfold, allowing perceptions and realizations of God and transcendent levels of consciousness. Ego-sense diminishes with increasing Self-realization. Normal activities and relationships are enjoyed without compulsion. One at this level may be able to easily understand the usefulness of Kriya Yoga practices, and commit to discipleship and extended durations of meditative contemplation. Characteristics of fourth chakra awareness.

• *Cosmic Consciousness* – Partial or complete knowledge and awareness of universal processes and insight into the fact that the field of nature is a play of cosmic forces. When meditating, perceptions and realizations are transcendental. Intellectual powers are keen. Intuition is pronounced. Comprehension of primordial nature as the Word (Om), cosmic particles, space, and time. Normal activities and relationships are enjoyed with higher understanding. Characteristics of fifth chakra awareness.

• *God Consciousness* – Partial or complete realization of God and transcendental realities. If some mental conditionings remain, their influences are weakened by the superior influences of refined superconscious forces and will be removed or dissolved. Natural living and knowledgeable actions prevent the further accumulation of conditionings. At this level, with more realizations to unfold, one is liberated from delusions and attachments. Characteristics of sixth chakra awareness.

• *Full Enlightenment* – Complete knowledge-realization of God and universal processes. Liberation of consciousness. When meditating, realizations are transcendental. When relating to mundane realms, enlightenment remains undiminished and all actions are spontaneously appropriate. Characteristics of seventh chakra awareness.

By honest self-evaluation of our attitudes, inclinations, preferences, and behaviors, we can determine our present spiritual status and choose mental states and behaviors which are more compatible with the levels we aspire to actualize. By such self-responsible actions we can experience adjustments of states of consciousness and facilitate our spiritual growth.

People who live wholesome, purposeful, uncomplicated lives experience spontaneous, progressive spiritual growth because of the soul's inclination to awaken from unconscious and self-conscious states. What is not generally known is that spiritual growth can be more rapid when intentional endeavors to eliminate obstacles to its unfoldment are removed and aspiration to enlightenment is constant. Regular, correct practice of Kriya Yoga meditation techniques more quickly facilitates psychological transformation and refinement of the nervous system so that flows of soul awareness are less obstructed.

Readers sincerely interested in being initiated into these meditation practices are advised to carefully study the information presented in this book, meditate on a regular schedule, and do their best to live constructively with intentional purpose.

A few decades ago, when I was much younger, I actually

thought that, with the unfoldment of the current era, many more people than are presently involved would be attentive to dedicated spiritual practices. Today, although there are many millions of people who are looking for meaning in life and desire spiritual awakening, first, second, and third levels of soul awareness are more commonly demonstrated in the mainstream of society. What is important for the individual who aspires to personal fulfillment and spiritual growth, however, is knowledge of the fact that awakening to higher understanding and having a conscious relationship with God is always a personal, inner process independent of external conditions. Our choices and actions, along with God's grace, determine our circumstances and our ultimate, knowledgeable freedom.

Glossary

An understanding of the meanings of the following English and Sanskrit words will be helpful in the study of the text of this book. Comprehension will improve as you become familiar with the words and your awareness clears as a result of progressive spiritual growth.

Absolute. Unmodified, Supreme Consciousness. The transcendental field. The field of pure consciousness.

actualize. To make real or to bring into manifestation. We actualize our capacities when we express or demonstrate them. Goals are actualized when they are achieved. Purposes are actualized when they are accomplished or fulfilled.

advaita. Nonduality. The teaching that everything in manifestation is an expression of one Life, Being, Substance, and expressive Power of Supreme Consciousness.

ahamkara. Personal illusion of independent existence resulting in a veiling or clouding of awareness and a deluded sense of being separate from God. Ahamkara is the basis of egoism. Because of this, the soul feels itself to be independent of its origins and identifies with objective realms, unable to comprehend the subjective ones. See *delusion* and *illusion*.

akasha. The first of five material element manifestations comprising the field of manifested nature. Sometimes translated into English as ether, or space comprised of fine substances which are not-yet-matter but have the potential to manifest as matter. The four other element influences are air, fire, water, and earth which express as their corresponding material manifestations.

ananda. Bliss. Unadulterated soul joy of awareness of pure being, rather than mental happiness or an emotional mood.

asana. Posture or pose. Yogasanas are the various postures assumed when practicing Hatha Yoga. Sitting postures are used for meditation and contemplation. For meditation practice any stable, comfortable asana is suitable.

ashram. A quiet, secluded abode for study and spiritual practice. An ashram should provide a supportive environment in which residents can live close to nature, without distractions. Only elevating influences should prevail, to nurture soul qualities and encourage their unfoldment.

astral realm. The sphere of life forces and electricities. Souls come into physical incarnation from the astral realm and return to it between earth sojourns. Spiritually advanced souls may pass through the astral realms, or transcend them, to continue their awakening in finer spheres or to completely awaken from involvement with all aspects of primordial nature. See *causal realm*.

atman. The permanent essence of every person and creature. The divine Self which is to be consciously experienced by the seeker on the spiritual path. When realization is complete, one knows the True Self, God, to be cosmic. Paramatman (*para*, beyond) is nonindividualized Supreme Consciousness. See *soul*.

avatar. The emergence of divine power into human form. A full incarnation of God for the purpose of infusing planetary consciousness with divine influences. Avatars sometimes play outwardly dramatic roles; at other times their spiritual state is unrecognized by those with whom they associate. Their redemptive work is in accord with God's will (evidenced by the innate inclinations of evolution). The "universal avatar" concept should also be understood: God dwells equally *in* and *as* every soul. To the degree that divine capacities are actualized through all human beings, so collective human consciousness and planetary consciousness becomes illumined.

avidya. Literally, not knowledge, in contrast to *vidya*, full knowledge of Consciousness and its categories of manifestation.

Ayurveda. *Ayur*, life, and *veda*, knowledge. India's several thousand year-old system of wellness. According to folklore, this knowledge was taught to man by the gods. Chinese Medicine is also said to have been taught to man by the gods, and there is a similarity between their procedures. Both include a total examination of the patient—pulse, temperature, skin condition, eyes, psychological characteristics, behavior, and other factors—when making a diagnosis. Ayurveda uses diet, herbs, water therapy, massage, attitude training and behavior modification, detoxification regimens, and meditation, along with other procedures to encourage restoration of the body to a condition of balance. The basis of therapy is to balance the three subtle element-influences (space-air, *vata*; fire-water, *pitta*; and water-earth, *kapha*) which govern physiological functions and influence psychological states. The *Charaka Samhita*, a basic Ayurvedic text, lists over five hundred herbs and describes their medicinal uses. Knowledge of Ayurveda passed from India to Mediterranean countries, and finally to the West. During the years of British rule, state patronage resulted in the decline of Ayurvedic practice in the urban centers of India, although it continued to be the treatment of choice among rural populations. There are several Ayurvedic colleges in India, and scientific research is progressing there and in other countries to investigate and validate these wellness procedures.

Babaji. *Baba*, father. *Ji* is a suffix used at the end of a name to indicate respect. In Asia, many saints who are venerated are referred to as Baba or Babaji. In this Kriya Yoga tradition the name *Mahavatar Babaji* is used to refer to the enlightened master who revived these teachings and practices and again introduced them into public consciousness. See more details in the opening paragraphs of the *Appendix*.

Bhagavad Gita. The Holy or Divine Song. From *bhaj*, to revere or love; and *gita*, song. A scripture treasured by millions of devotees in which the author portrays Krishna as a divine incarnation who teaches the philosophy of "the eternal way of righteousness" to his disciple, Arjuna. Frequent reading of the *Gita* can make a profound impact upon the mind and consciousness of a surrendered disciple on the spiritual path. It, along with the *Yoga Sutras*, is one of the basic study texts recommended to Kriya Yoga devotees.

Bhagavan. Lord, that which rules. Also, one who is endowed with the divine attributes of infinite spiritual power, righteousness, glory, splendor, knowledge, and renunciation.

bhakti. Fervent, devotional love for God which can result in God-realization and perception of God-as-nature. A common teaching is that love for God unfolds higher knowledge, and the cultivation of higher knowledge causes love to blossom.

Brahma. The expanding and projecting aspect of the Godhead which results in full manifestation of nature. *Vishnu* is the name given to the aspect of God which preserves and maintains the universe. *Shiva* is the name given to God's transformative aspect which dissolves forms and circumstances to allow new expressions.

Brahma Sutras. Also known as the *Vedanta Sutras*. Revelations and philosophical speculations of the seers of Vedic times. *Sutras* are concise statements or threads of concepts comprising a theme to be contemplated until the meaning is apprehended.

brahmacharya. From *brahma*, divine; and *acharya*, going. The regulation of vital forces, mental and emotional tendencies, and behaviors for the conservation and transmutation of energies, freeing them and the devotee's attention for intentional living and dedicated spiritual practices. A *brahmachari* is a person, usually a novice of a monastic order, dedicated to brahmacharya. The original meaning of *brahmachari* is one whose attention is fixed in God whether cloistered or living a responsible secular life.

Brahman. The Supreme Reality, the Absolute.

Buddha. A seer who lived in northern India about 500 B.C. Of royal birth, as a young man he became troubled when he learned of the sufferings of the average person in society. After marrying, and fathering a son, he left home to seek higher knowledge. Following a duration of ascetic yogic practice he adopted "the middle way" of controlled moderation. He attained illumination of consciousness; hence the name attributed to him—the Buddha, the enlightened one. After his illumination he walked through the Ganges Valley for almost half a century, preaching freely and forming a society of renunciates. He taught love, nonhatred, dedication to truth, the elimination of wishful thinking, and nondependence upon externals, including even religious ritual. Buddhism teaches that illumination is the realization of the True Self which is common to all, rather than merely a state of consciousness to be attained.

buddhi. From the verb-root *budh*, to know. The faculty of discernment, the intellectual capacity. When, by discernment, the totality of Consciousness is apprehended, one is a *buddha*, an enlightened being. Because all souls are expressions of Supreme Consciousness, all have a buddha nature. When the soul fully realizes its true nature, it is spiritually free.

capacity. The power or ability to receive or contain. The power or ability to do: to use skills and accomplish purposes.

causal realm. The sphere pervading the cosmos comprised of magnetism and electric properties which precede astral and physical manifestation. Souls reside here while awakening to celestial and transcendental levels. See *astral realm*.

chakra. Literally, *wheel*. Chakras are vital centers through which prana (life force) flows. In yogic literature, the primary chakras are designated as the crown chakra in the upper brain; the spiritual eye center between the eyebrows; and the five centers at the cervical, dorsal, lumbar, sacral, and coccygeal regions of the spine.

Chitta. Supreme Consciousness in its aspect of dynamic creative power.

chitti. Individualized consciousness, soul awareness. When movements and transformations which are characteristic of unenlightened awareness are quieted, Self (soul) illumination is spontaneously experienced or realized.

Christ. From Greek *khristos*, anointed; and *khriein*, to anoint. In common usage the word was used to mean the religious rite of anointing with oil. Early Christians, believing Jesus to be endowed with divine qualities, spoke of him as being a Christ (anointed) of God. *Christ Consciousness* is a term sometimes used to refer to the aspect of God universally expressive in creation. Vedic scriptures refer to this as *Kutastha Chaitanya*: *Kutastha*, the one on the summit, the Immutable Self or Reality which remains above changes; and *Chaitanya*, the omniscient Being that is both the source and the ruler of the universe.

consciousness. This word has two meanings: 1) consciousness as awareness which has an object or supportive relationship; 2) the entity of consciousness itself without an object, which requires no support—often referred to as pure consciousness.

cosmic consciousness. Sometimes referred to as unity consciousness, awareness of life as wholeness as an actual, experienced realization. It may be partial or it may be more complete. It may unfold gradually or suddenly, bringing with it knowledge which is self-revealed rather than acquired. Cosmic consciousness can be nurtured by renouncing egocentric attitudes and self-conscious behaviors, by aspiration to spiritual growth, prayer, meditation, and reliance upon the God. When superconsciousness is maintained during ordinary waking circumstances, cosmic consciousness increases.

Cosmic Mind. Cosmic Mind-Substance or Universal Mind. The omnipresent mental field of which all individualized minds are an aspect or part. Mind, whether Cosmic or individualized, is comprised of a field of awareness, self-sense, intellect or discerning aspect, and thinking (information processing) aspect. At the level of mind identification we are in relationship with Cosmic Mind. Our mental states (including our thoughts, desires, intentions, and karmic conditions) interact with Cosmic Mind which is responsive to our mental states.

darshan. Literally, to see, to discern the truth. The blessing and insight one has as a result of looking upon any aspect or manifestation of divinity whether objectively or subjectively perceived. To visit a pilgrimage site or be in the company of a saint, is to have the opportunity for darshan. To apprehend higher realities when meditating or during an interlude of transcendence is to experience darshan.

delusion. An erroneous or invalid belief or opinion due to intellectual error or defective discernment. The initial error of the intellect is considered to be that of mistakenly believing the Self (soul) to be mind or matter. All other delusions, and their consequences, result from this. See *ahamkara* and *illusion*.

deva. A shining one, a god. Gods, *devas*, and goddesses, *devis*, are spiritually radiant souls which dwell in subtle or celestial realms.

dharma. That which upholds and maintains; that which supports creation and contributes to evolutionary processes. To live in harmony with evolutionary processes is to be righteous, appropriately correct, or *dharmic*. To be in accord with life processes and one's destined path is to fulfill one's dharma.

dhatu. Dhatus are the body's supporting tissues: plasma, blood, muscle, fat, bone, bone marrow, and reproductive essence which result from orderly food transformation. See *ojas*.

diksha. Yoga initiation, during which meditation instruction is given and the guru transmits spiritual force to the disciple. Instruction is usually determined by the capacity of the initiated person to comprehend and to practice what is taught, and the philosophical tradition represented by the guru.

dosha. In the Ayurvedic system, regimens are recommended for the purpose of balancing the three primary governing influences (*doshas*) which regulate physiological and psychological characteristics. See *Ayurveda*.

God. The Supreme Being. The outward manifestation of Supreme Consciousness in the direction of universal manifestation. The Oversoul, the Cosmic Soul.

guna. A quality or attribute of consciousness expressing as a cosmic influence that regulates nature's forces which are in proximity to it. There are three gunas. *Sattva* contributes to purity and luminosity. *Rajas* contributes to movement and transformation *Tamas* contributes to heaviness, inertia, and darkness.

guru. That which removes darkness or inertia. The light and reality of God is the true guru; when expressing through an illumined teacher, it removes darkness from the mind and consciousness of the disciple. Such a teacher is a *Satguru*, a truth revealer.

heaven. Originally a cosmological term that identified a region of the universe but which also came to function as a vehicle of religious idealism. In ancient Near Eastern thought, heaven identified a region of the observable cosmos which pointed beyond itself to a realm or field of transcendence. In ancient Greek mythology, Zeus dwells on Mount Olympus. The Old Testament refers to heaven as God's abode from which he exercises his sovereign rule and to which he finally welcomes the faithful righteous. The New Testament reflects a modified version: heaven is God's creation in which he resides as well as a condition of blessedness experienced by the spiritually prepared. Various sects have their own concepts of heaven and its opposite place or condition, hell. Illusion-free understanding allows us to directly experience the truth: that our degree of Self-knowledge and God-realization determines our circumstantial conditions.

Holy Spirit. The active, enlivening, vitalizing, and animating aspect of God expressive in creation.

illusion. Misperception; failure or incapacity to see what is objectively or subjectively present to be observed. We may then assume that we know when, in fact, we do not know. Our illusions and delusions distort awareness and contribute to mental and emotional conflict. When renounced or removed, soul awareness is restored to wholeness. See *ahamkara* and *delusion*.

imagination. The ability to image, visualize, or mentally picture what is not present to the senses. Creative imagination differs from daydreaming or fantasy only in degree. Controlled imagination enables one to clearly define mental concepts.

Ishwara. *Isvara*. The personalized aspect of God which governs and regulates creation. Referred to as the lord or ruling influence.

japa. Repetition of any of the names of God for the purpose of cultivating devotion and improving meditative concentration. A *japmala* is a string of beads used to count the repetitions or to more completely involve the meditator's attention during contemplation.

jivanmukta. One who is soul, *jiva*, liberated, *mukti*, while embodied. Traces of karma may yet remain, but the soul is inwardly free because Self-realized. Future actions of a liberated soul are then determined, not by karmic compulsion, but by the soul's innate intelligence and its responsiveness to God's guiding grace. A *paramukta* is one who is supremely liberated: without delusions, illusions, or karmic compulsions, and no longer subject to any influences of cosmic forces. See *salvation*.

jnana. Knowledge, especially knowledge of God.

jyotish. The study and application of knowledge of astronomy and astrology. In an ancient text, the *Kaushitaki Brahmana*, are indications that, in 3100 B.C., Vedic scholars had knowledge of astronomy for determining favorable times for religious and astrological ceremonies. Vedic astrology calculates planetary positions in relationship to fixed signs. Certain gemstones are believed to radiate forces similar to those of the major planets, hence the reason for recommending the use of gemstones to counteract, or strengthen, planetary influences. In this system the recommended gemstones are ruby for the sun's influence; pearl or moonstone for the Moon influence; red coral for the influence of Mars; emerald for the influence of Mercury; yellow sapphire for the influence of Jupiter; diamond for the influence of Venus; blue sapphire for the influence of Saturn; and onyx and cat's eye for the influences of the nodes of the Moon. It is recommended that gems for therapeutic or other helpful purposes be prescribed by an enlightened astrologer. The recommended weights are usually two or more carats. They should be obtained under favorable astrological circumstances, set in a ring or pendant at a chosen time, purified by the use of herbs and other substances, offered to one's chosen aspect of God, appropriate mantras should be chanted, and the item of jewelry worn beginning at the appropriate time of a prescribed day. The gems should also be set in a prescribed metal, such as gold or silver, as metals are also considered to impart their special influences.

kalpa. A duration of time. See *yuga*.

karma. From the verb-root *kri*, to act, do, make. The principle of causation. The thoughts we habitually think, our mental states, our states of consciousness (levels of soul awareness), and the actions we perform determine our experiences. Karma also refers to the accumulation of influential mental and emotional conditionings in the mental field and body. See *samskara*.

kaya-kalpa. An Ayurvedic process prescribed for physical rejuvenation. Regimens for internal cleansing and for balancing the governing principles of the body, prolonged rest, vitalizing diet, and extended periods of meditation. To ensure seclusion, the patient usually remains in a carefully prepared dwelling removed from social activities. Vitalizing substances and herbs may be prescribed. Care is taken to provide circumstances and regimens that allow nature's healing forces and one's spiritual capacities to be influential. It is reported that by this process, some saints have retained their physical bodies for hundreds of years. The most nourishing influences result from sustained, meditative superconsciousness (samadhi). See *Ayurveda* and *rasayana*.

kriya. Action, activity, process, procedure, practice. Self-chosen kriyas are actions implemented to facilitate wellness, success, fulfillment, and restoration of soul awareness to wholeness. Spontaneous kriyas are transformative actions which occur due to the soul's innate impulse to awaken and express.

kundalini. Dormant potential in nature and in the body. When kundalini awakens in nature, life forms emerge and are enlivened. When it awakens in human beings, soul qualities unfold, intellectual capacities are unveiled, intuition awakens, and adaptability and creativity are expressed.

Lahiri Mahasaya. Disciple of Mahavatar Babaji and guru of Sri Yukteswar. He made Kriya Yoga practices accessible to truth seekers in secular life. (September 30, 1827—September 26, 1895.) See biographical account in the *Appendix*.

linga. Sign, symbol, indicator, or mark. Example: an egg-shaped, metal or stone icon, a *shivalinga*, is used as a symbolic representation of consciousness coming into form from the unmanifest field, or flowing from form to formlessness. When the meaning of the symbol is known, merely seeing it reminds one of the essential aspects and characteristics of consciousness.

love. The attracting influence of God is the supreme expression of love. It unveils the mental organs of perception and releases the soul from bondage to matter. People speak of love of country, love of mankind, love for each other, and of emotional affection and attachments as love. All personal expressions of love are aspects of the soul's love for God. Love is purifying because it calls forth our innate qualities, and demands of us surrender to the highest and best in any relationship.

mahasamadhi. Conscious transition from the body. *Maha*, great, *samadhi*, oneness, is experienced when the soul's awareness is removed from relative identifications and awakens to freedom in God. The term is also used to refer to a shrine which may be built over the tomb of an enlightened yogi.

mantra. From *manas*, mind, and *tra*, to protect. A meditation mantra serves as an attractive focus for our attention, displacing awareness from mental processes and thus allowing pure consciousness to be directly experienced.

maya. The primal substance of which nature is formed. The components are creative force, space, time, and fine particles which are not yet matter but which can manifest as matter. One characteristic of maya is form-producing; hence the designation Mother Nature or Divine Mother. Another characteristic is truth-veiling: when a soul identifies with the field of nature it may experience a diminishing of intuitive and intellectual capacities, and become deluded. Maya is illusory, but is not an illusion.

meditation. Undisturbed flowing of attention to one's object of concentration. Meditation results in contemplation. In accord with the meditator's intention, contemplation can result in: 1) awareness of oneness with the object contemplated; 2) transcendence of the object to realize pure consciousness.

metaphysics. From Greek *meta*, beyond or after; and *physika* (Aristotle's treatise so titled), hence, after or beyond physics. The word is now used to refer to philosophical theories that deal with matters outside of physical realm operations and sciences.

moksha. Liberation of soul consciousness. Liberation is accomplished when awareness is devoid of delusions and illusions. *See jivanmukta and salvation.*

mudra. A symbolic gesture. Also, a yogic procedure used to regulate the body's life forces and provide control of involuntary processes.

nadi. A channel or pathway through which prana flows in the body at the astral level. *Ida* is the left channel along the spinal pathway, the lunar influence. *Pingala* is the right channel, the solar influence. The central channel is *sushumna*, the pathway through which the yogi's vital forces are directed when practicing Kriya Pranayama and other similar procedures.

nadi shuddhi. Purification of the nadis by pranayama or when prana flows spontaneously after kundalini is awakened.

Nirguna-Brahma. Supreme Consciousness *without* attributes or qualities. *Saguna-Brahma* is Consciousness *with* attributes.

ojas. The most refined form of energy-as-matter that strengthens and
vitalizes body and mind and enhances spiritual awareness. See
Ayurveda, brahmacharya, and *dhatu.*

Om. Aum. The sound current from which all manifestations of nature
are produced. The purest meditation mantra to contemplate

omnipotence. Unrestricted power, the power of God.

omnipresence. Present everywhere.

omniscience. Consciousness-knowing everywhere.

parabda karma. Residual karmic impressions which can cause
effects. They can be allowed to express if their effects are known to
be harmless, or they can be neutralized and dissolved by prayer,
meditation, the application of specific yogic procedures, and the
superior force of God-realization.

paramahansa. From *param*, beyond or transcendental, and *hansa*,
swan. One considered to be a spiritual master; a free spirit no longer
bound by rules. As the swan has an earthly abode but can soar free
in the sky, so a paramahansa dwells in the world but is not influenced by or confined to it. Also, according to mythology, the swan
supposedly is able to extract milk from water, thus a paramahansa
is able to partake of the divine essence from the realm of matter.

Paramahansa Yogananda. Disciple of Sri Yukteswar and guru of Roy
Eugene Davis. Paramahansaji lived in the United States for thirty-
two years (from 1920) to teach Kriya Yoga and establish the Self-
Realization Fellowship. (January 5, 1893 to March 7, 1952.) See
biographical account in the *Appendix.*

prakriti. The field of nature, consisting of elements and qualities.
Purusha is the divine force which enlivens nature.

prana. Life force which pervades nature. Prana expresses as various frequencies to perform specific life support functions. When pranas are in harmony, health prevails; when they are not in harmony, disease is possible. *Pranayamas* regulate the force and circulation of prana in the body, usually by regulated breathing.

prayer. Reverent petitioning to or communing with God, the results of which are demonstrated as desired circumstances or satisfying states of consciousness. Prayer can be as simple as pure aspiration, verbal or mental prayer, or attention given to cultivating an awareness of the Presence and Reality of God. It is a volitional act of turning away from self-sense to allow a more comprehensive realization of soul qualities and divine states to be actualized. Devout people of all faiths have experienced the transformational effects of surrendered prayer. Some have realized God directly by prayer without knowledge or practice of any other technique or procedure.

rasayana. *Rasa* can be translated to mean taste, juice, elixir, or essence; *ayana*, pathway, to circulate, or to have a home, place, or abode. In Ayurveda, rasayana treatment is a means of restoring the immune system so that body fluids circulate to find their places harmoniously. Herbal compounds are usually prescribed for rasayana therapy and are many and varied. One preparation contains: raw sugar, clarified butter, Indian gall nut, Indian gooseberry, dried catkins, Indian pennywort, honey, nutgrass, white sandalwood, embrella, aloewood, licorice, cardamom, cinnamon, and turmeric. The purified ashes of certain metals and gemstones may also be used. See *Ayurveda* and *Kaya-Kalpa*.

reincarnation. The doctrine of return, of being born into another body after a duration of rest in the astral realm. The soul can be drawn back to physical realms so long as there are attachments to them. Even casual interest in relating to circumstances may cause a soul to reincarnate because personal involvements tend to follow flows of attention.

renunciation. Relinquishment of attachments to things, circumstances, emotional states, and actions, while selflessly involved in relationships, work, service, and soul-awakening practices.

rishi. A seer; one who is enlightened.

sadhana. One's spiritual practices and involvement with processes which effectively remove inner restrictions and allow harmonious environmental relationships so that Self-realization can be more efficiently actualized.

salvation. The spiritual condition of being liberated from the effects of causes of pain or discomfort because of Self-knowledge, the absence of delusions and illusions, the overcoming or removal of karmic conditions, and God's grace.

samadhi. From the verb-root *sam*, to put together. When *vritties*, mental modifications, no longer fragment or disrupt the flow of soul awareness, awareness is restored to wholeness and samadhi is experienced. Samadhi is not an unconscious or trance state. It is a state of clear, unfragmented awareness.

samkalpa. Determination, will, or intention, to cause a thing, event, or circumstance to manifest.

samkhya. To enumerate, or number. Samkhya philosophy describes the categories, stages and processes of universal manifestation. *See part one of the text.*

samsara. The continuing transformation of nature. Unenlightened people who are involved in its shifting currents experience constant changes. Enlightened souls flow with changes while remaining established in Self-knowledge and God-realization.

samskara. Mental impression, imprint, a memory. Perceptions, whether of objective circumstances or of subjective incidents such as thoughts, feelings, or subtle insights, result in impressions or memories. If influential, they can disturb mental and emotional peace by agitating the mental field and field of awareness. They can be with potential for pain or pleasure, or be neutral. Kriya Yoga practice effectively erases or removes samskaras, as do the constructive influences of superconscious realizations. See *karma.*

samyama. Perfected or accomplished contemplation: when concentration, meditation, and identification with the object of concentration is simultaneous.

Sanatana Dharma. *The eternal way of righteousness*. The impulses which incline the actions of nature to be harmonious and fulfilling, being innate to consciousness, are beginningless. As knowledge of the eternal way of righteousness is revealed or discovered, life is lived effectively with the full support of nature and of our innate spiritual impulses.

Sanskrit. The refined, perfected or polished root language from which approximately one hundred Indo-European languages, including English, are derived. Prominent in Vedic times in India and still used today by some scholars and students of philosophy. The Sanskrit alphabet is considered to be a mantra, a sound-phrase of spiritual significance and power which reveals the seed-frequencies of creation. Every word or sound (*shabda*) has a power (*shakti*) which conveys the sense which is inseparably related to the sound. Sanskrit word-sounds have an innate power to convey their inner meaning. The sound-element behind the audible sound is the fundamental sound (*sphota*). Audible or written Sanskrit can accurately reveal the meaning of what is read or heard, and contemplation of the subtle sound-element or seed power reveals its true essence. Sanskrit mantras are taught as being unique for the purpose of facilitating a meditator's spiritual awakening. All mantras derive their potency from *Om*, the primordial sound current emanating from the Godhead and expressive throughout the universe.

sat. Reality, absolute truth.

Self-realization. Conscious knowledge-experience of one's true nature. The real Self of every person and creature is pure consciousness. When identified with mental processes, and the body and its sensations and sense objects, the Self becomes outwardly involved and forgets its true nature. Self-remembrance, ordered living, and spiritual practice facilitates soul awakening and Self-realization—the restoration of awareness to its original, pure state.

shakti. Cosmic creative force which enlivens nature. Also, the aspect of kundalini which, when aroused, vitalizes the body and contributes to psychological transformation, physical vitalization, and progressive spiritual awakening and growth.

shaktipat. The transmission of shakti from one person to another, usually from guru to disciple. Also, the spontaneous awakening of shakti as the result of devotion, yogic practice, prayer, or grace.

siddha. A perfected or accomplished yogi; a master of yoga.

siddhi. Innate spiritual power or ability which can unfold and be instrumental for fulfillment or accomplishment of purposes.

spiritual eye. Ajna chakra, in the forehead, between and above the eyebrows; the reflected light from the medulla oblongata center. Through the spiritual eye the meditator moves awareness into subtle realms to have mastery of space and time.

Sri Yukteswar. Disciple of Lahiri Mahasaya and guru of Paramahansa Yogananda. (May 10, 1855 to March 9, 1935.) See biographical account in the *Appendix*.

swami. A member of the ancient monastic order reorganized by Shankara in the eighth century. A swami is one who has renounced all attachments to live in the Spirit.

tantra. From *tan*, to extend or expand. The word is commonly used to refer to writings which explain the processes of creation and dissolution of the universe, various methods of relating to universal forces and accomplishing the goals of life, how to awaken and express innate abilities, and meditation approaches for unfolding ultimate Truth-realization.

tapasya. Spiritual endeavor by means of concentrated discipline, austerity; ardent devotion to the ideal. From the verb-root *tap*, to burn. Kriya Yoga practice, intentional living which includes dedicated spiritual practice, effectively removes all physical and mental obstacles to spiritual growth.

tattva. The true or inner essence of a thing. The essence of anything can be discerned through *samyama*, perfect contemplation.

Transcendental Field. The field of pure consciousness.

turiya. The fourth state of consciousness transcending the three commonly experienced states of deep sleep, dream state, and ordinary waking state. Superconsciousness.

Upanishads. A collection of sacred texts with origins in oral traditions. Centuries ago, in India, the disciple would live with the guru in a retreat environment and sit near him to learn: *upa*, near; *ni*, down; *sad, to* sit. There are many upanishads. The ones for which Shankara wrote commentaries are termed the *greater upanishads* because of their wider accessibility. The *lesser upanishads*, which Shankara did not write about, contain yogic instruction meant for those qualified to be taught. Among the latter is the *Shandilya Upanishad* compiled by one of Lahiri Mahasaya's ancestors; some Kriya Yoga procedures are described in it.

vasana. Latent tendency. When inclined in the direction of actualization, vasanas cause movements in the psyche, resulting in experiences which may not always be anticipated. Latent tendencies with the potential to influence are neutralized by the practice of yoga.

Veda. Revealed knowledge. The Vedas contain the revelations of the ancient seers; the Upanishads offer philosophical explanations of the Vedas.

Vedanta. The summing up of the wisdom of the Vedic tradition. The final wisdom is that Supreme Consciousness is the Cause, Reality, and Support of all that is.

viveka. Discrimination; discernment of that which is changeless in contrast to that which is transitory.

vritti. Process, action, fluctuation, wave, or modification occurring in the mental field when *vasanas* (impulses arising from tendencies to action, or restlessness) stir them into motion. Vrittis are calmed by dispassionate observation of circumstances when engaged in ordinary activities and relationships, meditation practice, and superconsciousness. Their inclinations are returned to their origins by the practice of Kriya Yoga.

Vyasa. An ancient sage believed to have arranged many of the Vedic works in their present form. *Vyasa* is probably a name used by several sages over a period of several centuries.

yama. Restraint. By resisting, restraining, and regulating destructive impulses, their opposite characteristics are cultivated and perfected: harmlessness, truthfulness, honesty, constructive use of vital forces and soul capacities, and insightful renunciation which makes possible appropriate relationships and use of natural resources.

Niyamas, intentional practices, are also essential: inner and outer purity, soul contentment in all circumstances, disciplines to facilitate psychological transformation (see *tapasya*), study for Self-knowledge and contemplation of higher realities, and surrender in God by cultivating awareness of the Presence and Reality of God.

yoga. Some meanings are: 1) to yoke or bring together all aspects of body, mind, and personality; 2) any of the various systems used for this purpose; 3) samadhi, the culmination of yoga practice—probably the original meaning of the word *yoga*. The culmination of samadhi is liberation of soul consciousness.

yuga. An Age or era. A 12,000 year Electric-Time cycle is comprised of *Kali Yuga*, a 1,200 year Dark Age during which most human beings are intellectually deficient and spiritually unaware; *Dwapara Yuga*, a 2,400 year Age during which intellectual powers and spiritual awareness increase; *Treta Yuga*, a 3,600 year Age when intellectual powers are keen and knowledge of God is common; and *Satya Yuga*, a 4,000 year Age when many on the planet can comprehend the reality of God—a true era of planetary enlightenment. We are currently in the early stages of an ascending Dwapara (the second) Yuga. *See chapter one of the text.*

zen. Japanese, from Chinese *ch'an* for Sanskrit *dhyana*: mental attention, alert meditative concentration.

ROY EUGENE DAVIS is the director of Center for Spiritual Awareness, an enlightenment movement with the publishing department and meditation retreat center in the mountain region of northeast Georgia.

He is a direct disciple of Paramahansa Yogananda and has been teaching in the Kriya Yoga tradition since his ordination by his guru in 1951. His many books, some in several languages, have inspired and encouraged thousands of readers to unfold their spiritual potential.

Mr. Davis has taught these philosophical principles and spiritual life-enhancement practices in over 100 North American communities, and in Japan, Brazil, England, Europe, West Africa, and India. He is the publisher of *Truth Journal* magazine and writes monthly lessons for students and disciples around the world.

Center for Spiritual Awareness is a global enlightenment movement with international headquarters and a meditation retreat center in the low mountain region of northeast Georgia. On an eleven acre site are administration and publishing offices, the main meeting hall and dining room, meditation temple, libraries, and guest houses for visiting members and retreat participants.

We teach that it is possible for every person, by right personal endeavor and God's grace, to experience a conscious relationship with the Infinite and to live a mature, meaningful, and fulfilled life. There are meditation centers in North America and in other countries.

Information about our retreats, publications and programs is available free upon request. There is no obligation.

Center for Spiritual Awareness
Lake Rabun Road, Post Office Box 7
Lakemont, Georgia 30552 (U.S.A.)

Tel: (706) 782-4723   Fax (706) 782-4560